AF575616

THROUGH A CHANGING LANDSCAPE

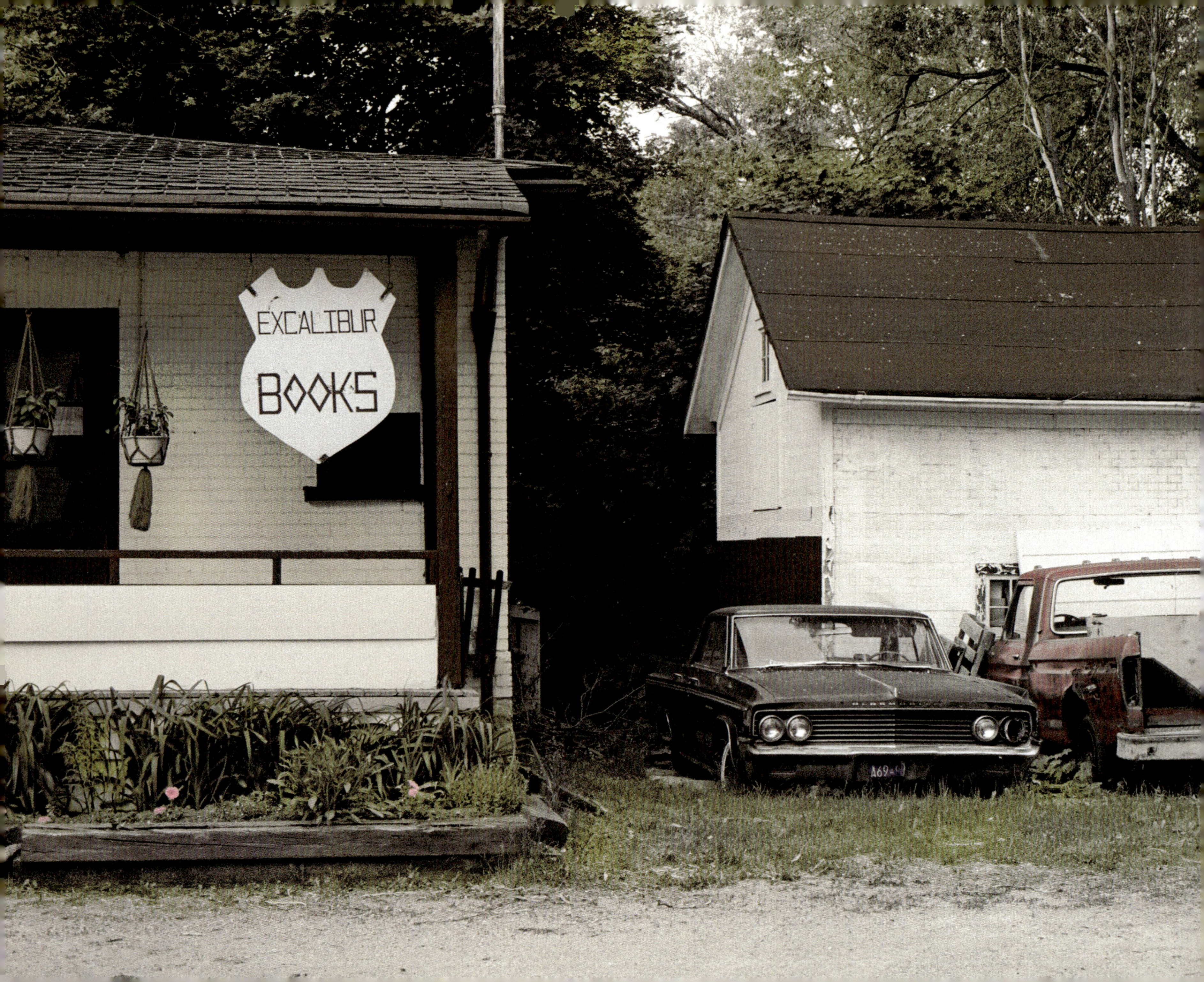
EXCALIBUR
BOOKS

THROUGH A CHANGING LANDSCAPE

Photographing Place and Community in Waterloo Region

PHILIPPE ELSWORTHY Interview and Afterword by Adam Crerar

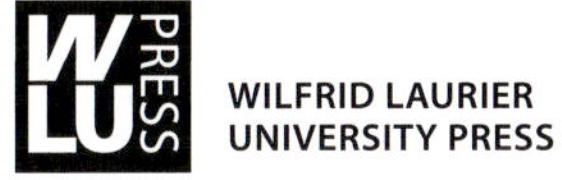

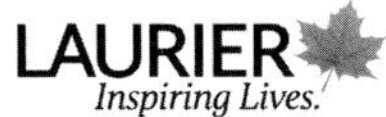

Wilfrid Laurier University Press acknowledges the support of the Canada Council for the Arts for our publishing program. We acknowledge the financial support of the Government of Canada through the Canada Book Fund for our publishing activities. Funding provided by the Government of Ontario and the Ontario Arts Council. This work was supported by the Research Support Fund.

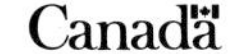

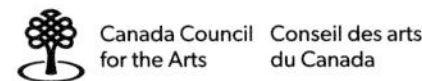

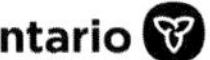

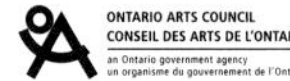

LIBRARY AND ARCHIVES CANADA CATALOGUING IN PUBLICATION

Title: Through a changing landscape: photographing place and community in Waterloo Region / Philippe Elsworthy; interview and afterword by Adam Crerar.
Names: Elsworthy, Philippe, photographer.
Description: Includes bibliographical references.
Identifiers: Canadiana (print) 2021033925X | ISBN 9781771125659 (hardcover)
Subjects: LCSH: Waterloo Region (Ont.)—Pictorial works.
Classification: LCC TR647 .E47 2022 | DDC 779.092—dc23

Cover and text design by Lime Design Inc. Front cover image shows Kmart, with two Seagram Distillery warehouses being demolished in the background, in what is now Waterloo Town Square in "Uptown" Waterloo, 1993.
Photo by Philippe Elsworthy.

This book is printed on FSC® certified paper. It contains recycled materials and other controlled sources, is processed chlorine-free, and is manufactured using biogas energy.

Printed in Canada

Wilfrid Laurier University Press is located on the Haldimand Tract, part of the traditional territories of the Haudenosaunee, Anishinaabe, and Neutral peoples. This land is part of the Dish with One Spoon Treaty between the Haudenosaunee and Anishnaabe peoples and symbolizes the agreement to share, to protect our resources, and not to engage in conflict. We are grateful to the Indigenous peoples who continue to care for and remain interconnected with this land. Through the work we publish in partnership with our authors, we seek to honour our local and larger community relationships, and to engage with the diversity of collective knowledge integral to responsible scholarly and cultural exchange.

The photographer's act is to see the outside world precisely, with intelligence as well as sensuous insight.

BERENICE ABBOTT, *The World of Atget*

...in real life only diverse surroundings have the practical power of inducing a natural, continuing flow of life and use.

JANE JACOBS, *The Death and Life of Great American Cities*

In an interview in 2000, architect Ralph Erskine was asked what it takes to become a good architect. He responded: "To be a good architect, you have to love people, because architecture is an applied art and deals with the frameworks for peoples lives." It is really as simple as that.

JAN GEHL, *Cities for People*

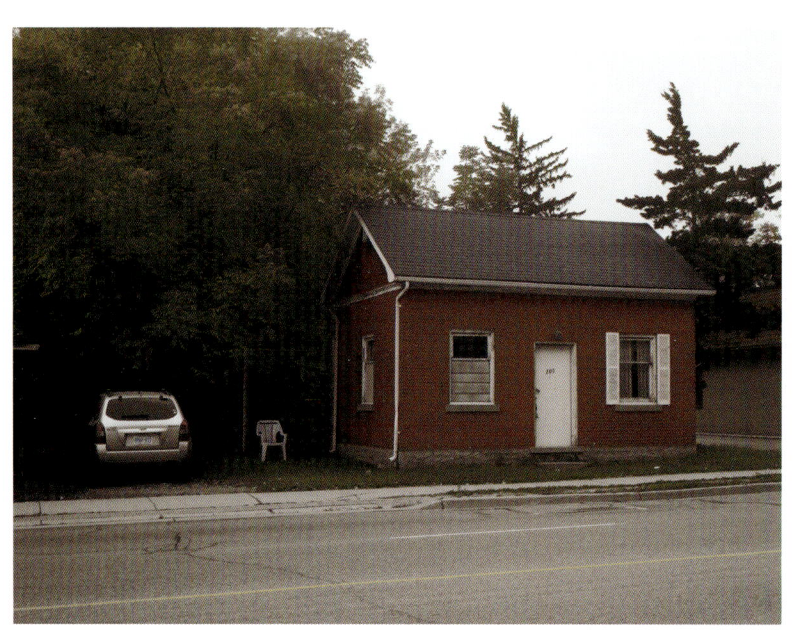

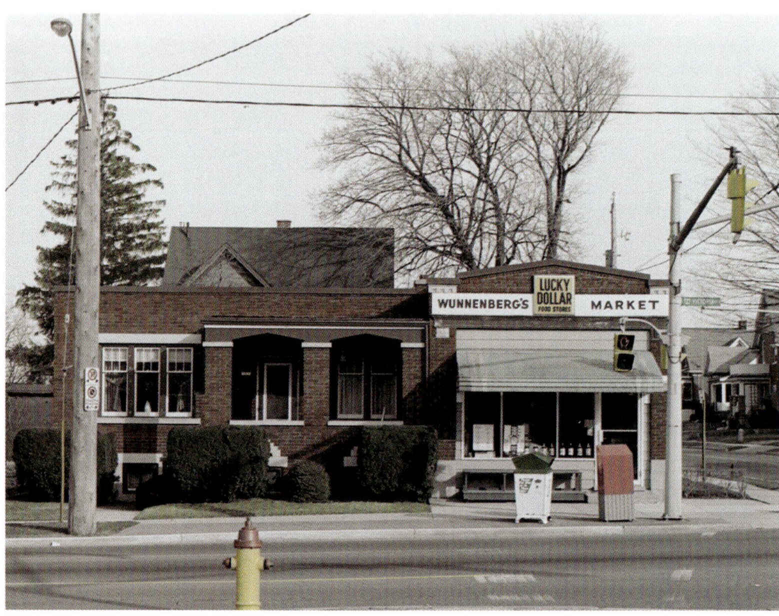
WUNNENBERG'S
LUCKY
DOLLAR
FOOD STORES
MARKET

CONTENTS

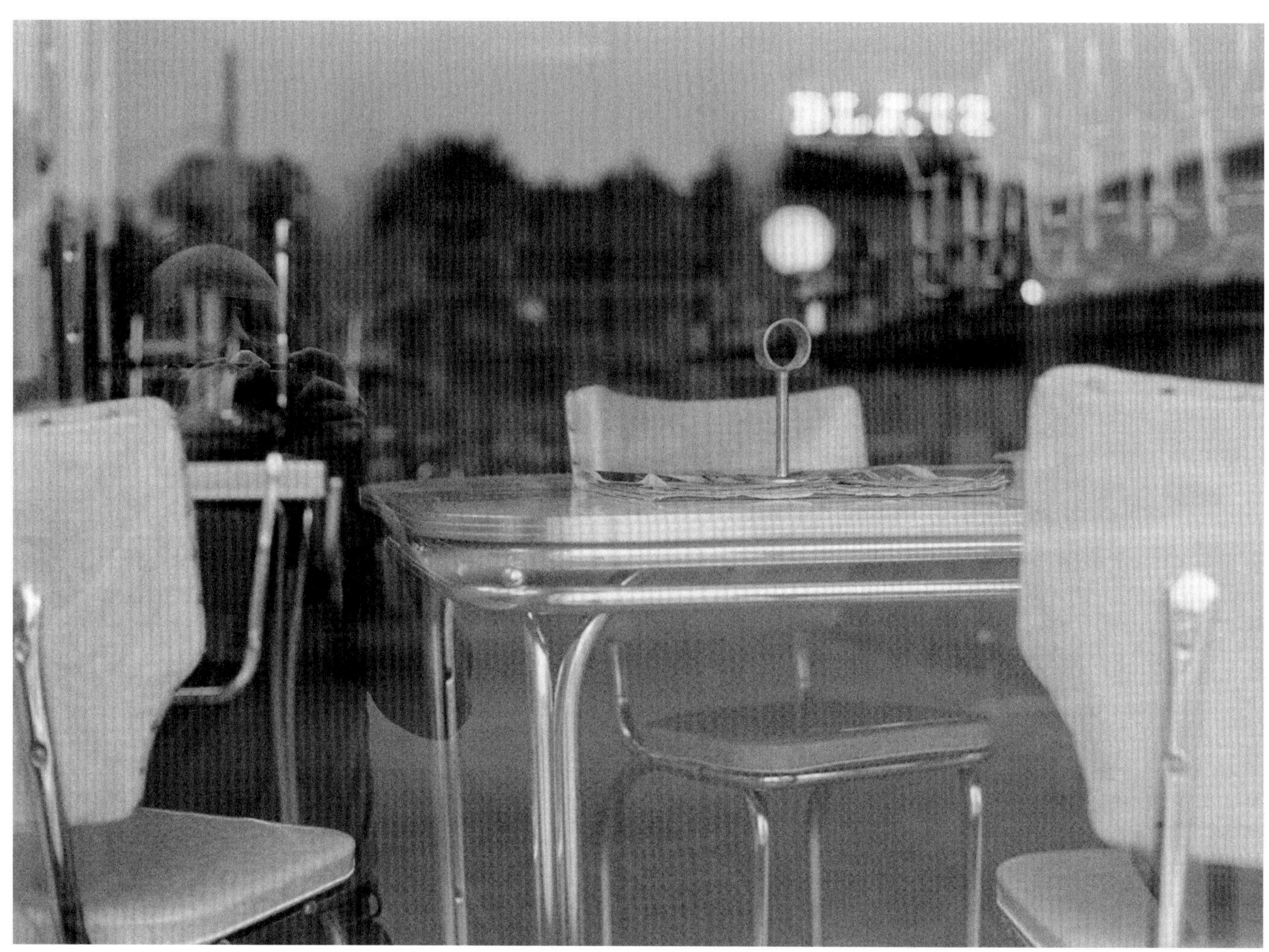

Author's reflection in the window of Ethel's Lounge, Waterloo. 1994

AUTHOR'S NOTE

Philippe Elsworthy

I have arranged this set of photos in a rough geographical form—Waterloo Region from north to south, following the course of what was called the Great Road long ago by the first settlers, known also as Highway 8 and King Street, and now the Central Transit Corridor. But there are some outliers. I have also tried to represent industrial, commercial, and residential buildings and streetscapes, and I have included a few photos in which I have attempted to show the landforms. I have referred to communities which are now part of Cambridge by their former names of Preston and Galt. The amalgamated City of Cambridge and the Regional Municipality of Waterloo were both formed in 1973. I refer to events including building constructions which

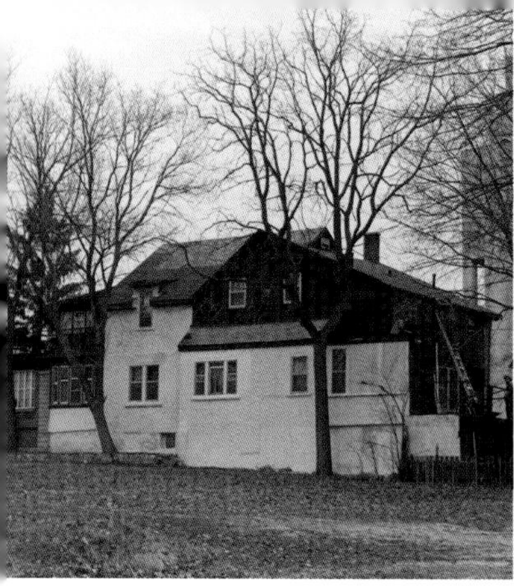

occurred before 1973 as taking place in Waterloo County. The images were originally recorded on black-and-white film, colour film, colour slides, and on several digital cameras. For consistency, since the majority started out as monochrome images, I have turned the colour images to monochrome, and then coloured them.

I have approached photography in much the same way as I have woodworking, which is to say, thinking of myself as a folk artist, and grasping opportunities as they appeared, without a lot of planning. Some images are the result of going to sites to capture specific scenes, such as a building about to be demolished, but I have almost always carried a camera with me, so most images are the result of a chance encounter with an appealing scene, whether walking to and from work, out for a bike ride exploring Kitchener-Waterloo, or driving to my parents' home in Galt, for example. As I continued to read and to study over the years, my knowledge has increased, and my ideas have become refined. My goal with these photos is to encourage people to look at their surroundings and to see them with a sharper eye.

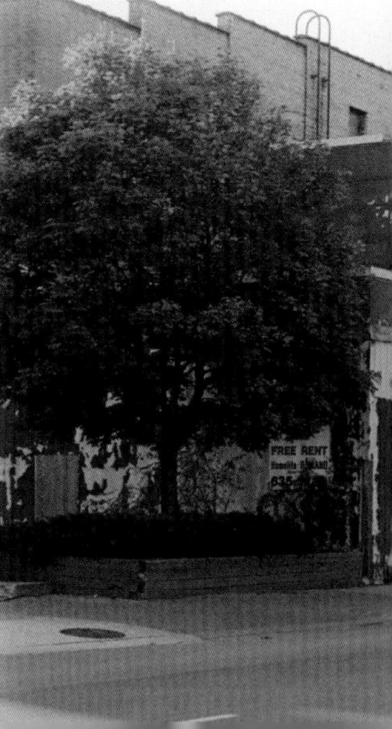

Although I haven't photographed people, I am preoccupied with the setting or place(s) that foster community, and in some cases, the places that hinder the flourishing of community (like the above-ground walkway on a Kitchener parking garage). I believe that community and place are intrinsically and vitally connected. A person's "sense of place," such as mine, for instance, is likely to be shared with many others, if only subconsciously. The sharing of place and life binds people together.

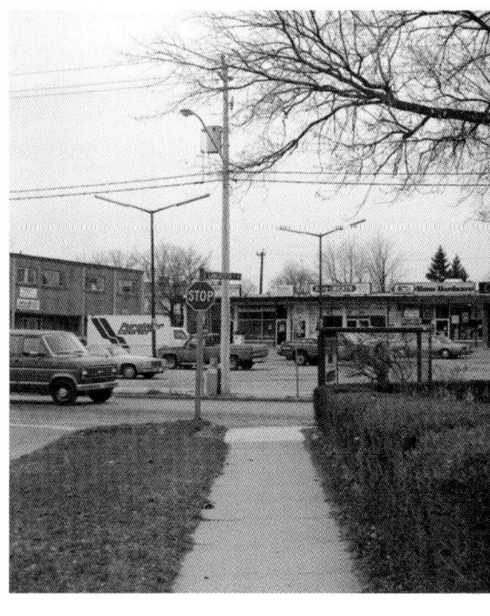

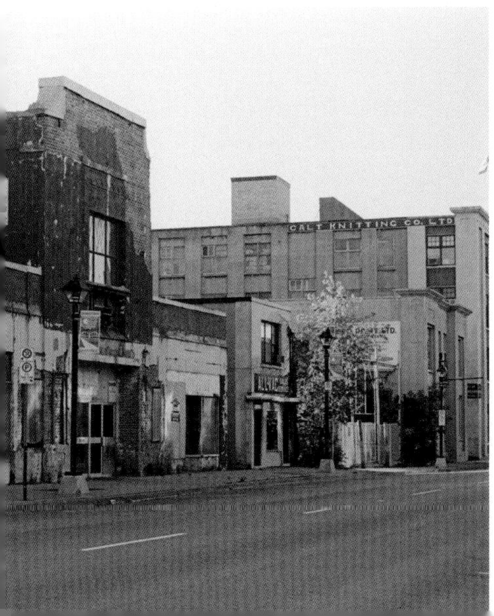

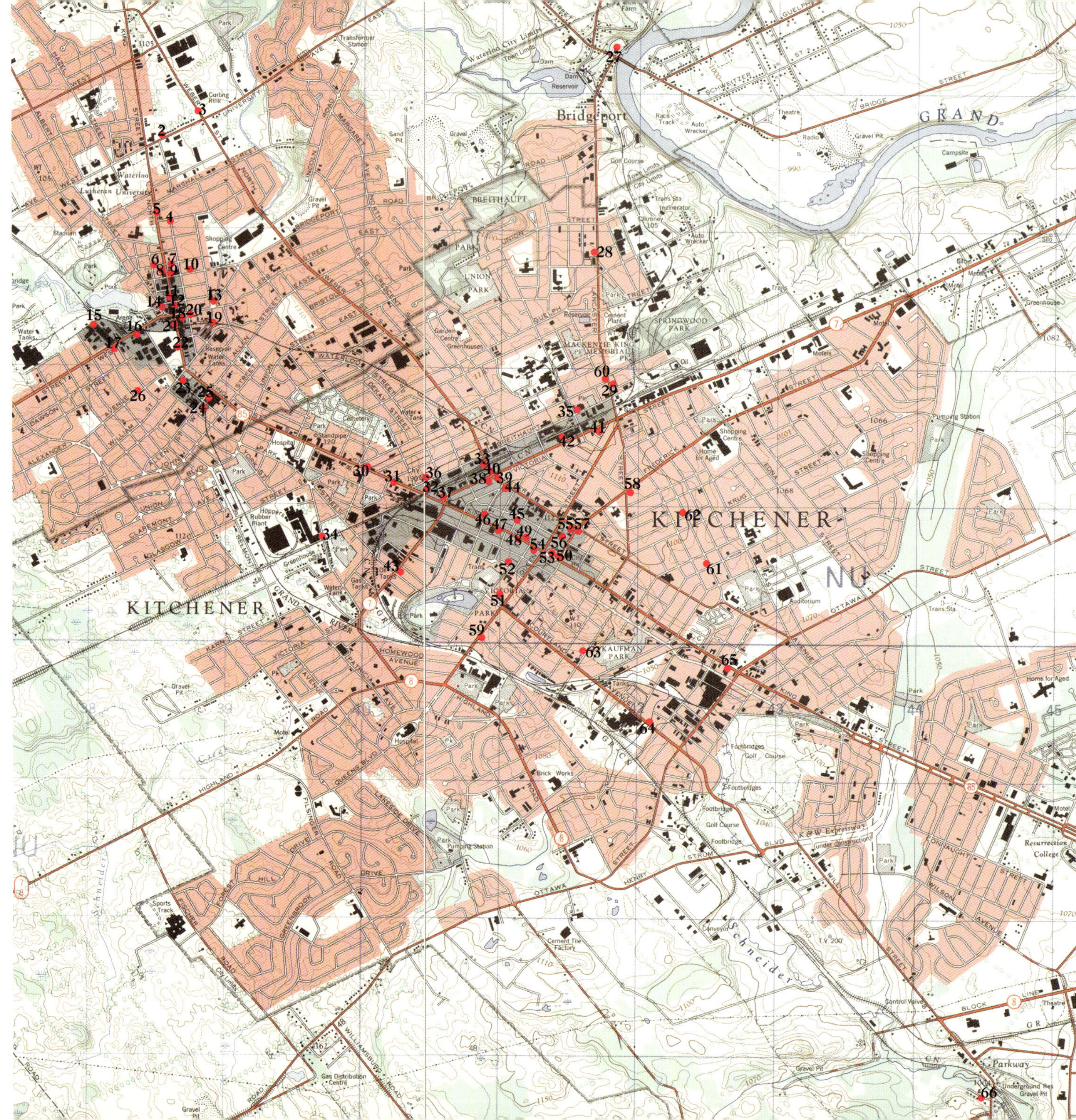

LIST OF PHOTOS / MAP 1

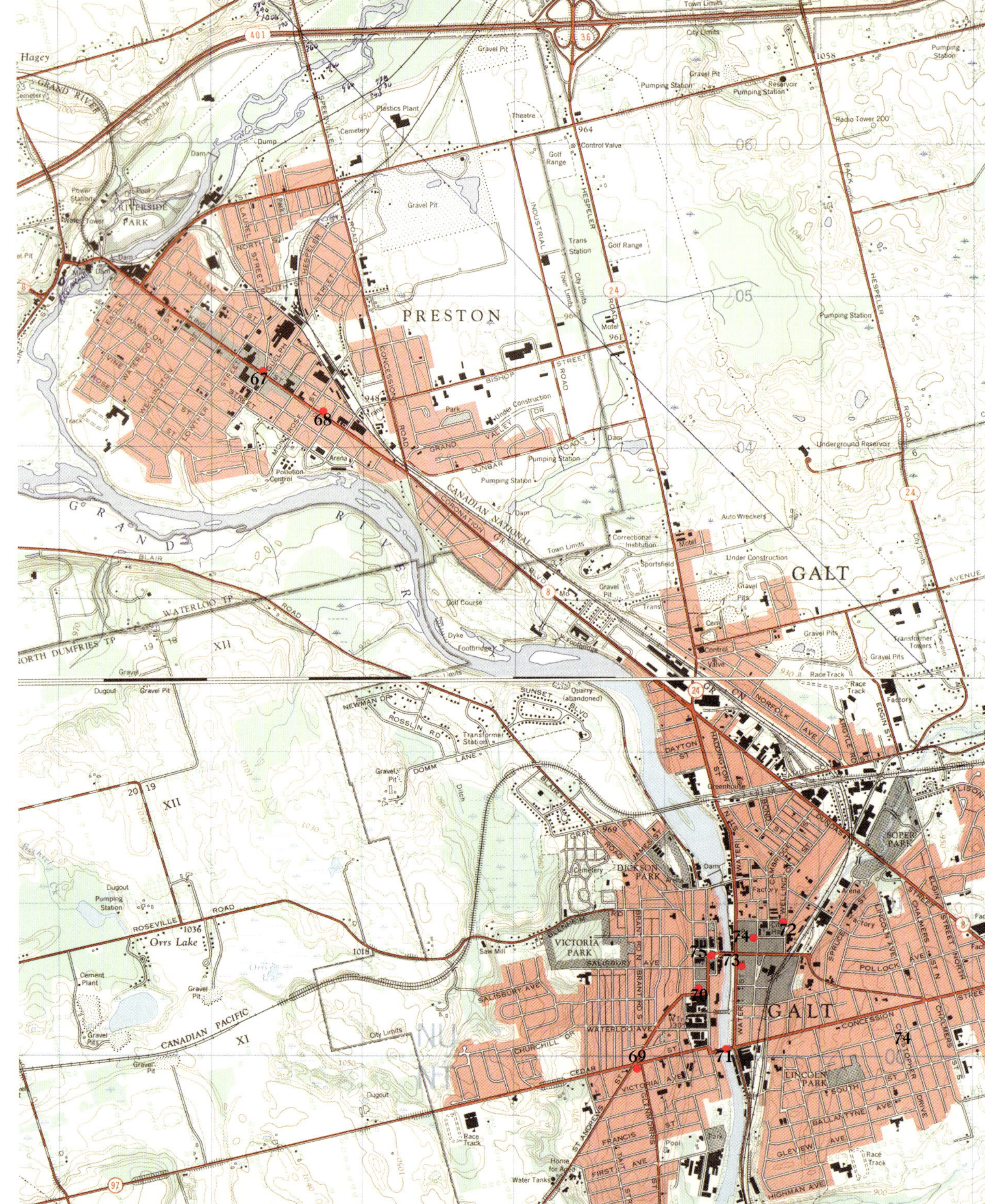

Base maps cropped from Surveys and Mapping Branch, Department of Energy, Mines and Resources, sheets 40P/7h, /8c, /8e, /8f, printed 1968 and 1969. Sourced from the University of Western Ontario Map Library.

LIST OF PHOTOS / MAP 2

PHOTOGRAPHS

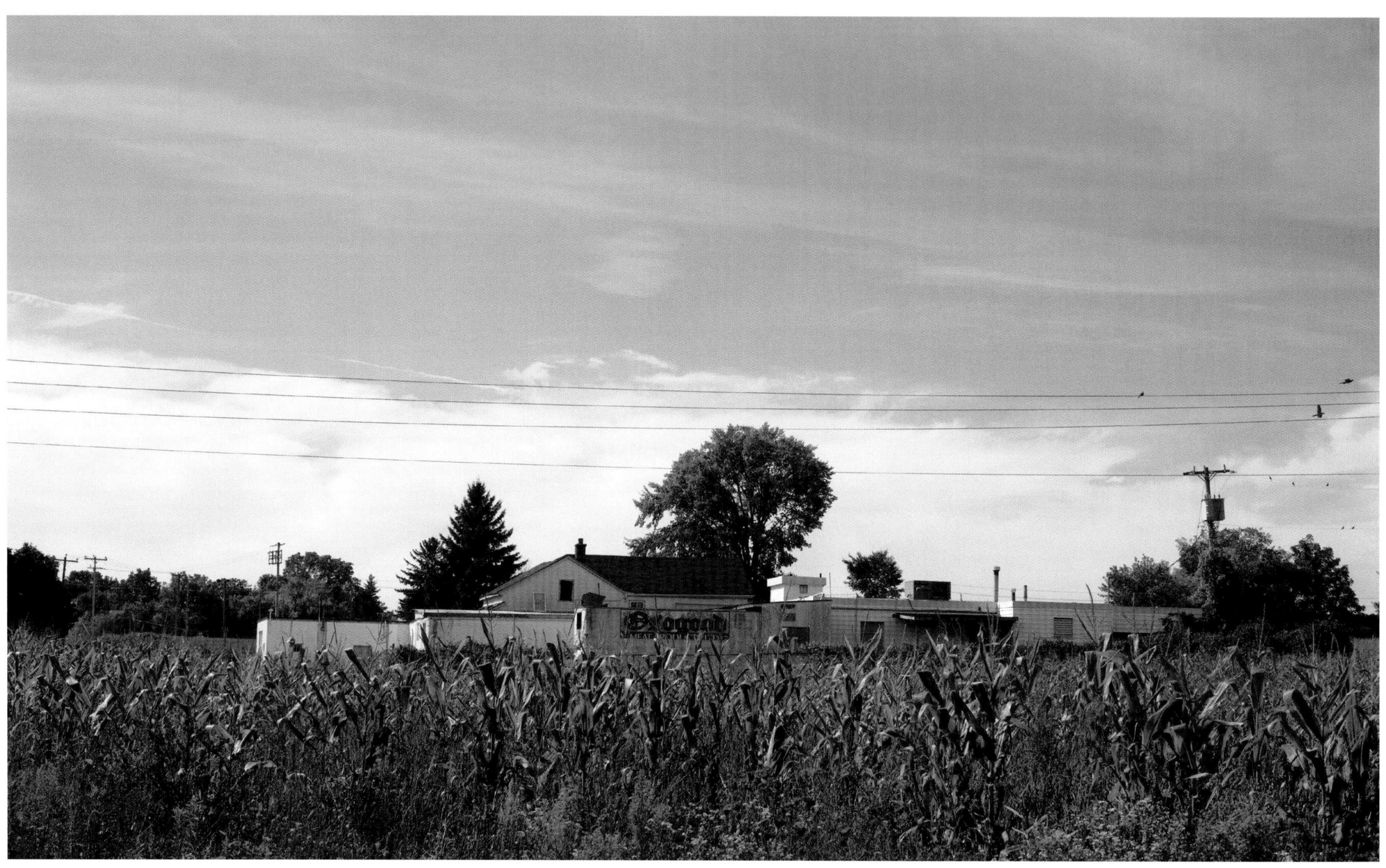

1 | **Osogood Meat Products** *(demolished) (not shown on map)*

Osogood Meat Products was established on Wismer Road in 1968 by Austrians Helen and Helmuth Koller, who had immigrated to Canada in 1961. They were at the Kitchener Market for forty years or so. In 1968 this was just off a rural county road, Woolwich Road, and the location was described as "vacant" rural land. Now it is being developed as suburbs. The company has been taken over by son Mike, rebranded as Nith Valley Butcher and Deli and moved to New Hamburg.

2014

2 | Dearborn Auto Refinishers

The Dearborn Auto Refinishers shop was located at the corner of what is today Regina and University. At the end of World War II this area was on the edge of town and was just being developed in the 1950s. Veterans' housing was being built on the northwest side of University and King, starting in 1947, and there were a few Victory houses along the former Schneider's Road, now University Avenue. Schneider's Road was undoubtedly named for Casper Schneider, who lived at the end of it. By 1951, when Dearborn Road, which ran west from Albert Street, was joined to Schneider's Road, the whole road was known as Dearborn for a while before being renamed University Avenue.

1995

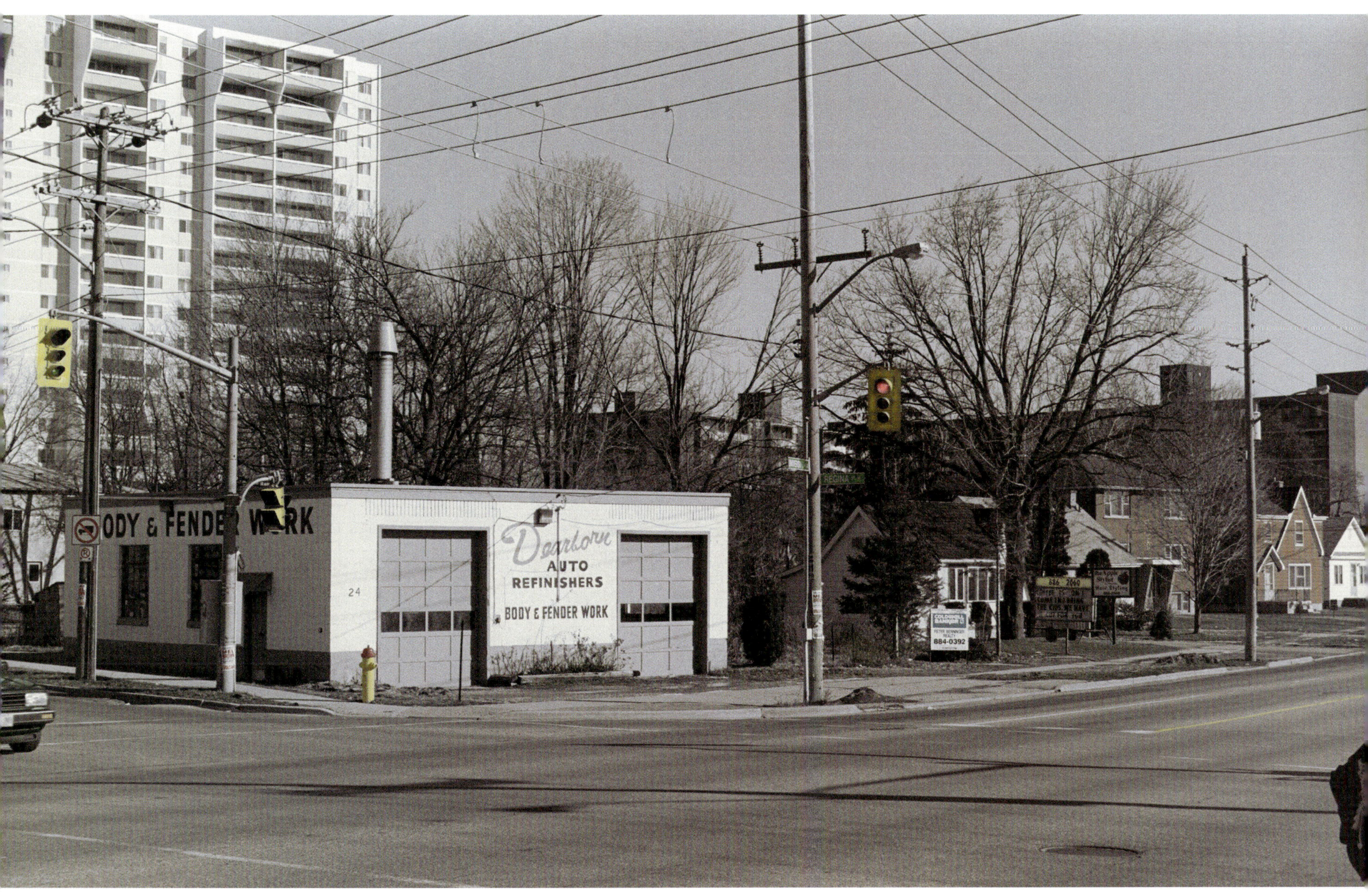

ODY & FENDER WORK
Dearborn
AUTO
REFINISHERS
BODY & FENDER WORK
24
884-0392

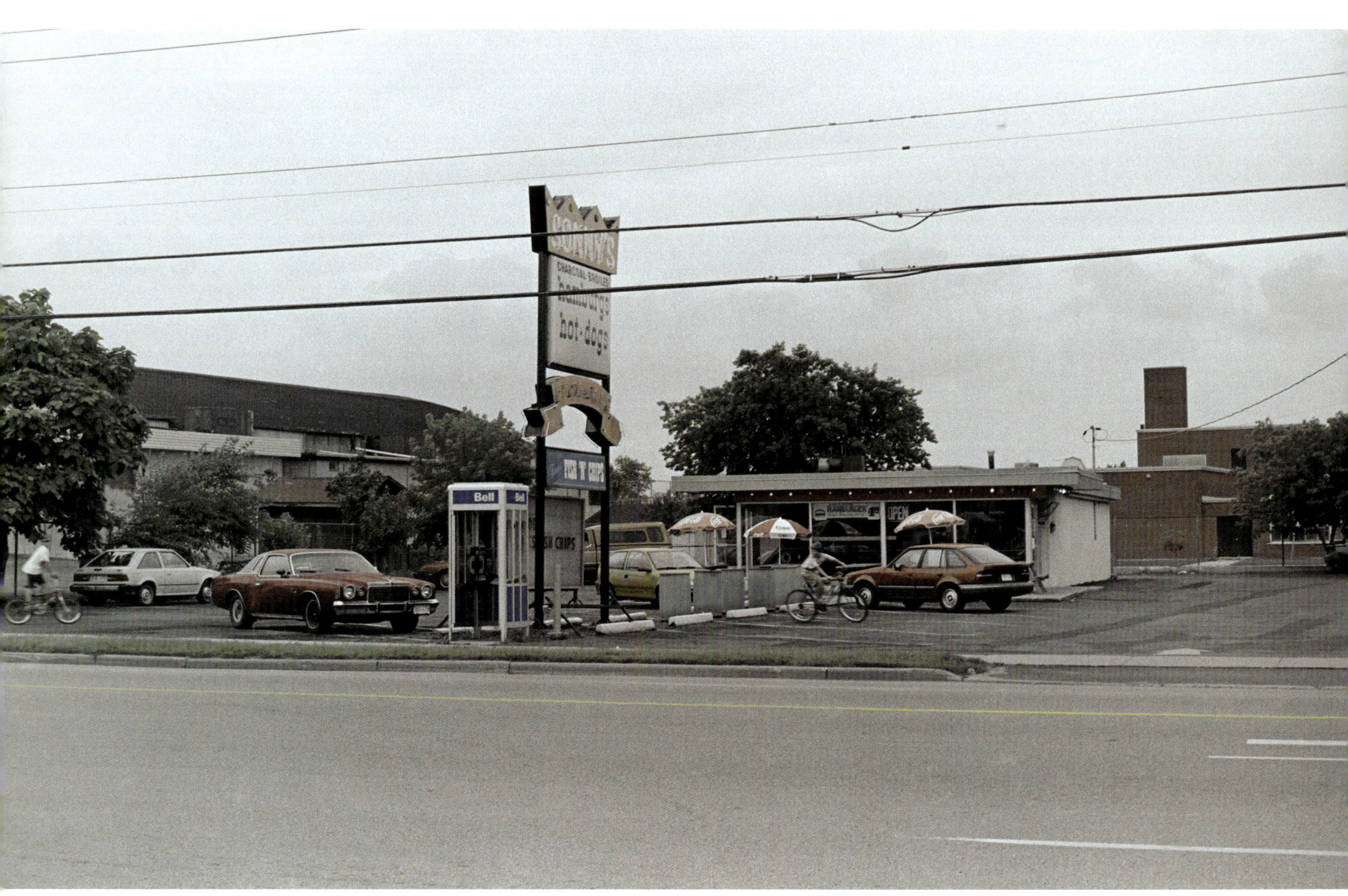
SONNY'S
CHARCOAL BROILED
hot-dogs
FISH 'N' CHIPS
Bell
Bell
OPEN
HAMBURGER

3 | Sonny's

Sonny's is still on Weber Street just north of University Avenue. At one time, before there was a Harvey's or McDonald's in Waterloo, Sonny's was the only drive-in fast-food joint near the universities where you could go for a late-night hamburger. Next door the Glenbriar Home Hardware, established there in 1977, was originally the Glenbriar Curling Rink. The phone booth is no longer there.

1993

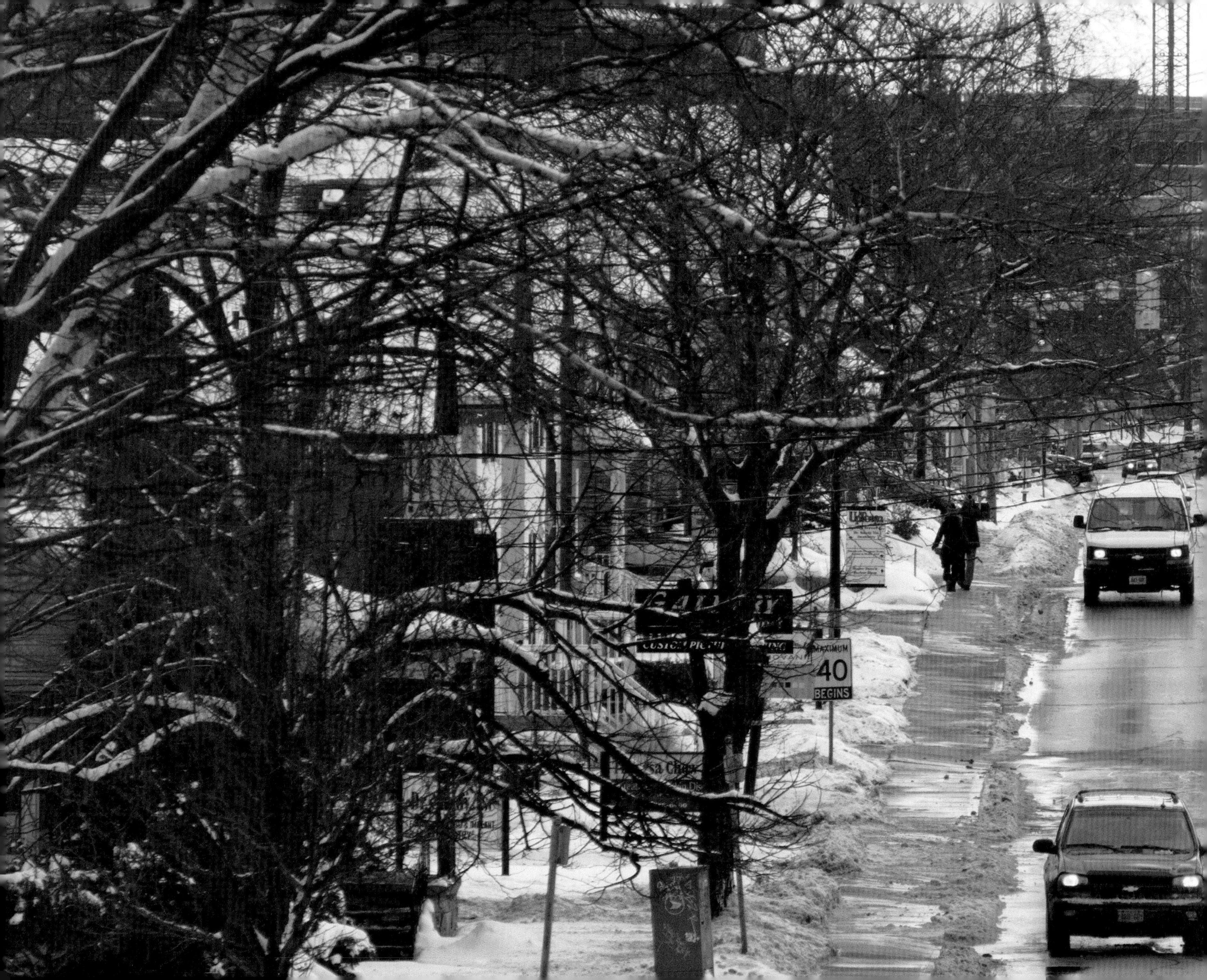
MAXIMUM
40
BEGINS

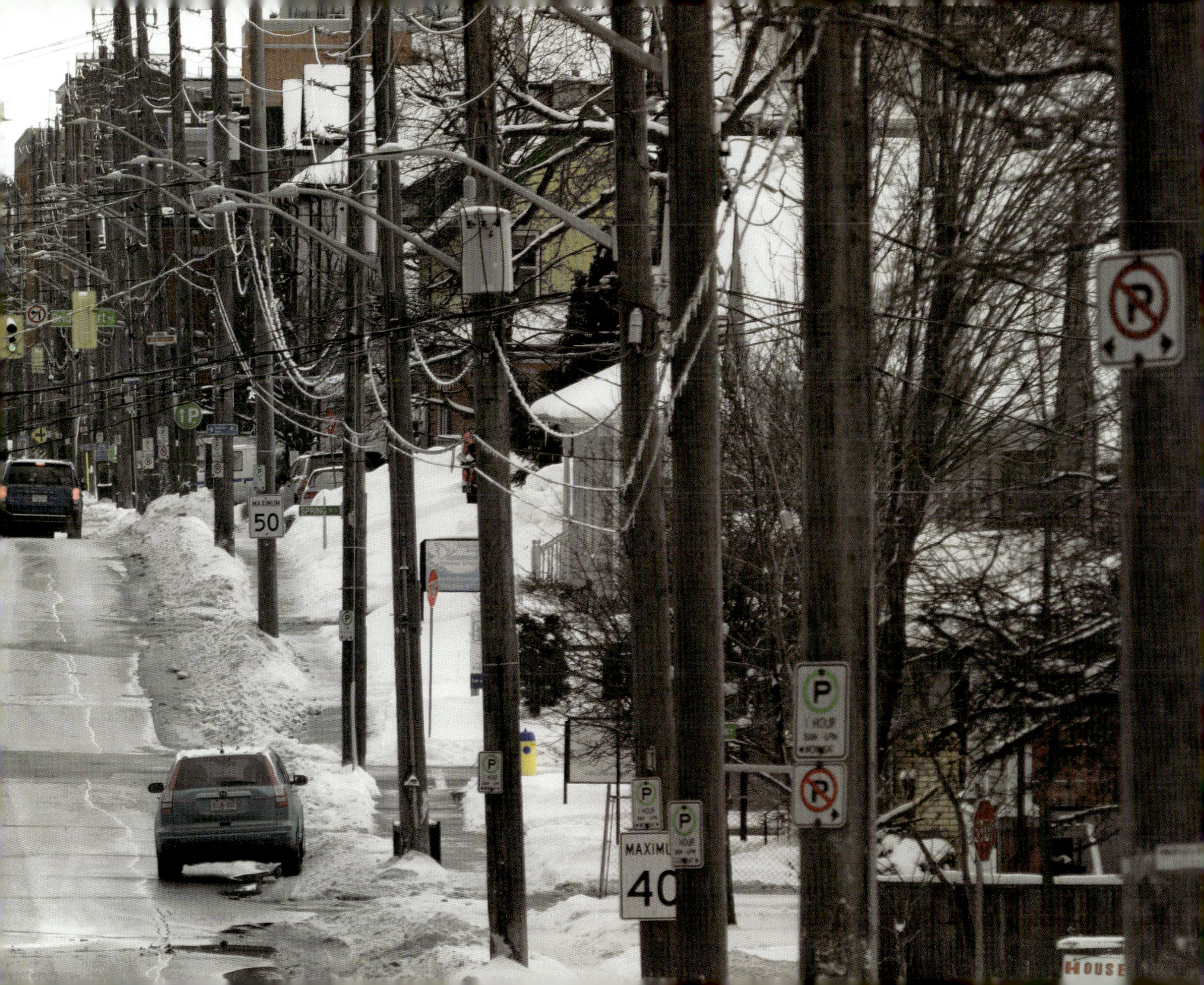
MAXIMUM
50
P
1 HOUR
40

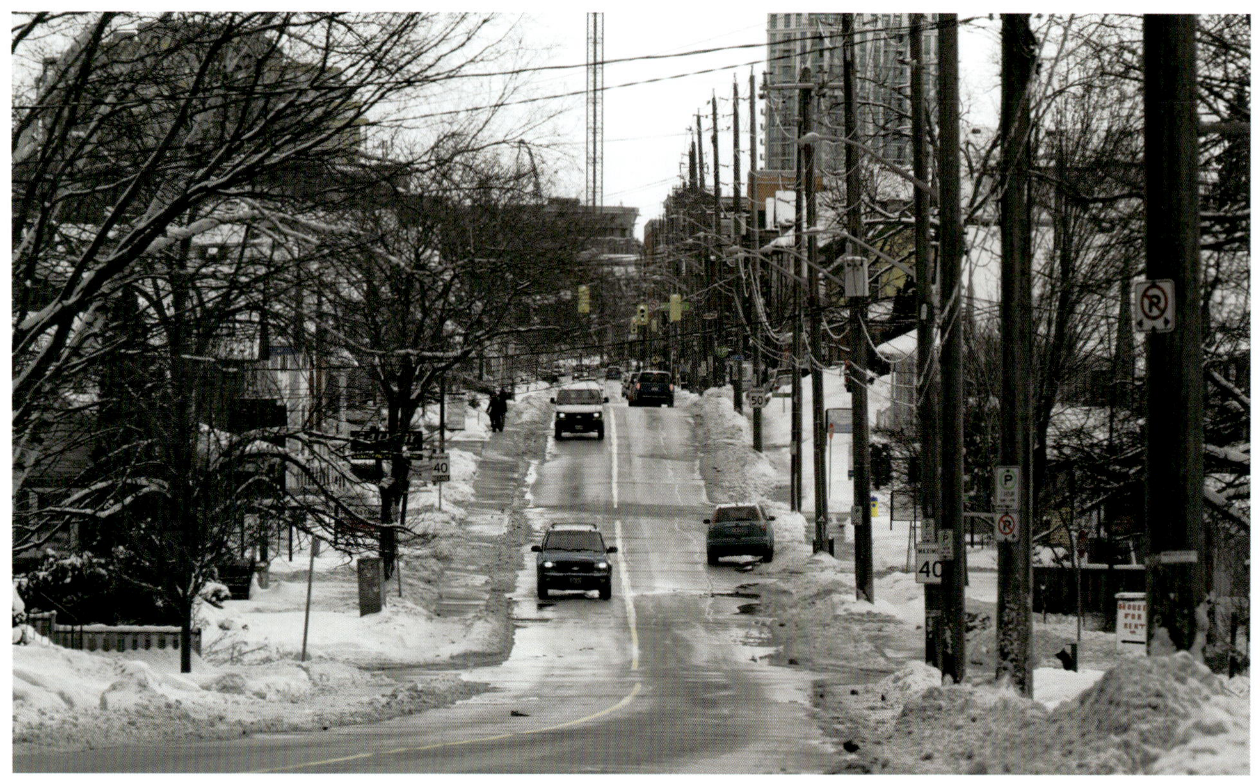

4 | Regina Street

The view south from the former end of Regina Street at Noecker shows the hilly terrain of uptown Waterloo. Regina Street, originally known as Queen Street, was part of Waterloo's first survey and first neighbourhood. To the east, between Laurel Creek and Regina, large "Park Lots" were surveyed and likely used as pasture land.

2018

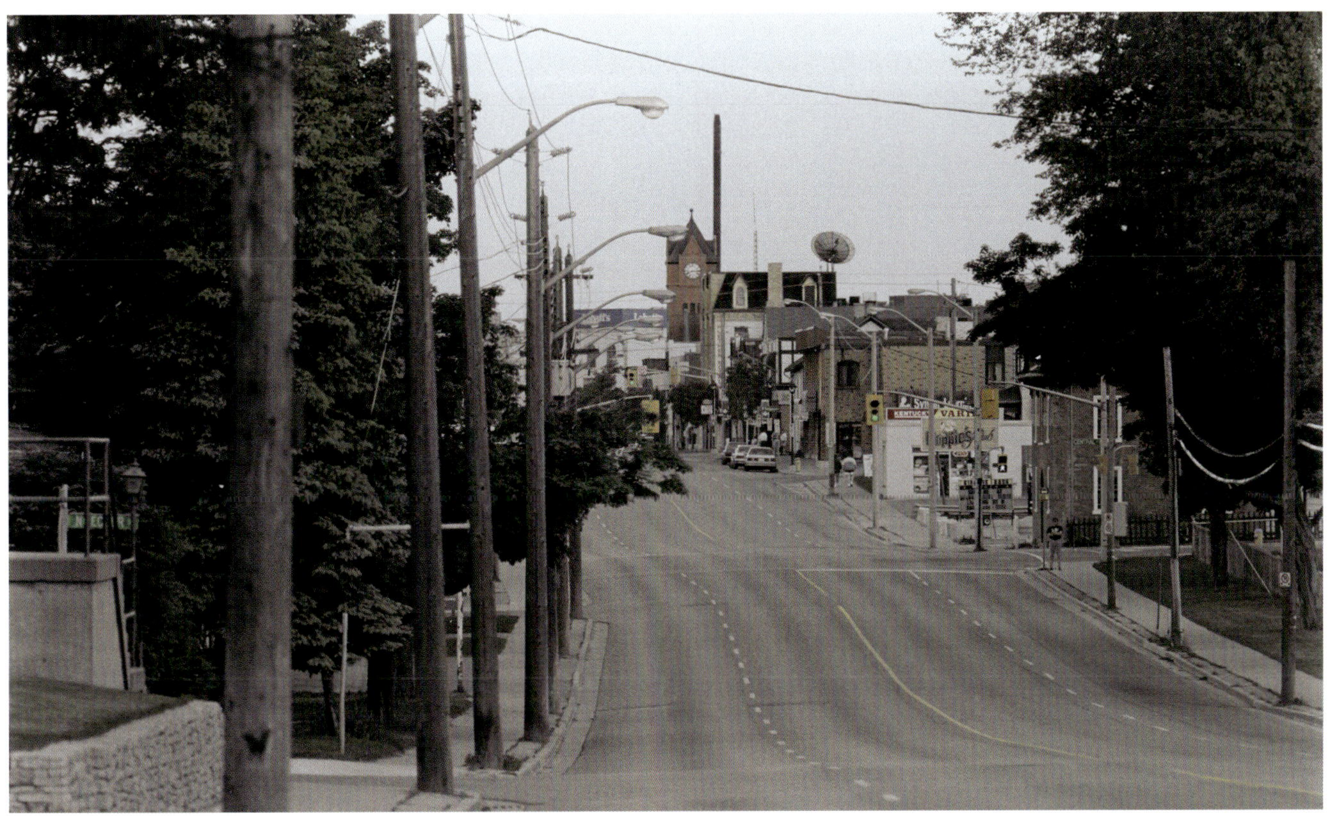

5 | Uptown: King Street from James

Looking south from James Street into the valley of Laurel Creek, you can just see in the distance the Labatt's brewery, formerly the Kuntz brewery (now the location of the Chartwell Terrace on the Square), which stood behind the old Hoffman's public square at King and William. A prominent landmark is the Huether Hotel with its mansard roof and dormers. Just beyond that, the clock tower of the old post office overlooks the city.

1993

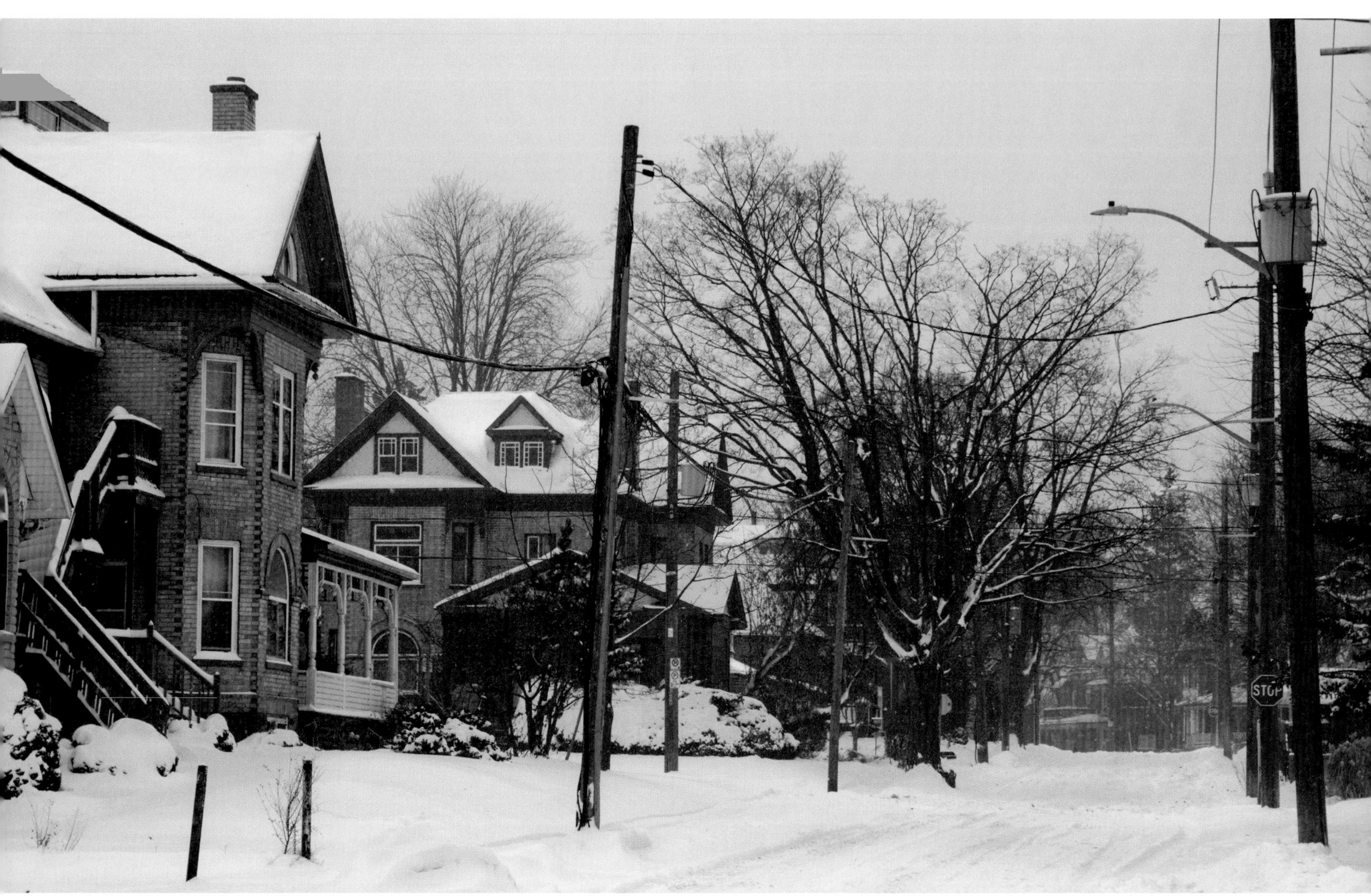
STOP

6 | Young Street West, Waterloo

Two grand Queen Anne houses on Dorset Street in Waterloo's oldest neighbourhood stand out among more modest homes, looking west towards Waterloo Park. This neighbourhood, now a Heritage Conservation District, was surveyed and settled from the 1830s and gradually infilled up to the present. On the far (west) side of Dorset, "Bon Accord" was built c. 1902, and on the near corner, "Braeside" was built c. 1896.

2017

7 | Young Street East, Excalibur Books

I would often visit this bookshop, but never found a treasure there. It was in the back of a grand Italianate house on Young Street, east of Regina. The white building behind may have been a coach house or stable. It was clad in sheets of galvanized metal pressed to look like brick. I think the car parked in back was a '63 Oldsmobile 88.

1994

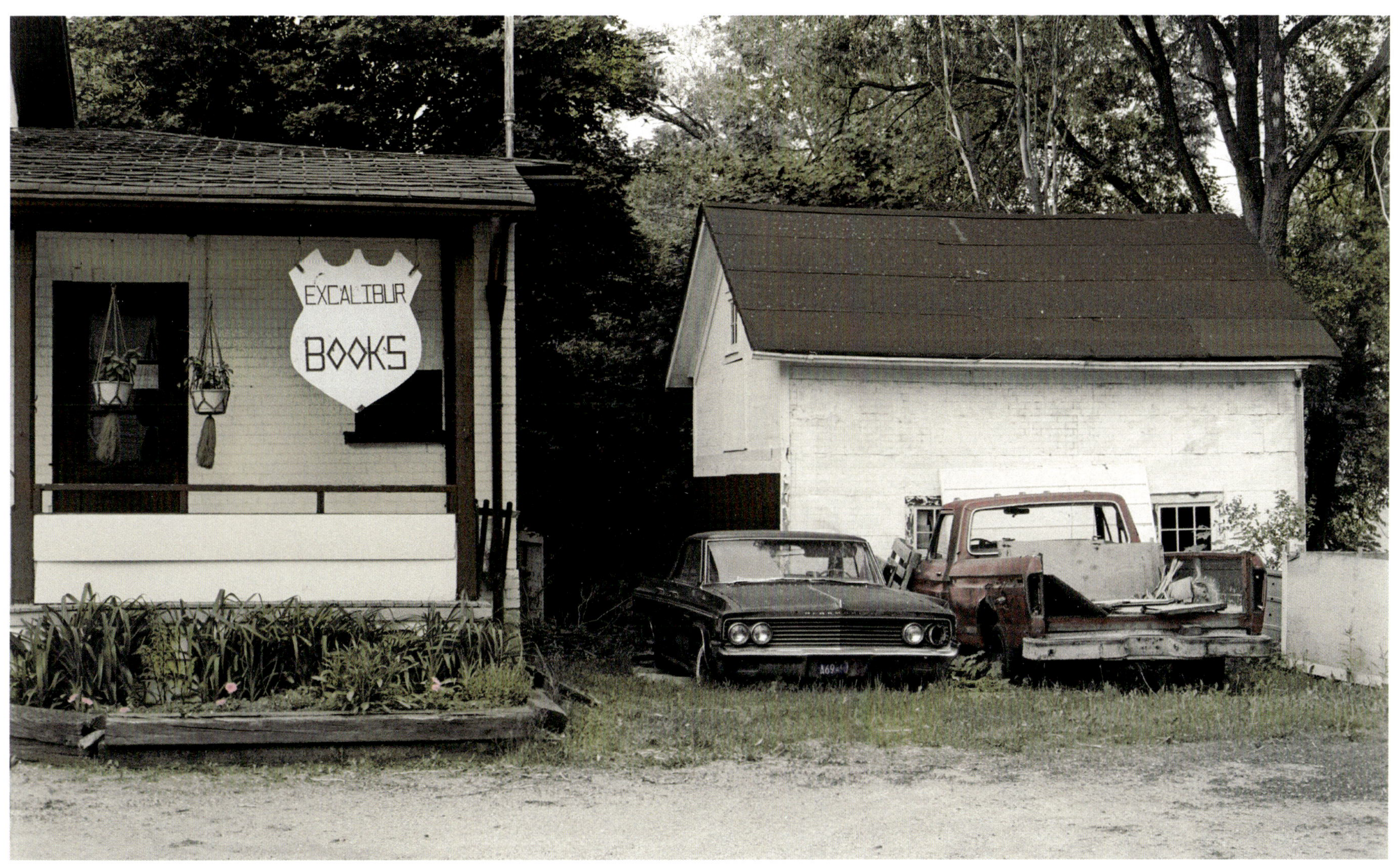
EXCALIBUR
BOOKS

8 | 85 King Street North

This is a rare remaining example of a banked building in the City of Waterloo and the region, built into the hillside behind it. The Pennsylvania Germans took advantage of the existing landscape form when able. A banked house will allow access to a basement which will stay cool in summer, while also providing access to a second floor from the outside. The surveyed lot was purchased in 1854 by John Seitz, a shoemaker. At the time of this photo it had just ceased to be a residence and was being converted to an Irish pub called Failte.

1997

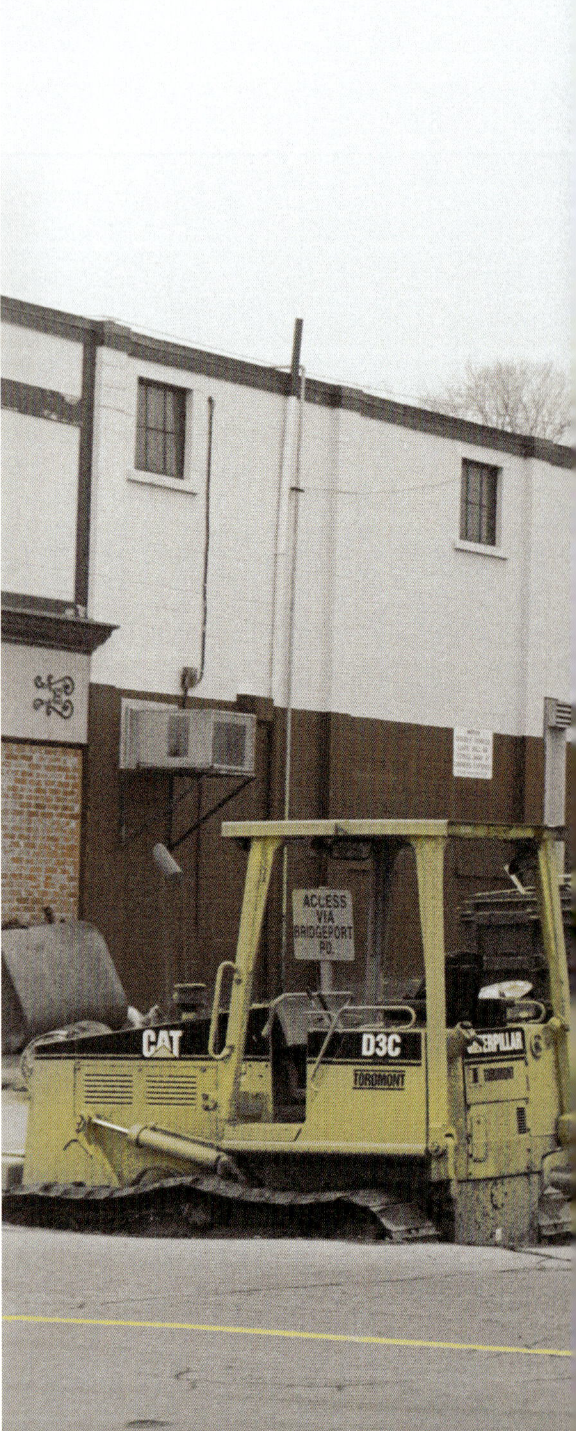

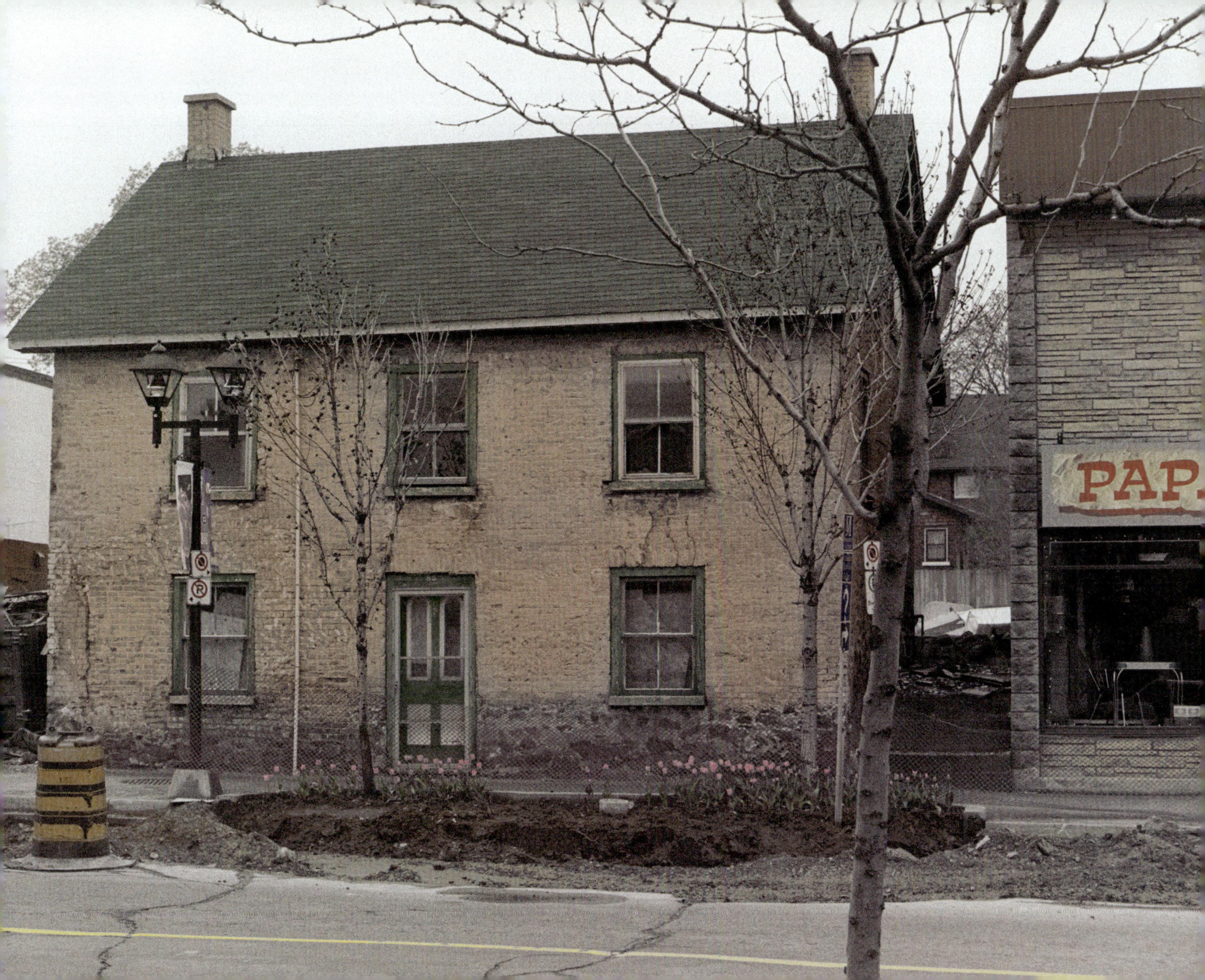
PAP

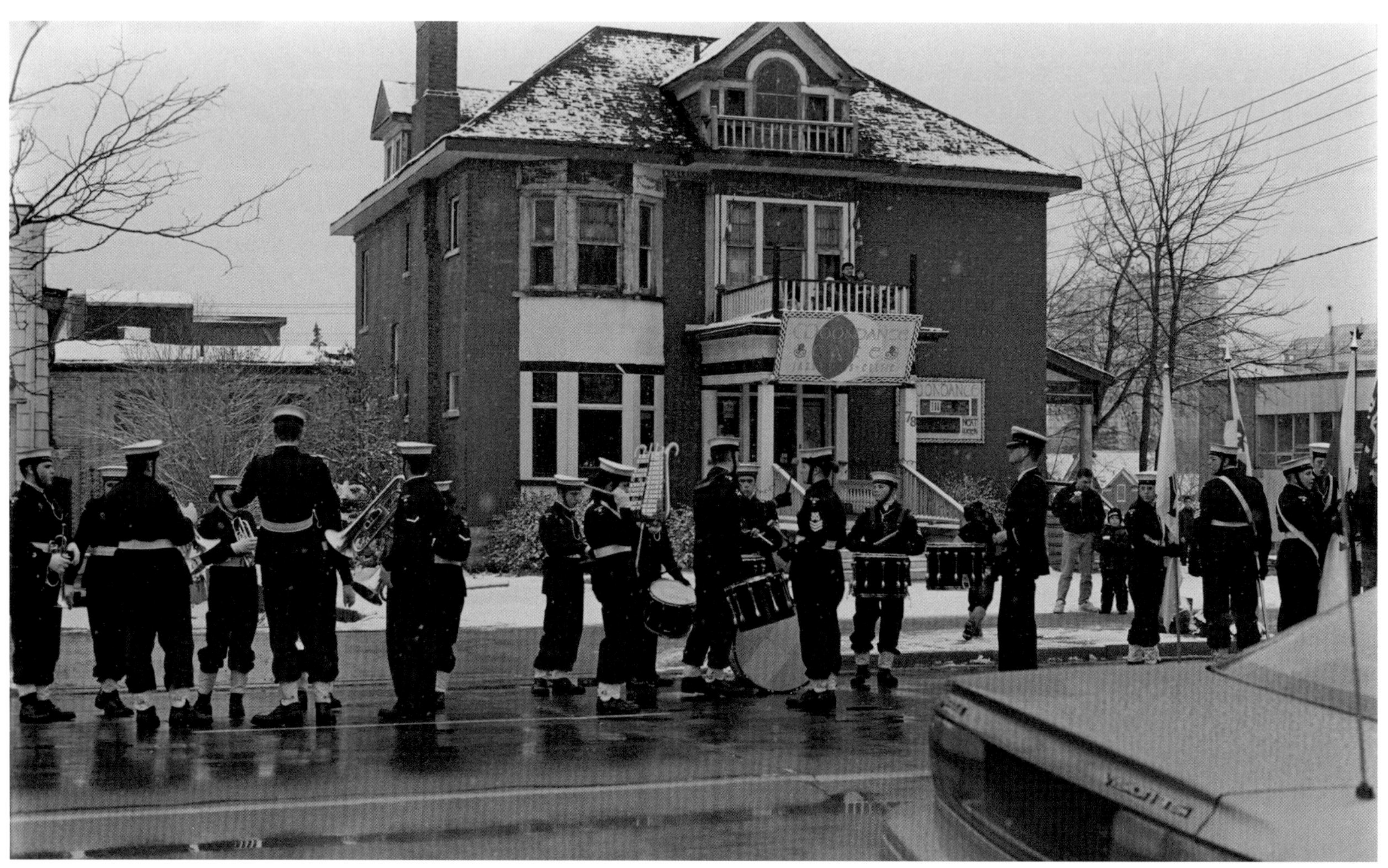

9 | Moondance, King Street at Bridgeport

For some years the Moondance Café was a centre for local music thanks to support of the proprietor, Lou Wright. Besides hosting jazz, it was the scene of the first traditional Irish music session in the region. This is Lot 13, East of King in the Jacob C and Elias Snider Survey. In 1906, Theresa Kuntz bought the property from John Letter, a well-known local house builder. She was the widow of Louis Kuntz, the brewer. On the street the naval cadets were organizing for the Santa Claus parade.

1995

10 | 34 Bridgeport Road East (*demolished*)

I missed seeing the demolition of the stuccoed Georgian building in the foreground. A typical four-bay Pennsylvania-German building, once the common building type in Waterloo County, it was wood under the stucco, according to fire insurance maps. Throughout Waterloo County buildings of this style were built of timber frame, stone, and brick.

1995

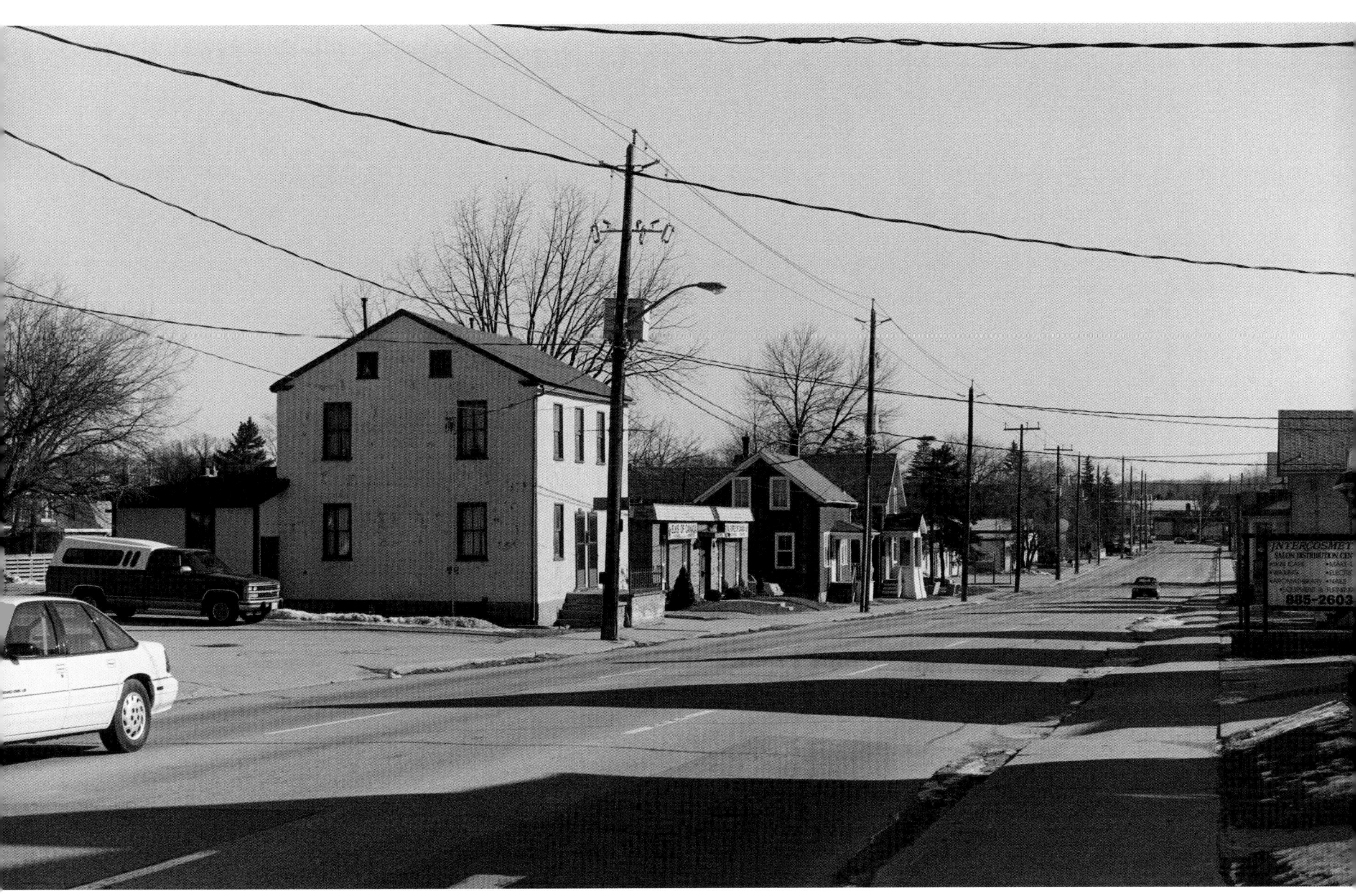
INTERCOSMET
885-2603

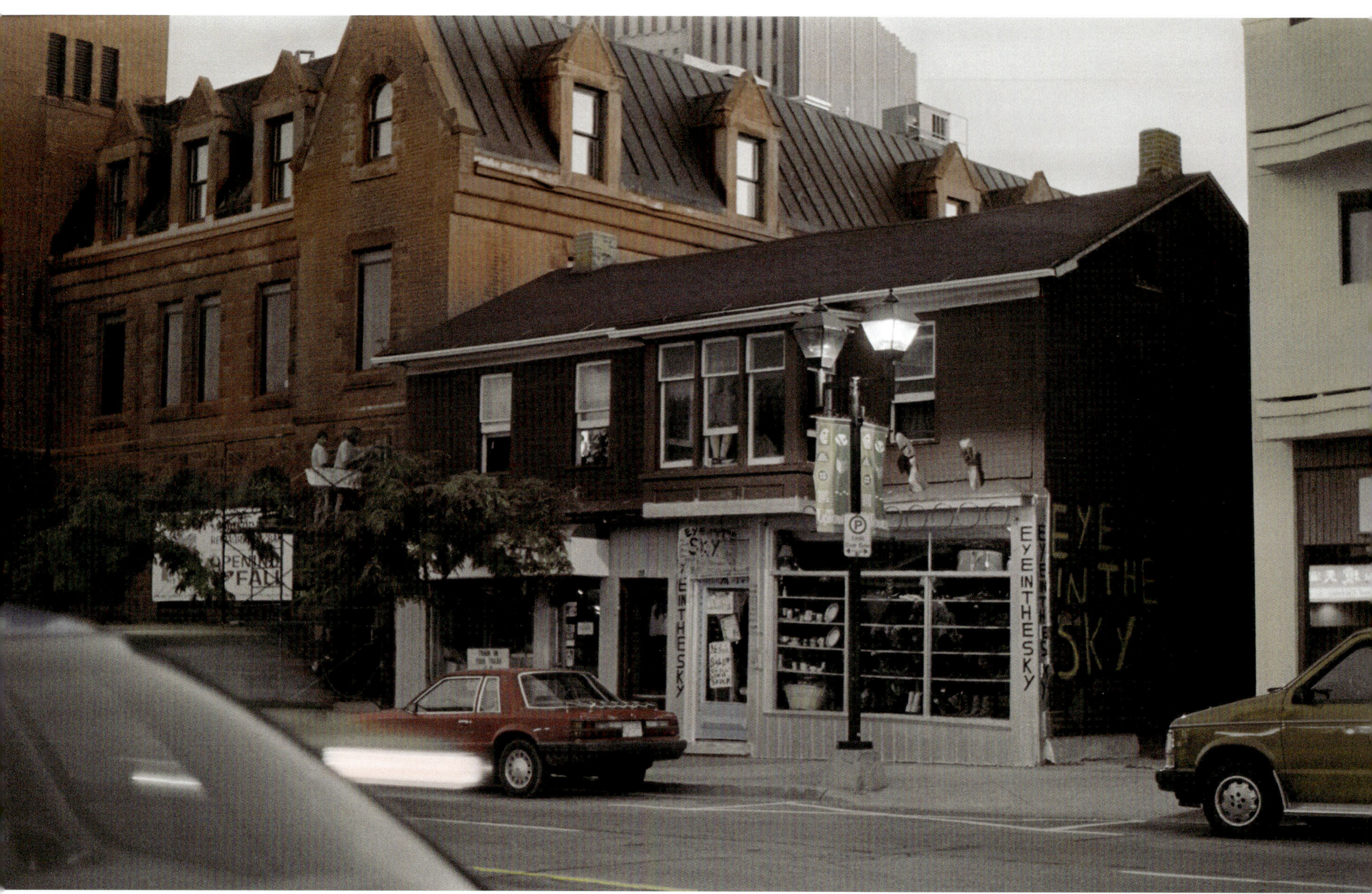
EYE IN THE SKY
EYE IN THE SKY
EYE IN THE SKY

11 | 37-41 King Street North *(destroyed by fire)*

This timber frame building at 37-41 King Street North was from an era when this was the typical building style in Waterloo. It has the paired attic windows common in Pennsylvania-German houses. When the site was cleared after the building was destroyed by fire in August 2012, it was apparent that there was no basement—just a small cold cellar. This is Lot 6, West of King in the Snider survey and was occupied in the 1837 Gore District assessment by John Hett. As yet, I've been unable to find land title records from that period.

1995

12 | Waterloo Theatre and Uptown Waterloo

It was a drizzly fall evening on my walk home from work. For 13 years I walked home from my cabinetmaking shop on Victoria Street North to Fountain Street. During that time I explored every possible route. This particular evening, I stepped into the doorway at 10 King Street North for a little respite from the rain. In the distance once again is the Huether Hotel seen from the south.

1991

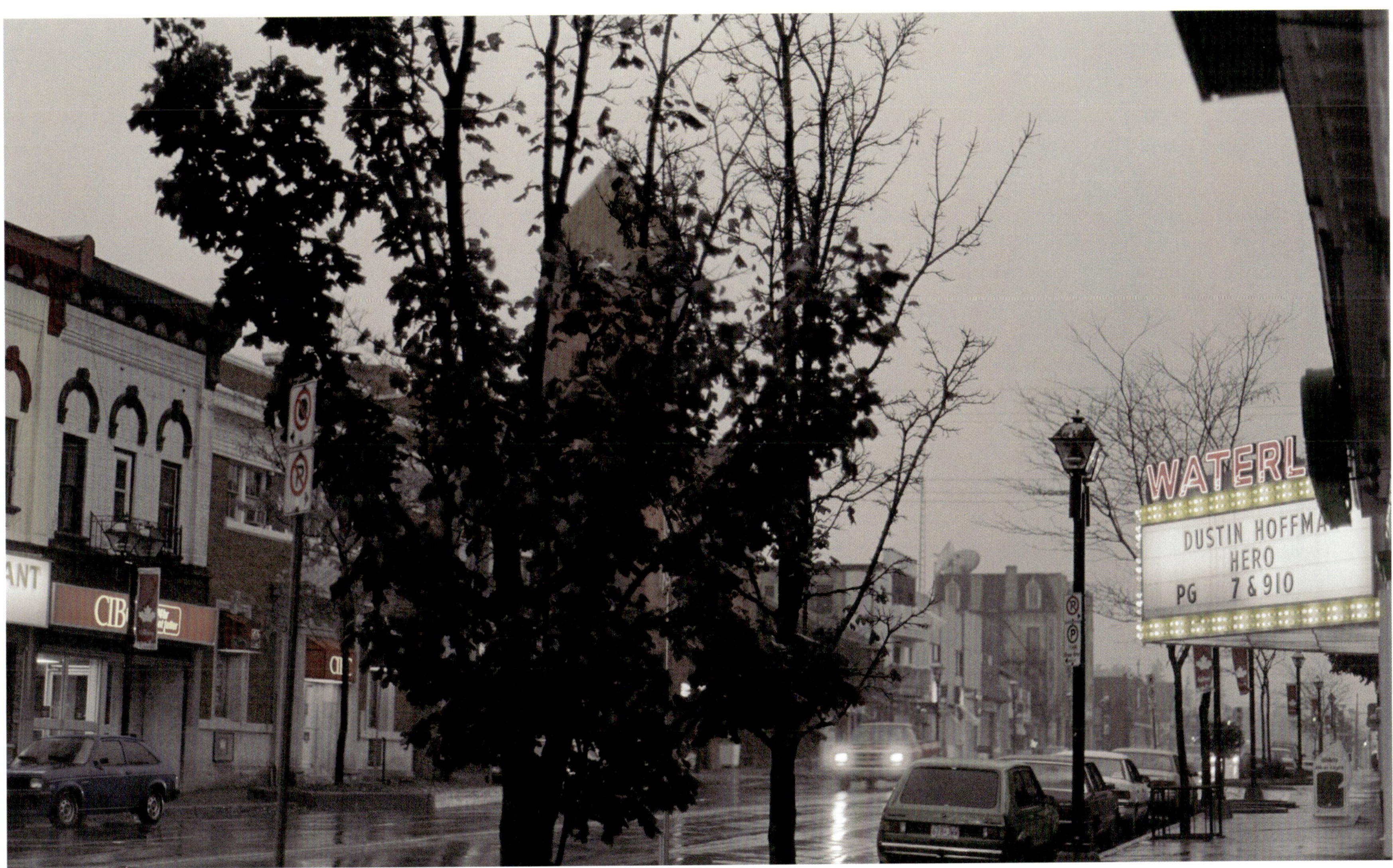

WATERL
DUSTIN HOFFMA
HERO
PG 7 & 910

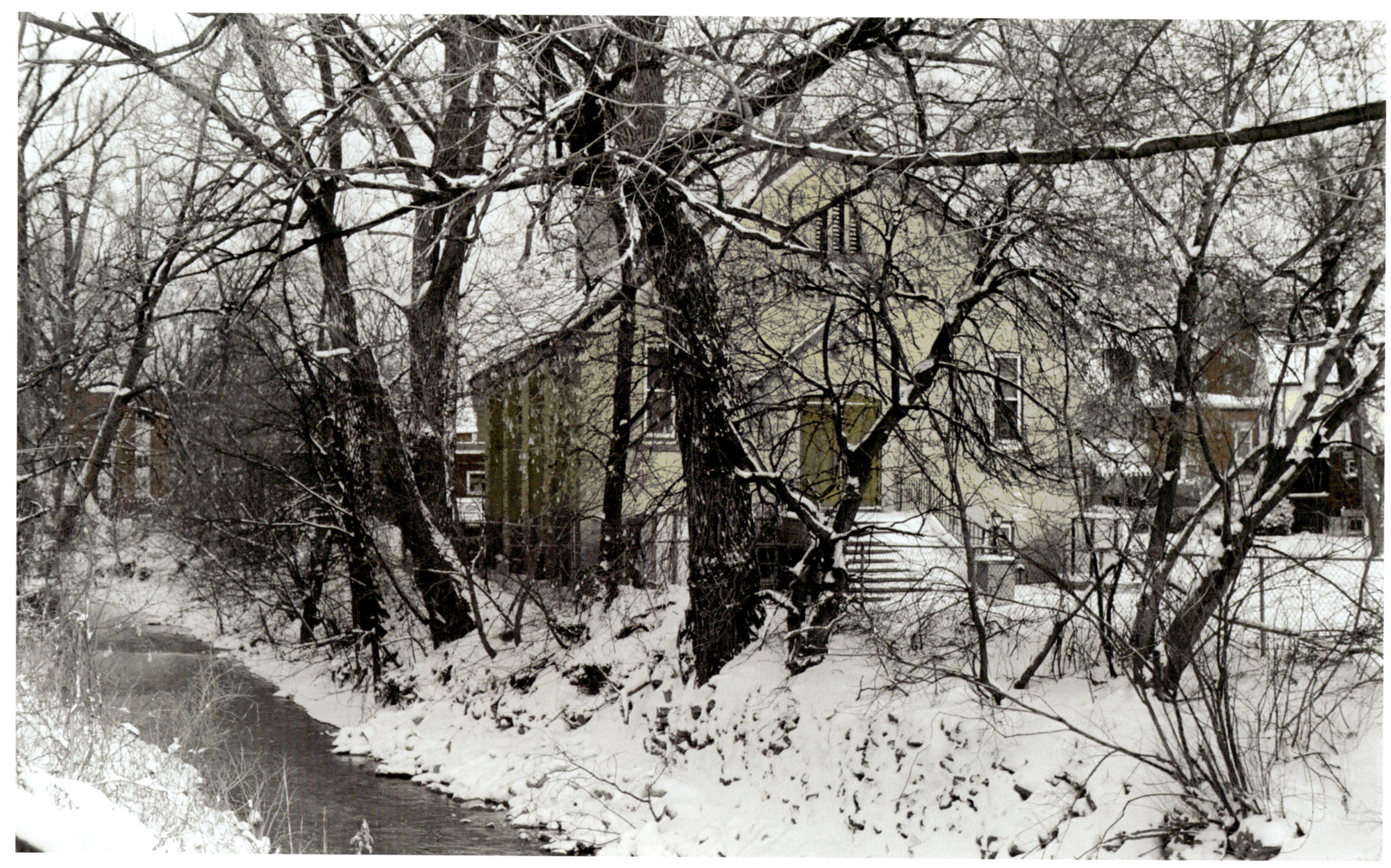

13 | Bethel Chapel on Laurel Street

When I took this photograph in 1992, this was the point at which Laurel Creek emerged from a concrete canalization into a more natural riparian area just north of Erb Street East. Recently the east bank in this area has been reinforced by a wall of large limestone blocks. Before the Waterloo Square shopping centre was built in 1960, Laurel Creek was open through Uptown. In 1971, when I worked for the City of Waterloo, the creek emerged in a natural state from underneath buildings on King Street.

1992

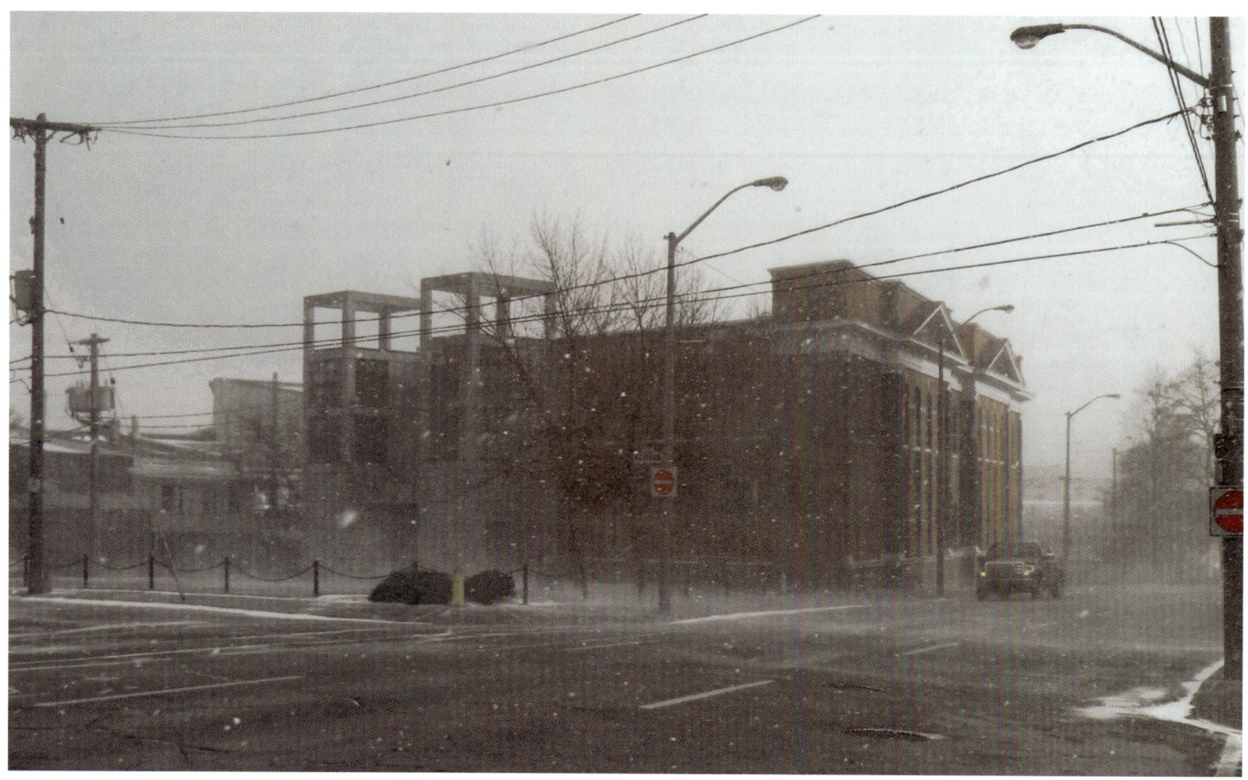

14 | Snow Squall, November

Lower Albert Street experiences a November snow squall. This is my answer to some of the glamorous publicity photos of Waterloo. It's not always sunny; in fact, sometimes it's quite windy, especially at this corner. Constructed in yellow brick by the town engineer Charles Moogk, this building started its life as the office of the Mutual Life Assurance Company of Ontario. It was enlarged considerably with brown brick to more or less its present form by the Dominion Life Assurance Company when they acquired it in 1912. The huge concrete bits on the back were added when the building served as the police station.

2013

15 | Globe Furniture *(demolished)*

Built on the north side of Erb Street about 1911, on land that was fairly wet a hundred years earlier, Globe Furniture was established with tax incentives. It was a landmark, and an employer of highly skilled wood craftsmen whose carving can still found locally, at the Church of the Holy Saviour on Allen Street, for example. It has a metal fire escape and a shaft for a lift between floors.

c.1985

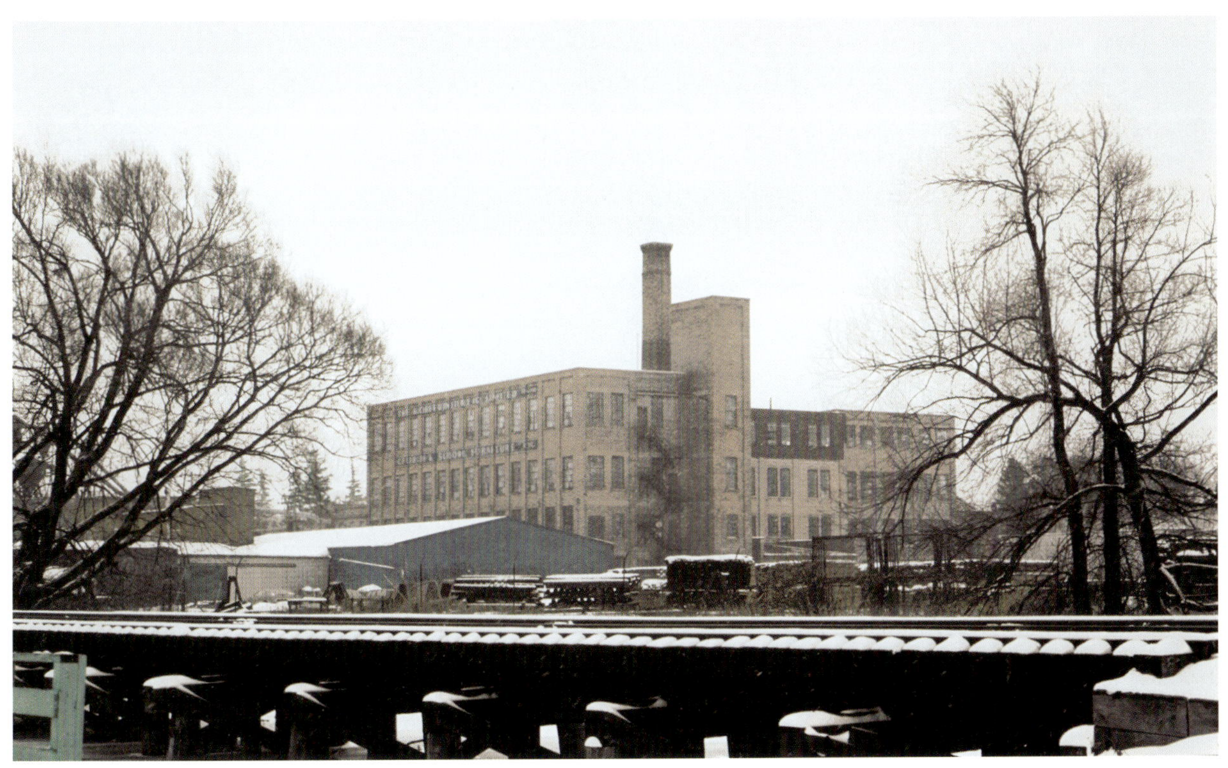

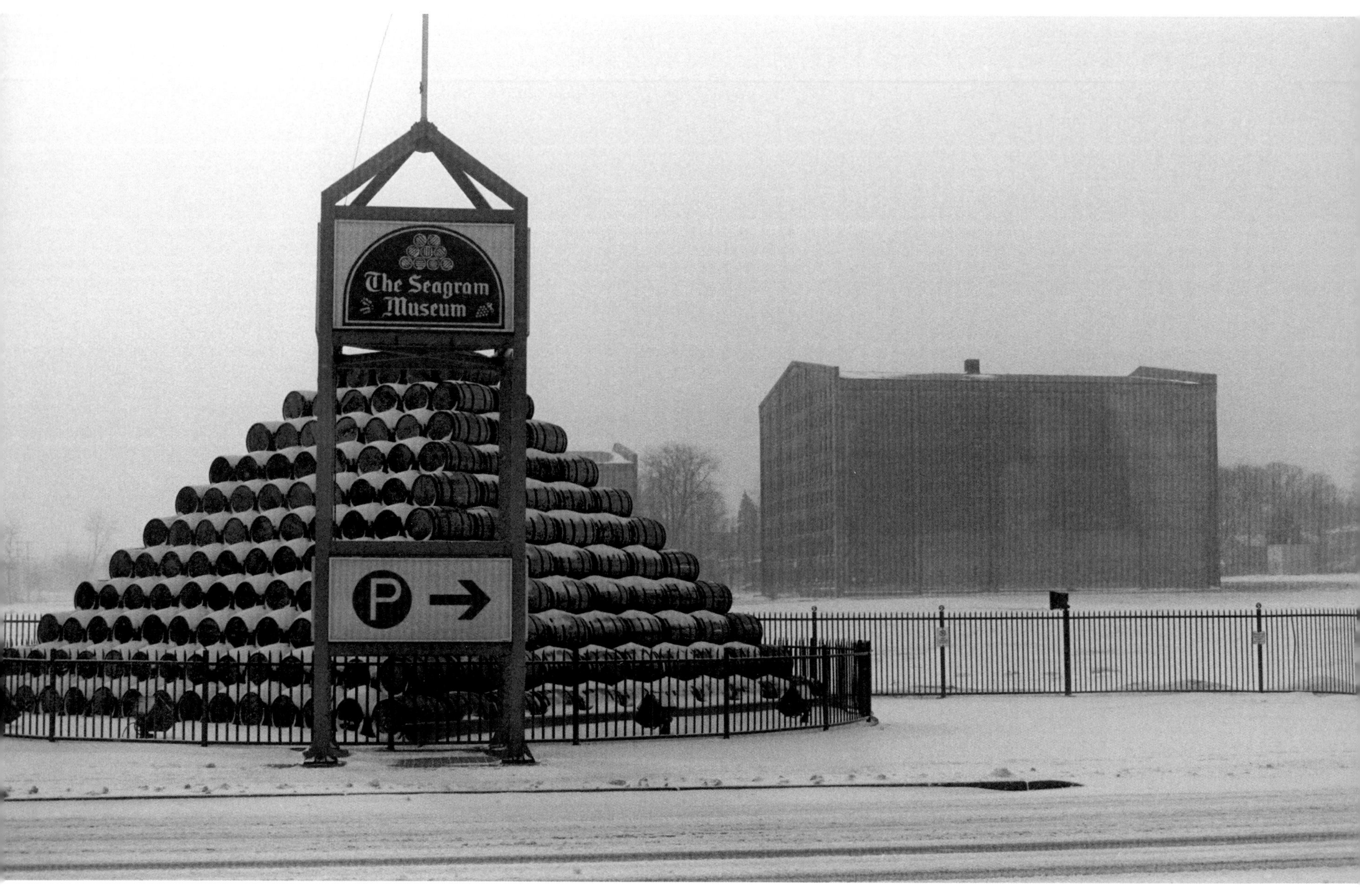
The Seagram
Museum
P

16 | The Seagram Museum Barrel Pyramid (*demolished*)

Built during the 13 years that the museum was open, the Seagram barrel pyramid became a landmark that people recognized and gave directions by. A huge crowd assembled in August 2009 when it was dismantled. Before the Granite Mills were established on the site by George Randall and William Hespeler in 1857, there was a spring-fed watering hole at this location. Joseph Seagram acquired full control of the company from Randall and Hespeler by 1883. The barrel warehouse in the background, now condominium residences since 1999, was constructed in the 1890s. Incidentally, this was also the location of Jacob C. Snider's farm of thirty acres, the first property that Waterloo founder Abraham Erb sold.

1995

17 | 103 Erb Street West

This is a very modest example of a now-decommissioned hydro house, or, in proper technical parlance, "residential substation." A particular, functional form of architecture, these buildings were designed to blend into their settings. Some of the electrical equipment was fenced in the yard behind. Some have been demolished, but a few remain, and some have been repurposed. They are as varied in appearance as the neighbourhoods they inhabit, and there are some very grand ones throughout the province.

2014

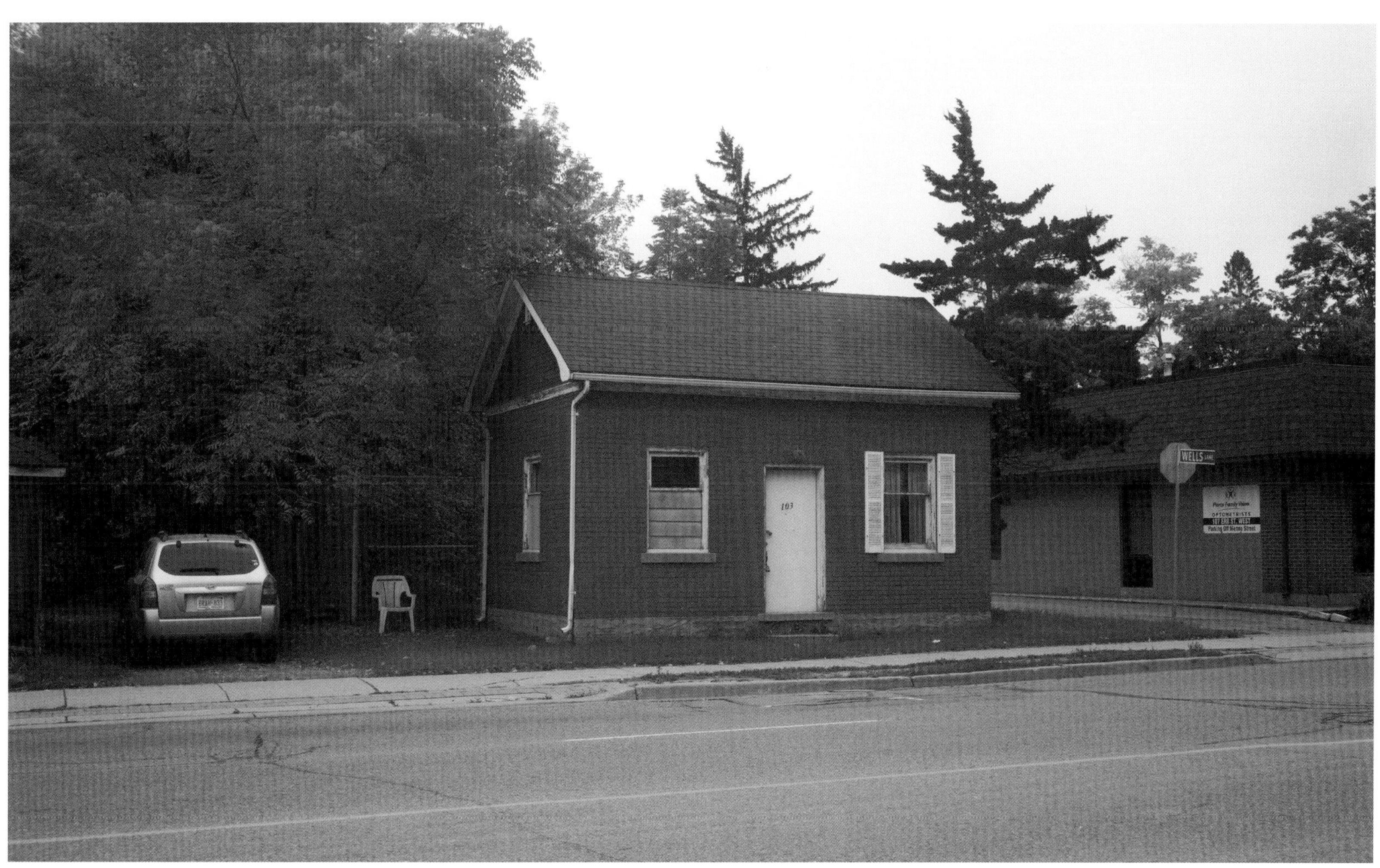
103
WELLS
OPTOMETRISTS

18 | Hughes Lane

The back of the Button Factory is visible down Hughes Lane looking south from Erb Street. This has been a well-utilized public lane, especially when King Street was closed for the construction of services associated with the light rail transit line. Many will remember the surprising discovery (to transit engineers) of the corduroy road in King Street, which necessitated the closing of King Street for many more months than anticipated. The lane was likely named in honour of Jeremiah Hughes, who was elected Mayor in 1898 and lived at 65 Albert Street.

1993

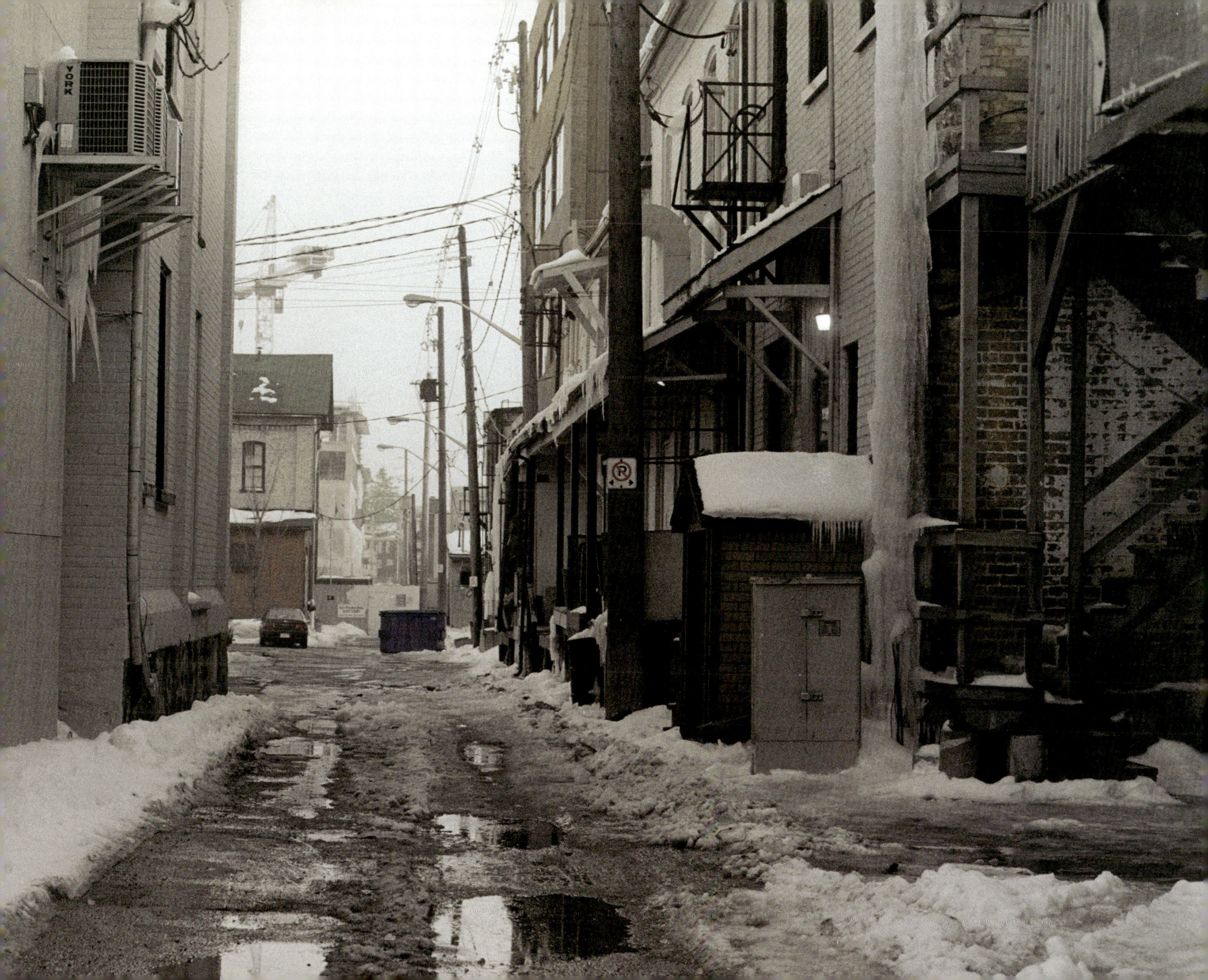
YORK

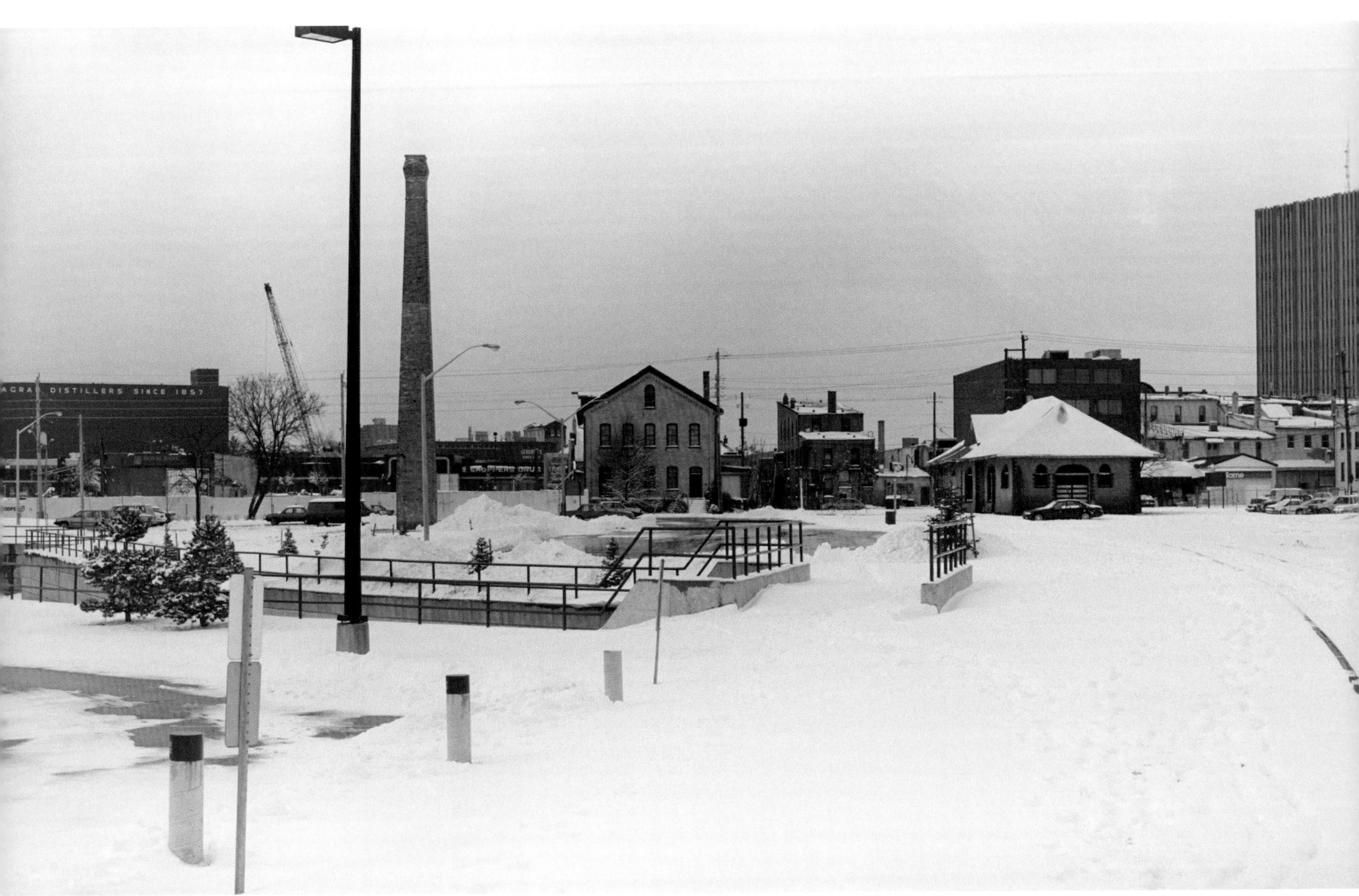
AGRA DISTILLERS SINCE 1857

19 | Mueller Chimney *(demolished)*

One can see the Seagram Distillery still intact on the horizon. Construction of the parking garage was just beginning. The chimney was the last remnant of the Mueller Cooperage which had moved to Erb Street West across from the Seagram Distillery in 1906. The cooperage was purchased by Seagram's in 1920 and renamed Canada Barrel and Kegs, and later Canbar. The area on the east side of Regina near the rail yards remained an industrial area until the 1980s when it was cleared out for parking. Although it was intended to commemorate an early local industry, the Mueller Cooperage chimney did not last for many years with no context and no signage to indicate its purpose.

1992

20 | Regina Street

The Button Factory Community Arts Centre, the city parking garage, and the Region of Waterloo Community Services building are on the west side of Regina Street South (right hand side of the frame). With financial help from the Town of Waterloo, the button factory was constructed for Richard and Rudolph Roschman in 1886 and operated until 1946. They used bivalve shells as the raw material. The property was designated under the Ontario Heritage Act by the city (the present owner) in 1982. The Waterloo Community Arts Centre was established there in 1994 with help from the City of Waterloo and is now an important cultural asset. When I took the photo, it was not late in the evening, but it seemed pretty forlorn. There were no curbs north of the tracks then.

1993

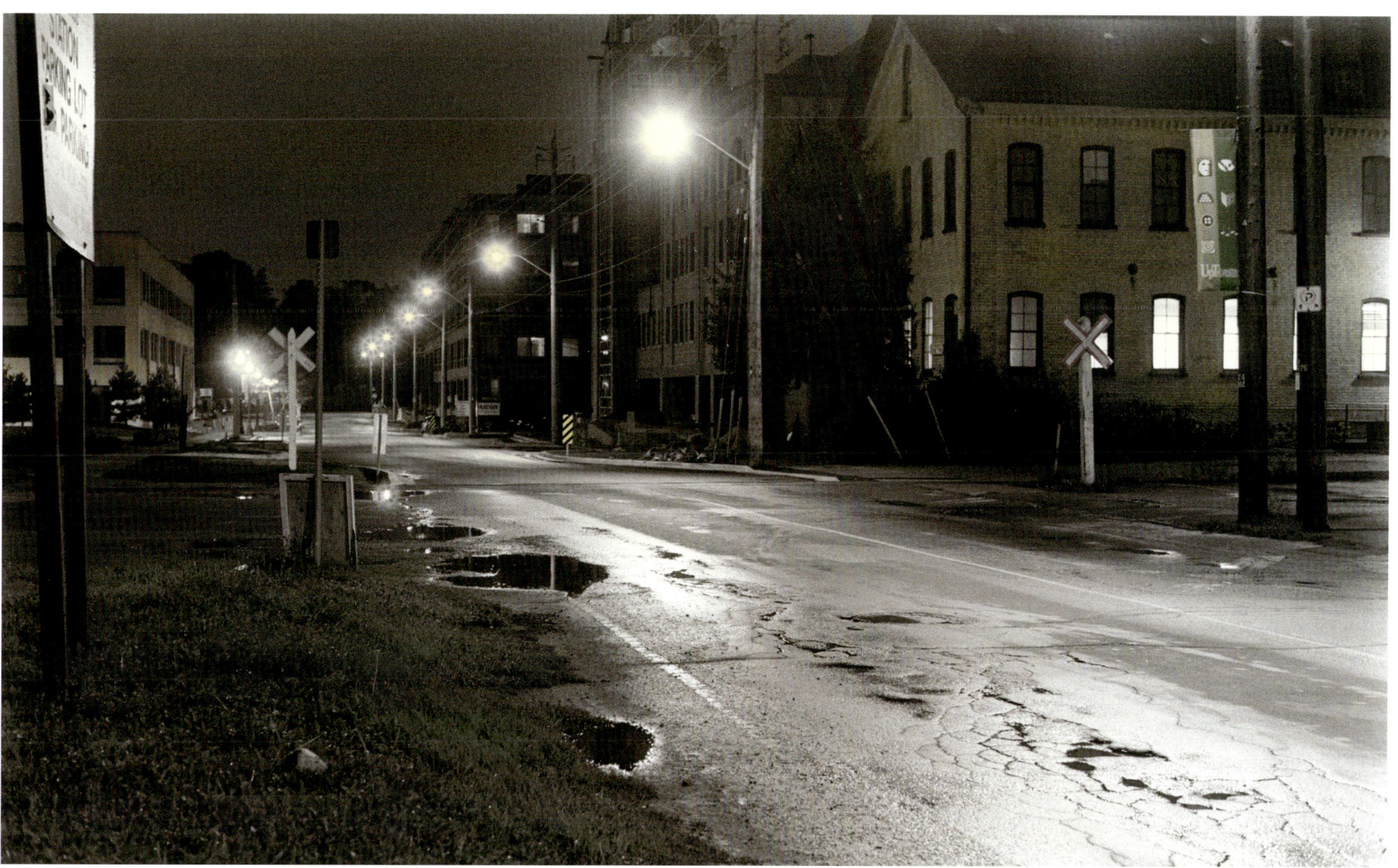
STATION
PARKING LOT
PARKING

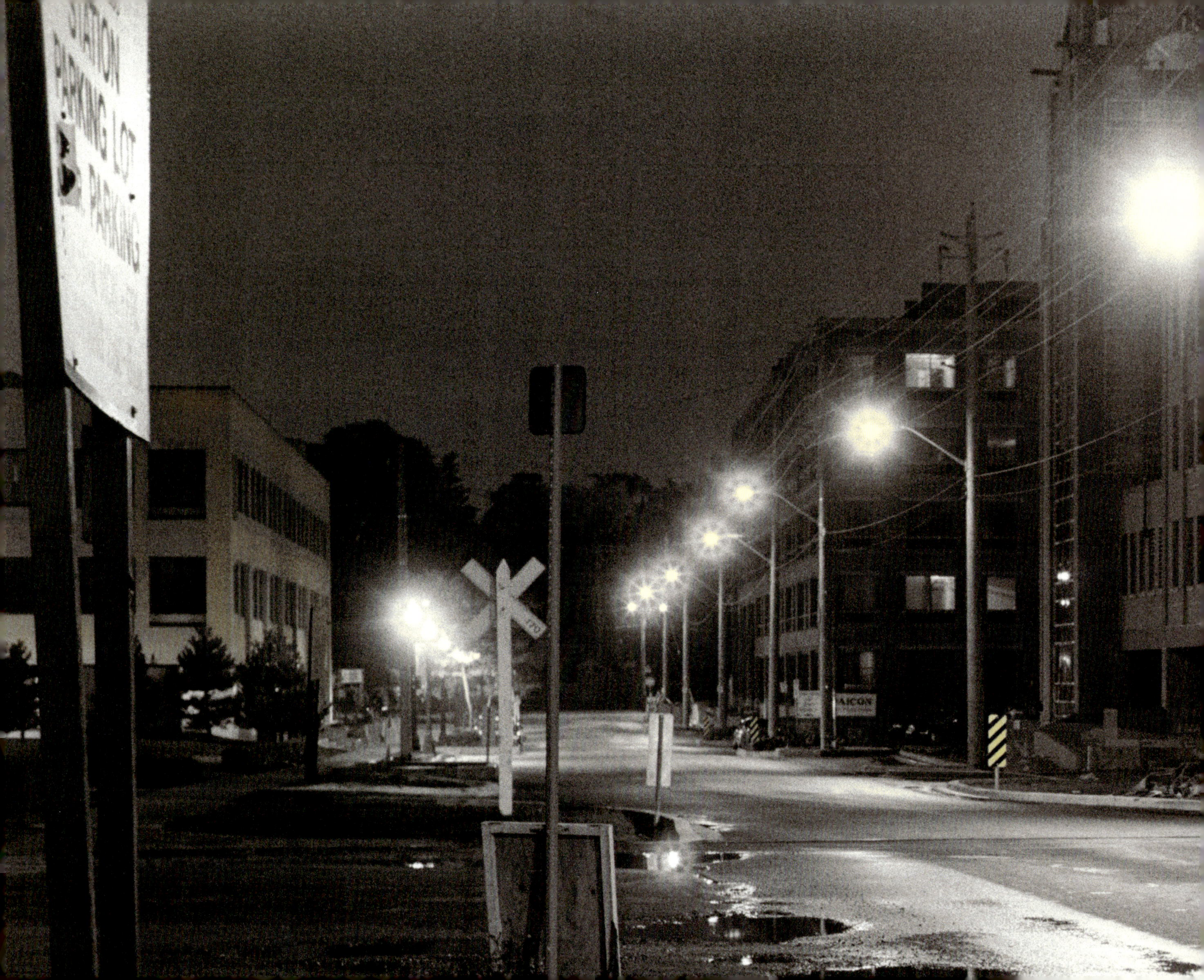
STATION
PARKING LOT
PARKING

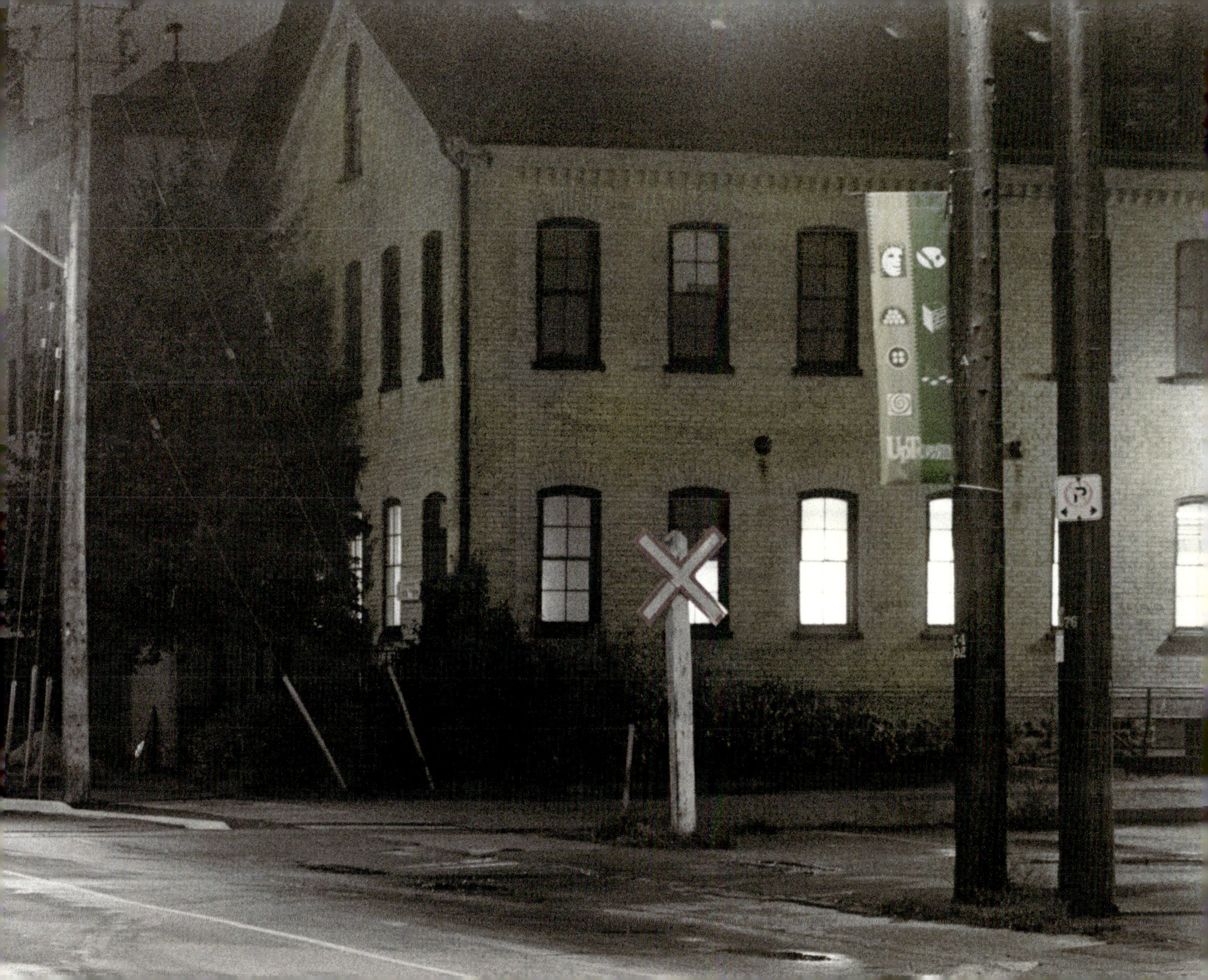

21 | **Bingo Hall** *(demolished)*

Located at approximately 19 King Street South, the bingo hall didn't have a sign, but its purpose was obvious. I worked bingos there for the Friends of the Joseph Schneider Haus when they were fundraising for a classroom addition. I had to hang my clothes up outside to air out when I got home. Prior to the 2006 Smoke-Free Ontario Act banning smoking in public places, nearly everyone in the bingo hall smoked, and there was only one "no smoking" table, in the back corner.

1995

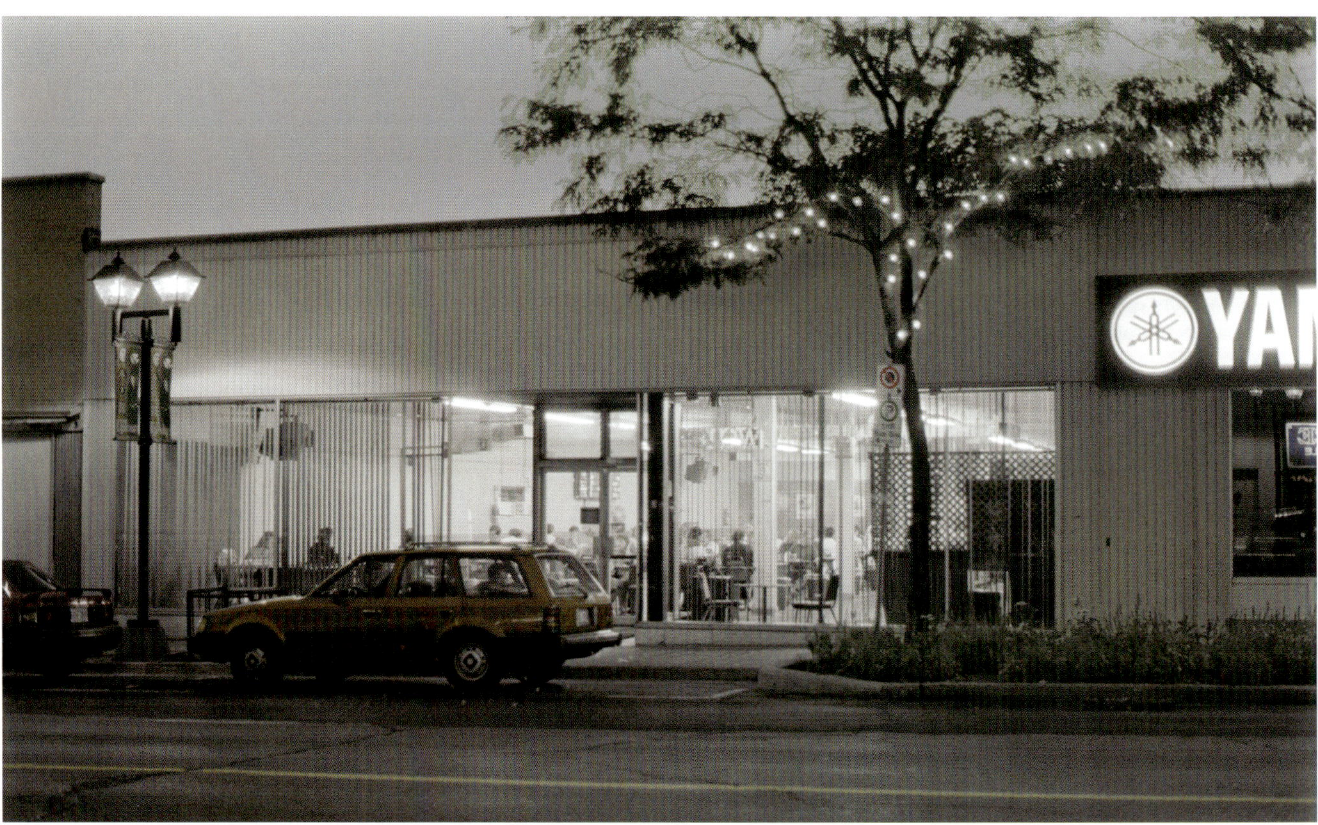

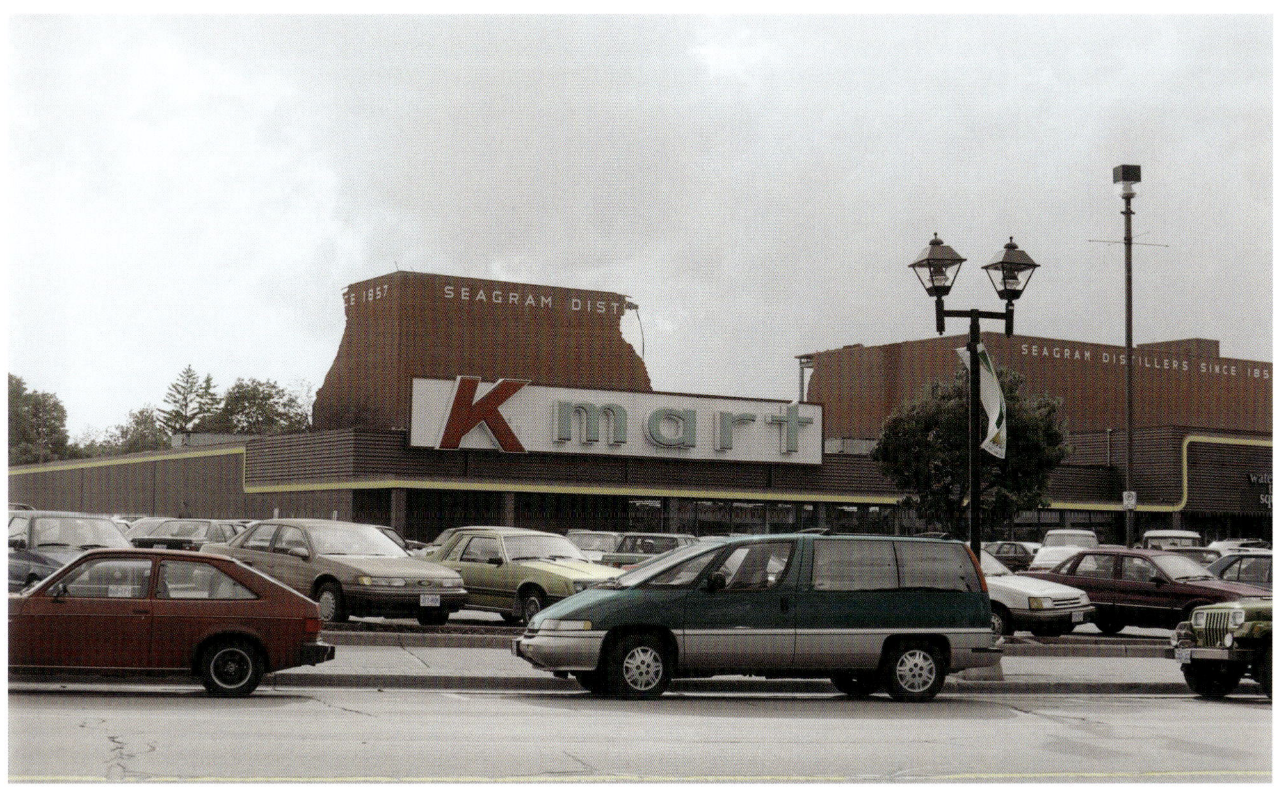

22 | Kmart *(demolished)*

This was Waterloo Town Square before it was upscaled. Kmart was a general merchandise department store that provided a wide range of goods for people uptown and beyond. Before 1960 this had been a site of heavy industry. The two newer Seagram Distillery warehouses were being demolished in the background. They had dominated the skyline of Waterloo for forty years or so. The first reference to rebranding the core as "Uptown" that I could find was in John Shortreed's council election ad in 1980.

1993

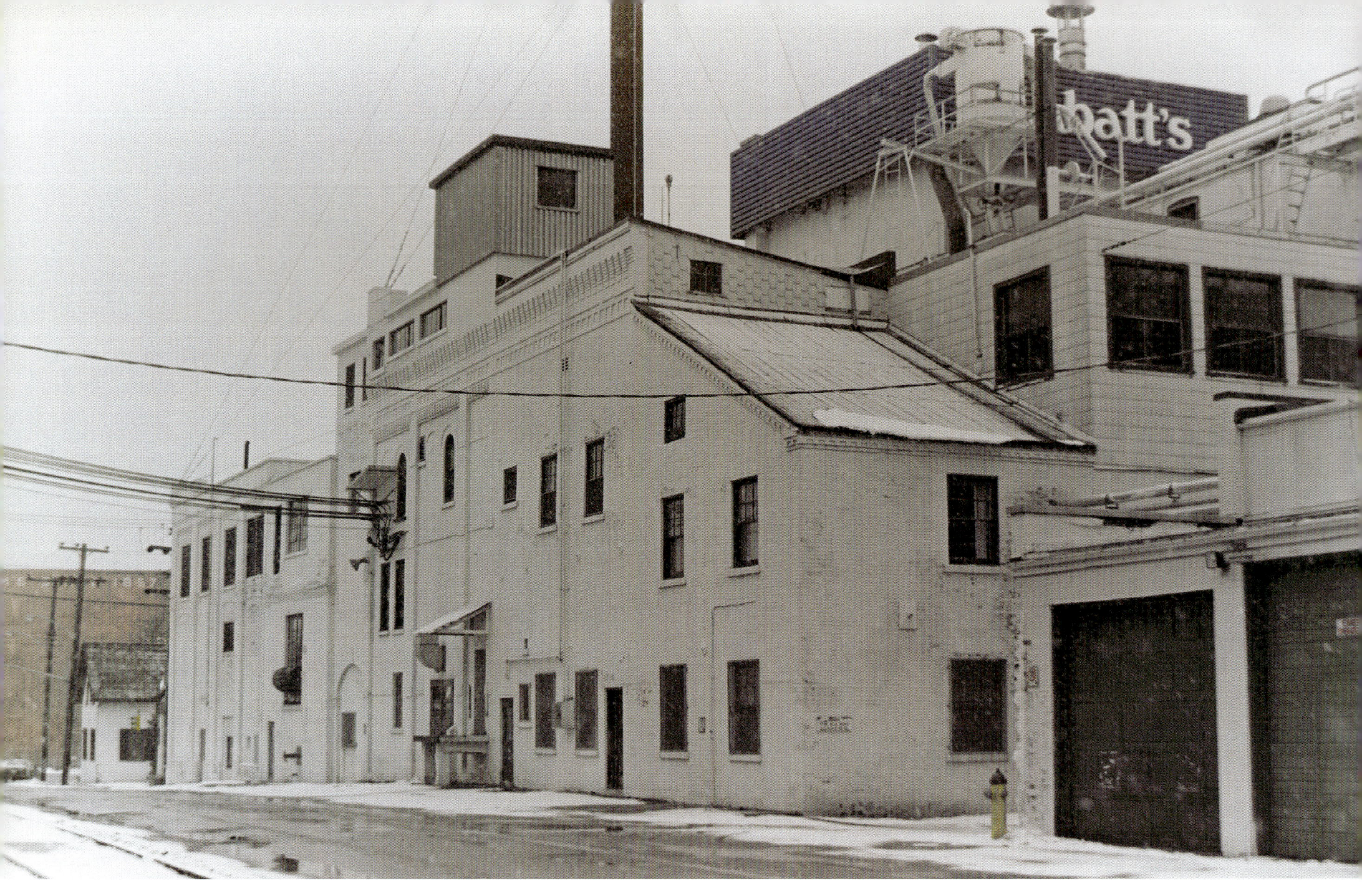
batt's

23 | **Kuntz Brewery** *(demolished)*

This is the back of the Kuntz Brewery on Caroline Street. It was acquired by Carling Breweries of London (owned by E. P. Taylor) in the 1920s and later by Labatt's. In the bottom left, the Grand River Railway, now the Iron Horse Trail, can be seen running on one side of the street. Some (especially cyclists) will remember that the railway track ran right up Caroline Street in the northbound curb lane to the Canbar barrel works factory and Globe Furniture. Caroline Street may have been named after the brewer Louis Kuntz's daughter.

1993

24 | Bauer Industries, Caroline Street, near Allen

(demolished)

On the right side of the frame is a little PUC hydro substation on Caroline Street. I recently realized that there is an identical building at Borden and Courtland which has the name Public Utilities Commission still affixed to it in bronze letters. This is the back of the Bauer Industries factory complex along Caroline Street, where Vincenzo's is now. Aloyes Bauer established the Shoddy Mills on land at King and Allen purchased in 1888. Incorporated in 1911 as Bauer's Ltd, the company made cotton felt and batts for mattresses, upholstery, and cushions.

2002

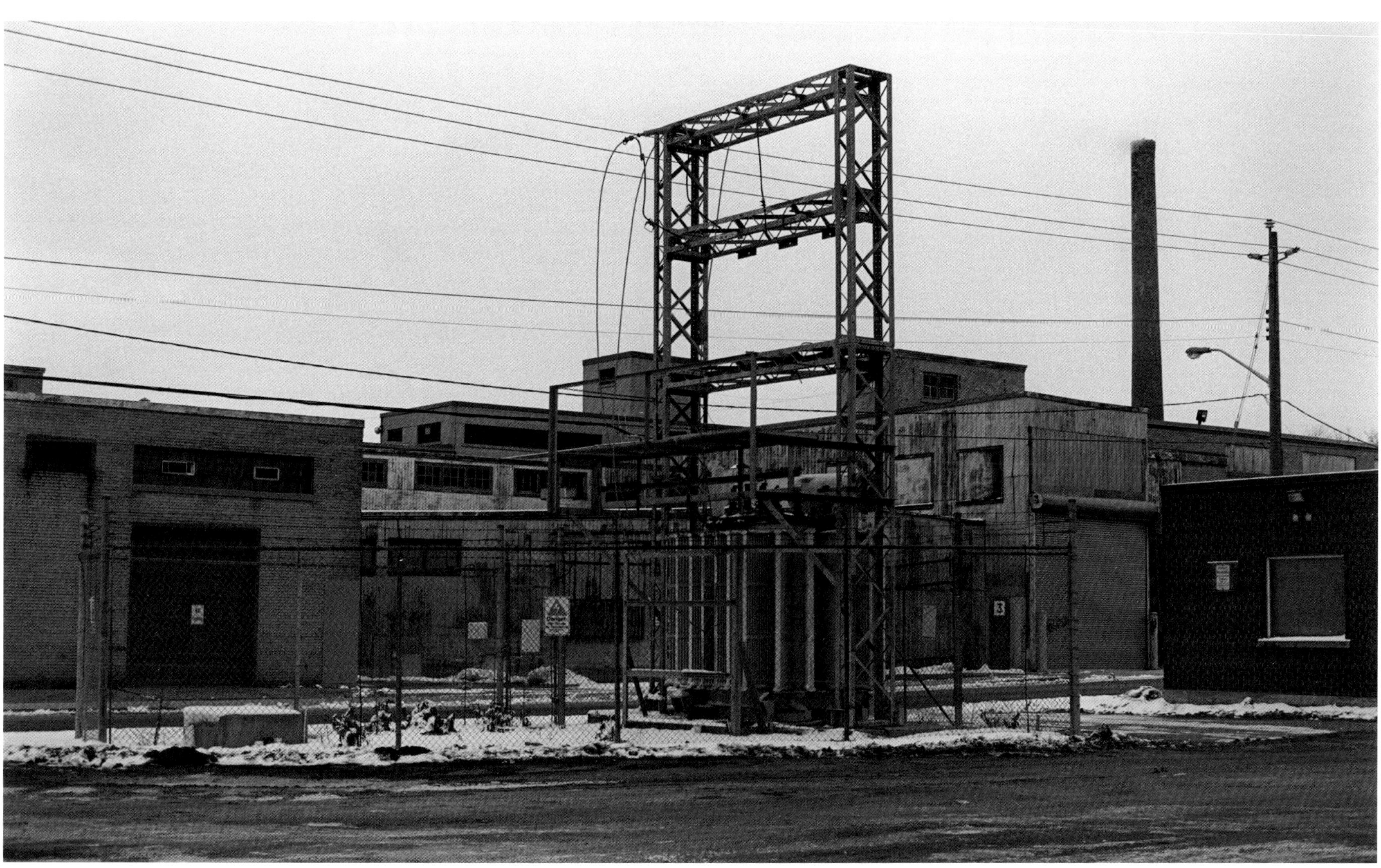

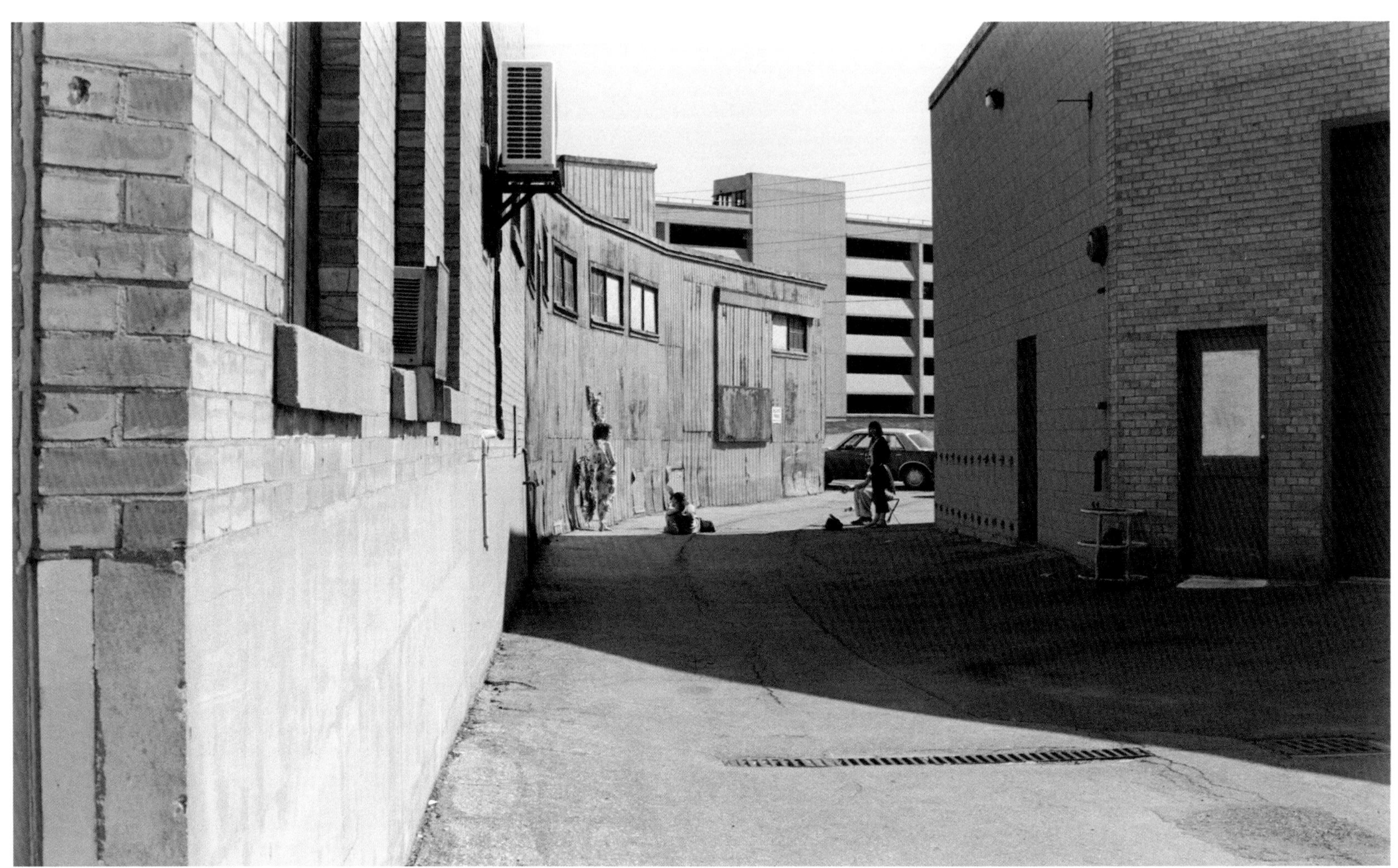

25 | Rail Siding

This was a random encounter with a fashion photo shoot. The directors were amused to find themselves the subject of another photographer. The location was a former rail siding of the Grand River Railway that ran into the Bauer property. Railway history is complicated, but the Grand River Railway ran from Galt to Waterloo, and the part from Ottawa Street to Erb Street since 1997 has been the Iron Horse Trail for cyclists and pedestrians. When I worked on this negative, I was uncertain of the exact location because all of the buildings in the foreground are gone. The only clue now to the location is the orientation of the Mutual Life (Sun Life) parking garage in the distance.

2001

26 | 70 Alexandra Avenue

70 Alexandra Avenue in Waterloo was being converted from a store into a residence. Judging from the windows and the brick, it was built in the late 1920s or 1930s like so many other neighbourhood stores. Corner or neighbourhood stores are an interesting phenomenon. The ones with datestones are usually from the early 1930s. This is the common form, with the residence above and shop on the main floor, so the shopkeeper could work long hours. Even when converted to dwellings, they can still be recognized.

1996

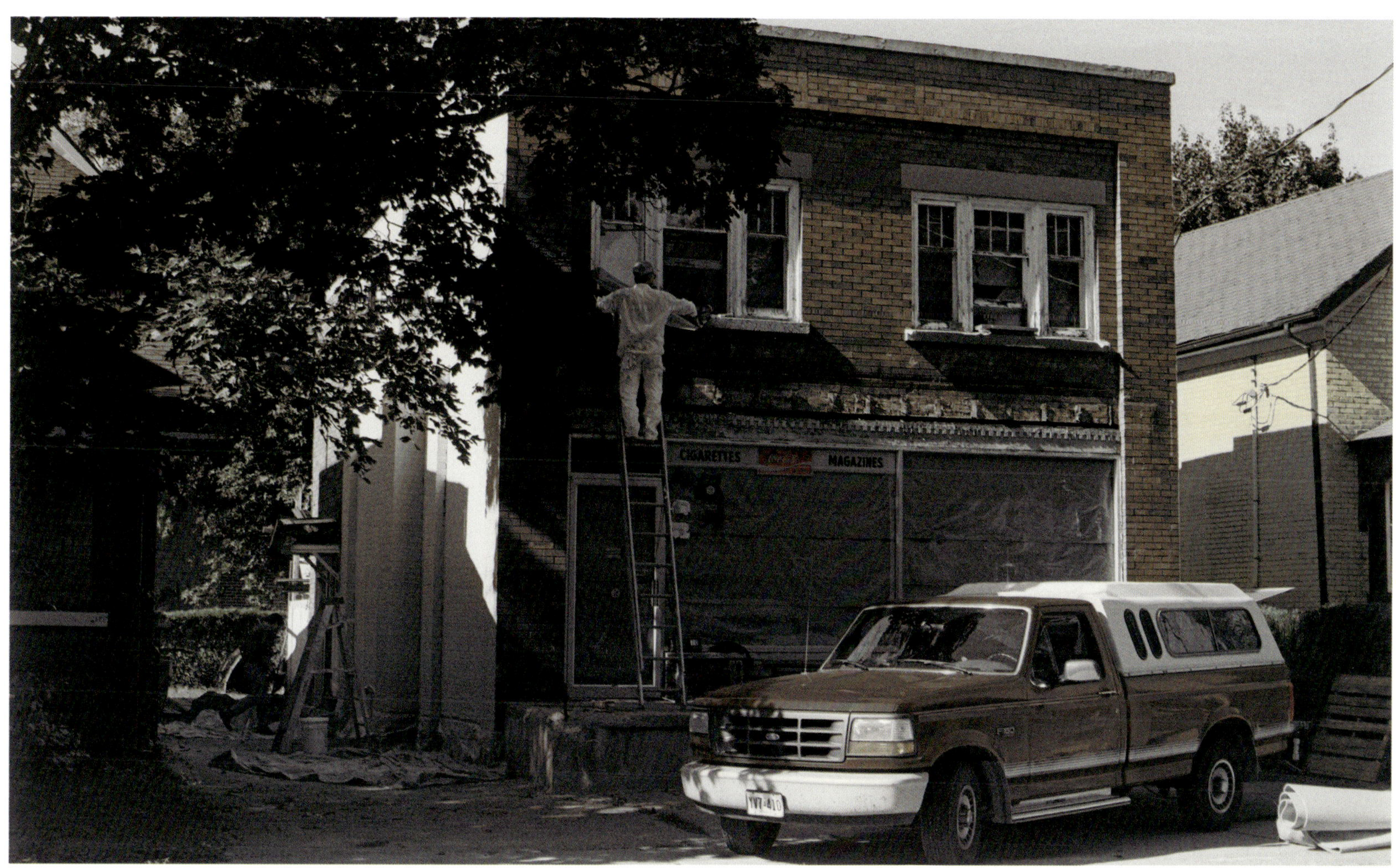
CIGARETTES
MAGAZINES

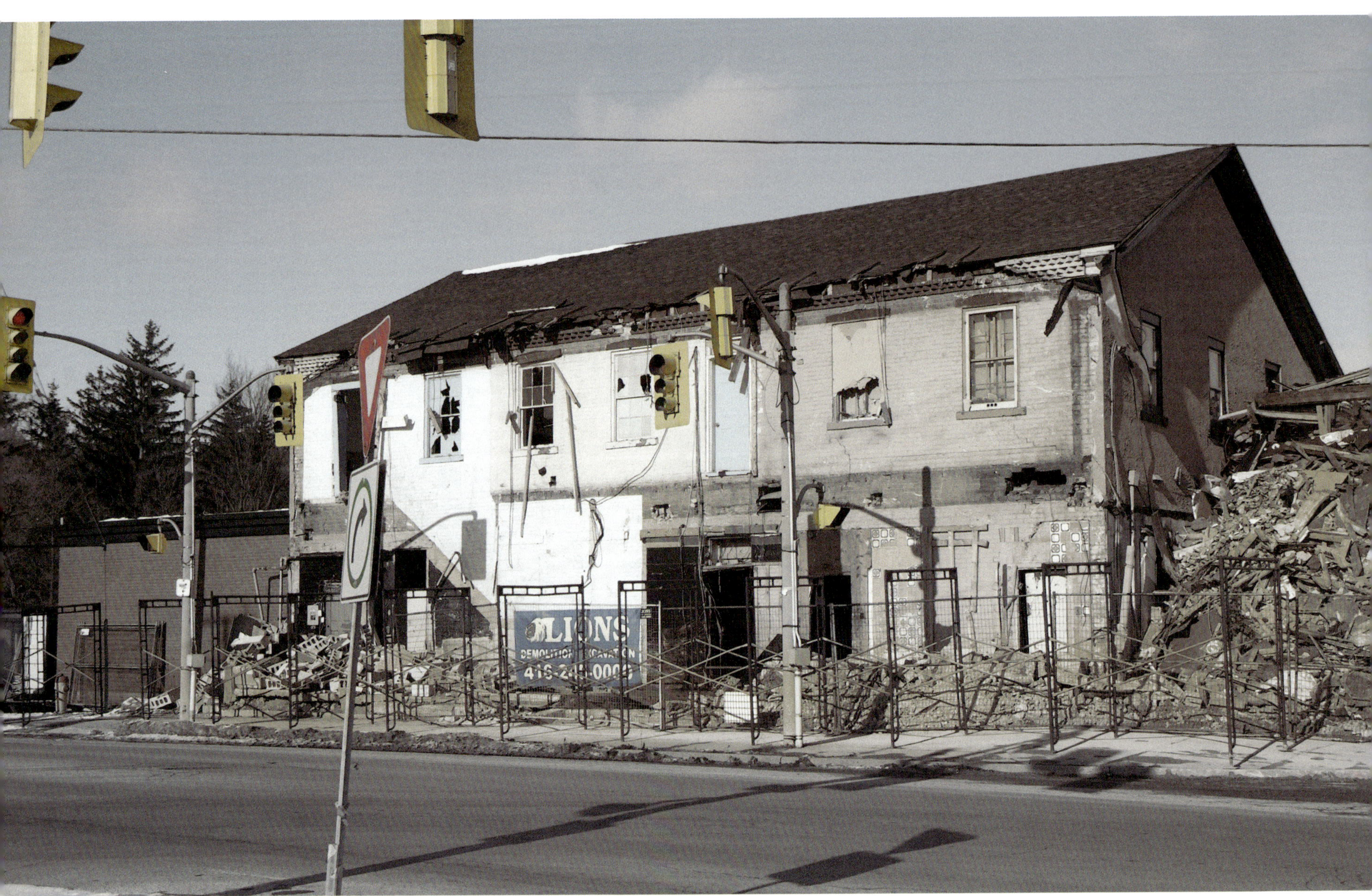
LIONS

27 | The Grand Hotel Bridgeport *(demolished)*

The Grand Hotel in Bridgeport was known to some as "Huggy's," due to the discotheque that occupied part of the space for a while. Over the course of a number of years it developed an unsavoury reputation which likely contributed to the enthusiasm with which demolition was approved. The front facade had been obscured by unsympathetic additions. Even though historic photos exist, some were surprised to discover that there was a fine Georgian hotel, built about 1860, underneath the facade of the building. The Bridge Street/Lancaster Street roundabout is now in this location.

2009

28 | Lancaster Plaza

This modest car-oriented plaza was built at the same time as the early post-war suburbs which surround it. According to the aerial photos, in 1945 there was a farm in this location. By 1955, the neighbourhood had been mostly developed.

1994

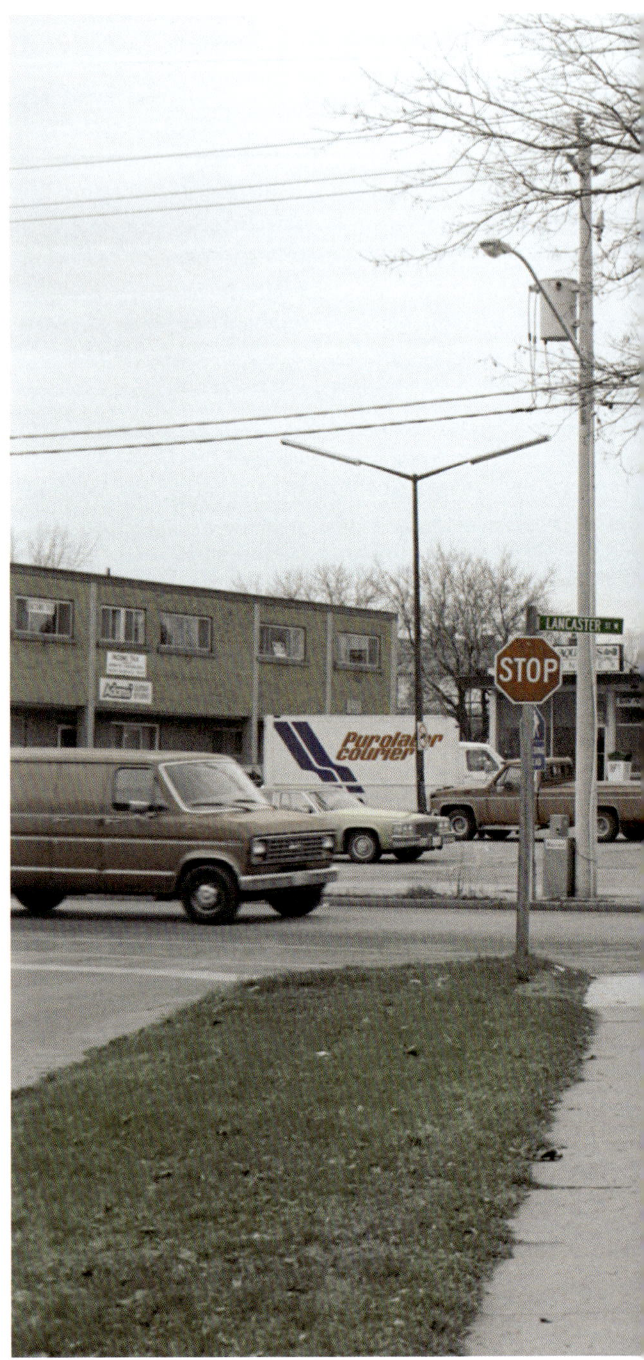

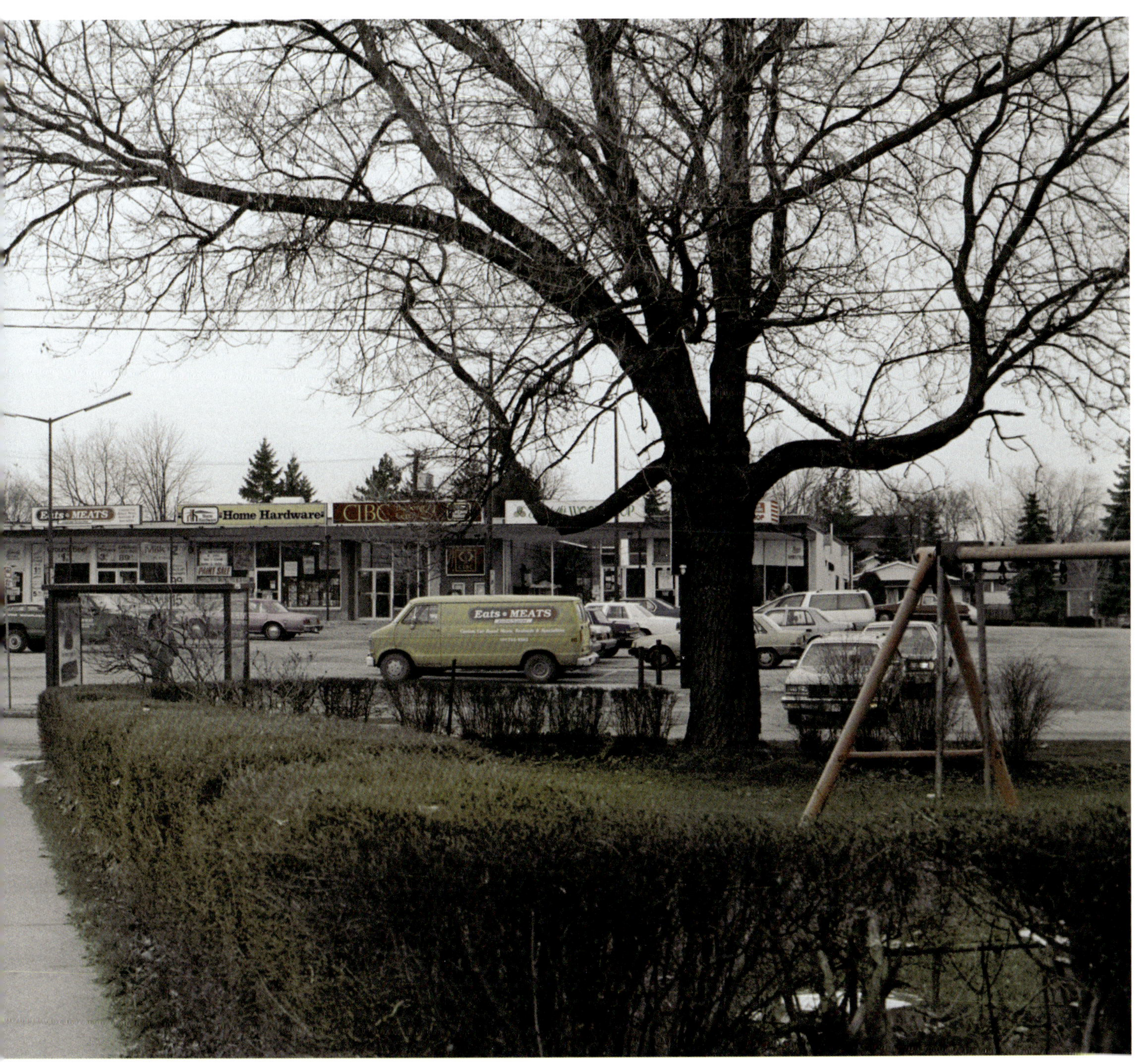
Eats • MEATS
Home Hardware
CIBC
PAINT SALE
Eats • MEATS

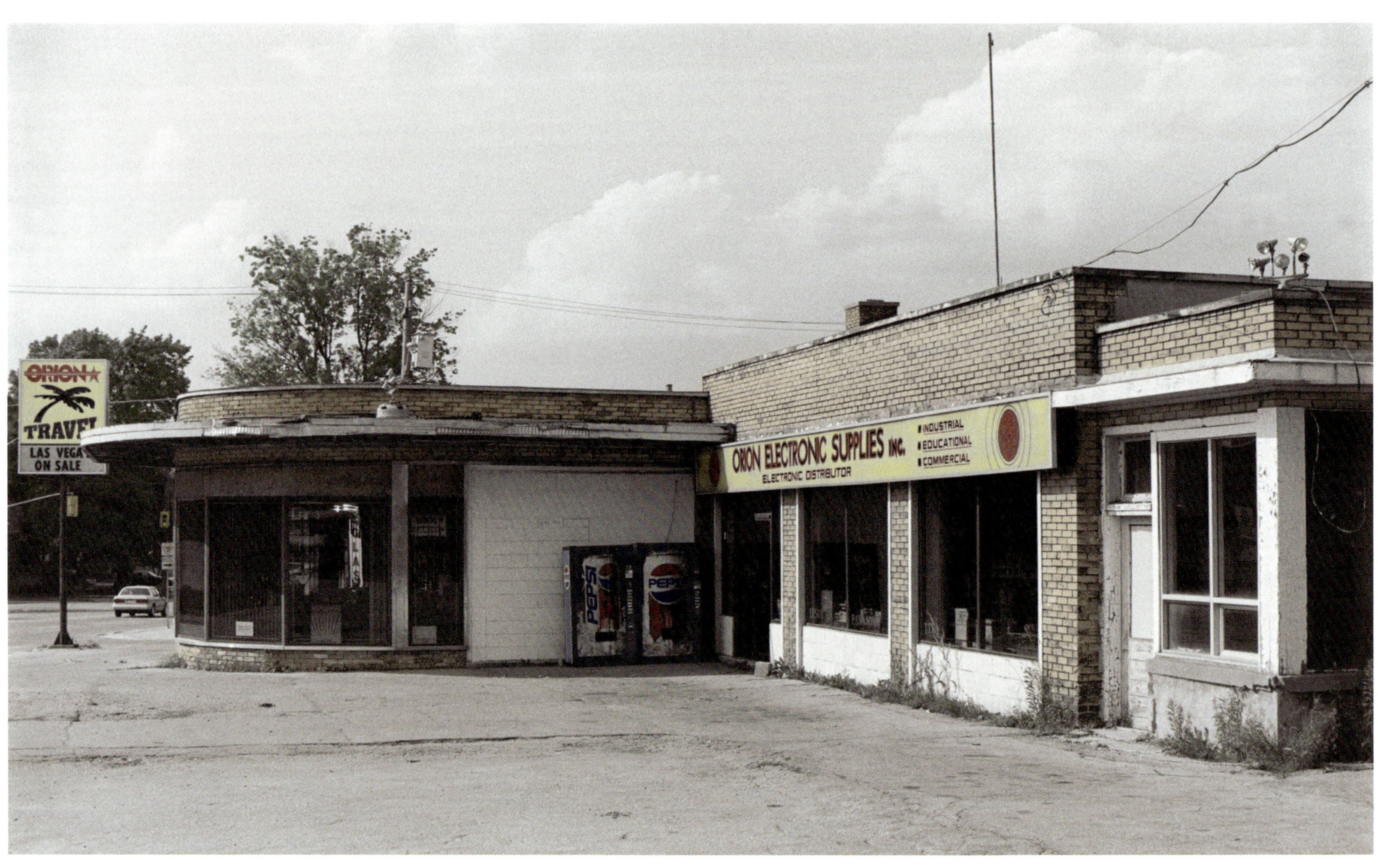

ORION
TRAVEL
LAS VEGAS
ON SALE
ORION ELECTRONIC SUPPLIES INC.
ELECTRONIC DISTRIBUTOR
INDUSTRIAL
EDUCATIONAL
COMMERCIAL
PEPSI
PEPSI

29 | Orion Electronics and Travel

Situated on Lancaster Street at the end of Breithaupt Street, not far from Victoria Street North and the railway tracks, this once-stylish building must have been a car dealership and garage. The car bays have been filled in and the once-glamorous canopy has become pretty shabby, although it has recently been repainted.

1993

30 | Lane opposite Agnes Street *(garage demolished)*

This unnamed lane between Shanley and Louisa runs northeast from King Street West opposite Agnes Street. The garage, when it was converted to residences, was no doubt affordable housing. The property has now been redeveloped for a mid-rise apartment building.

2012

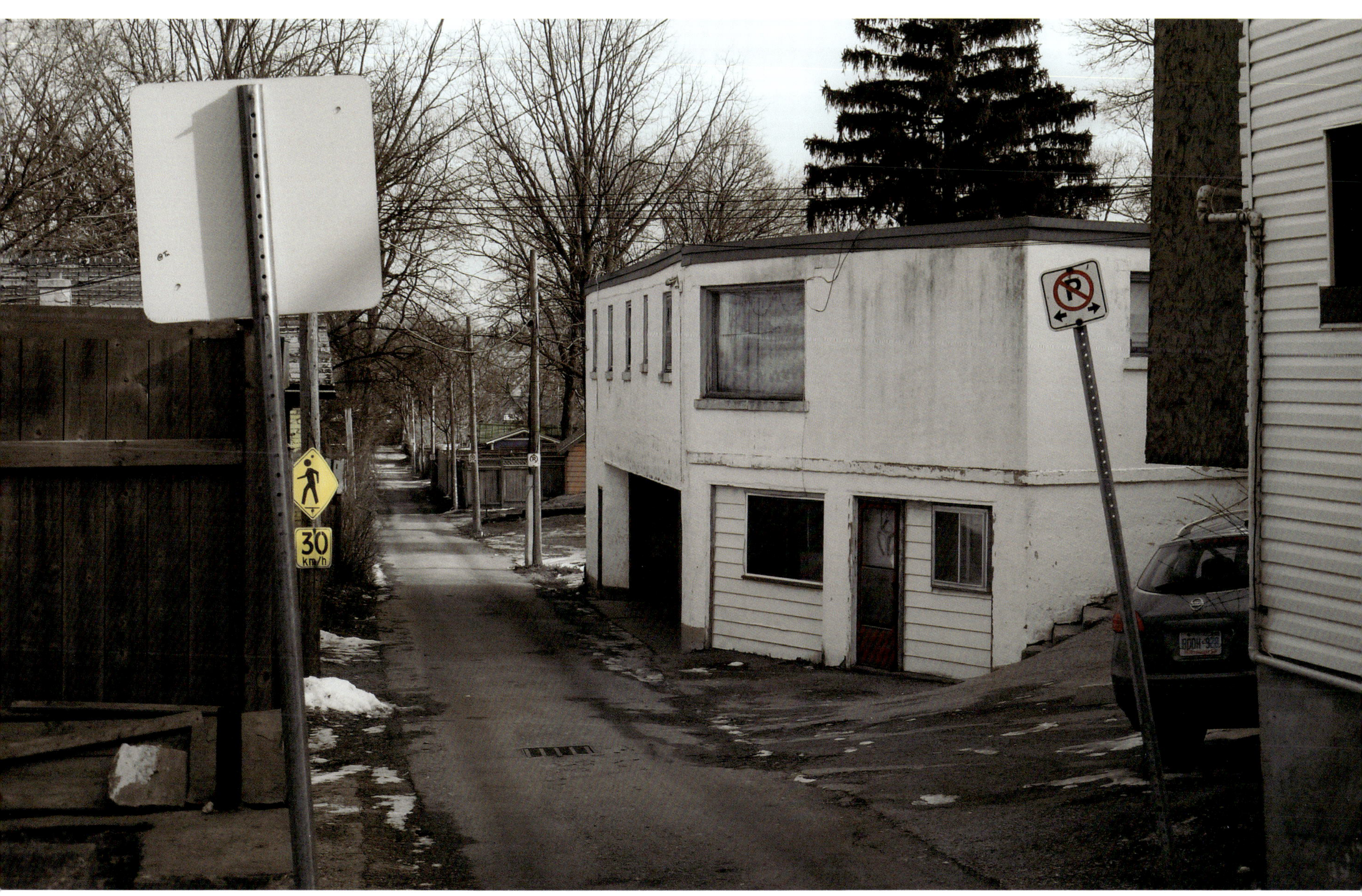
30
km/h

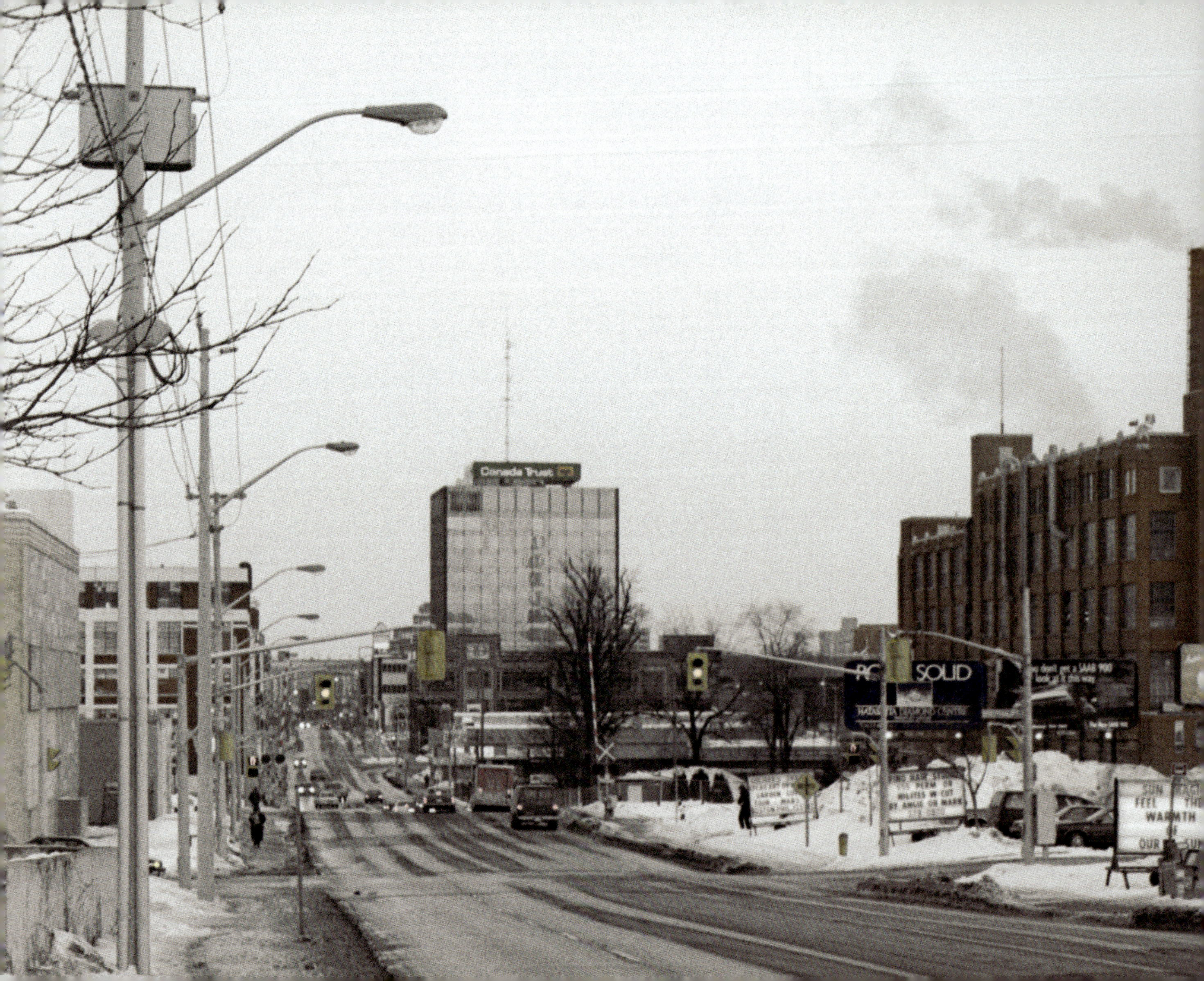
Canada Trust
SOLID
FEEL
WARMTH

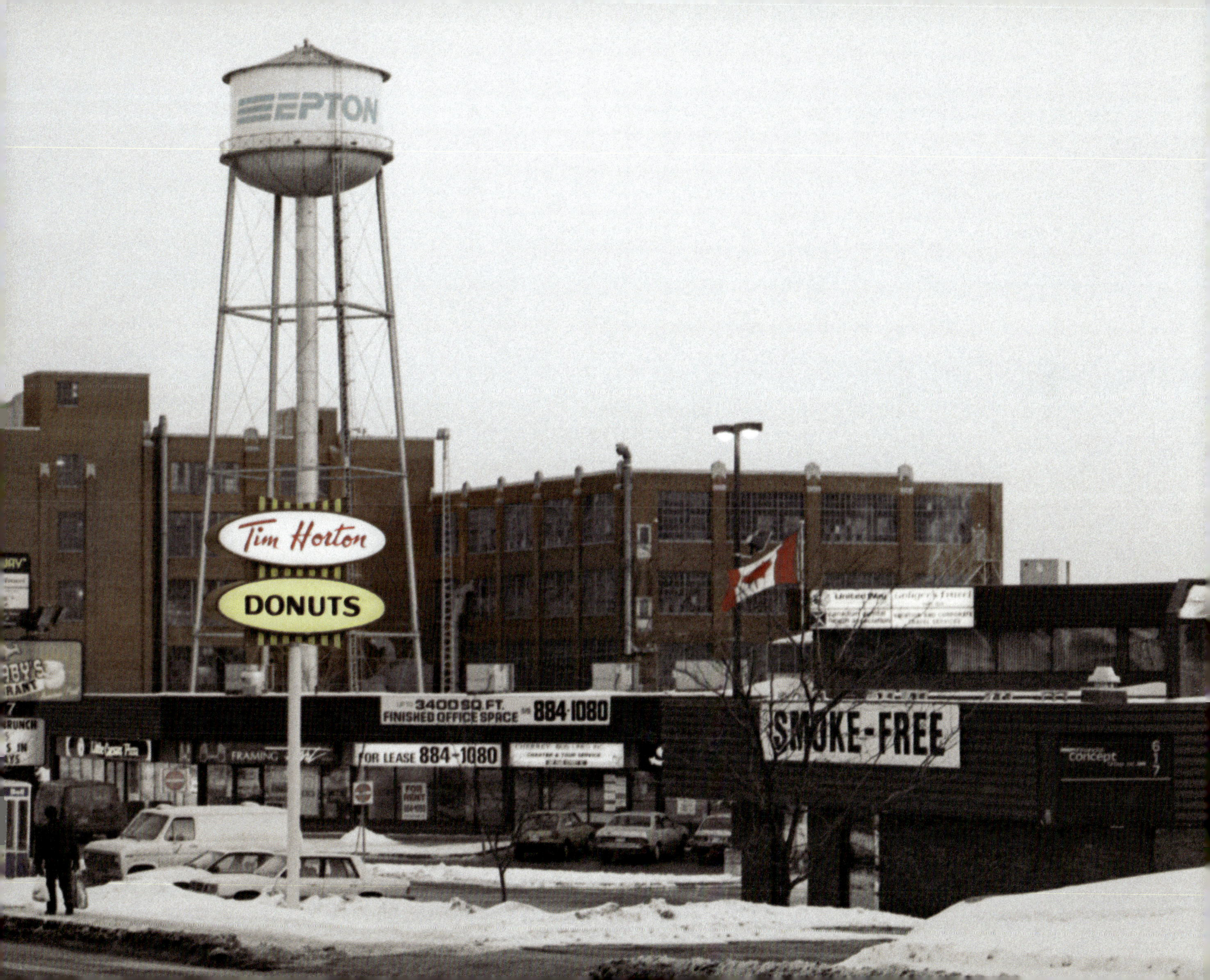

EEPTON
Tim Horton
DONUTS
3400 SQ.FT.
FINISHED OFFICE SPACE
884-1080
FOR LEASE 884-1080
FRAMING
SMOKE-FREE

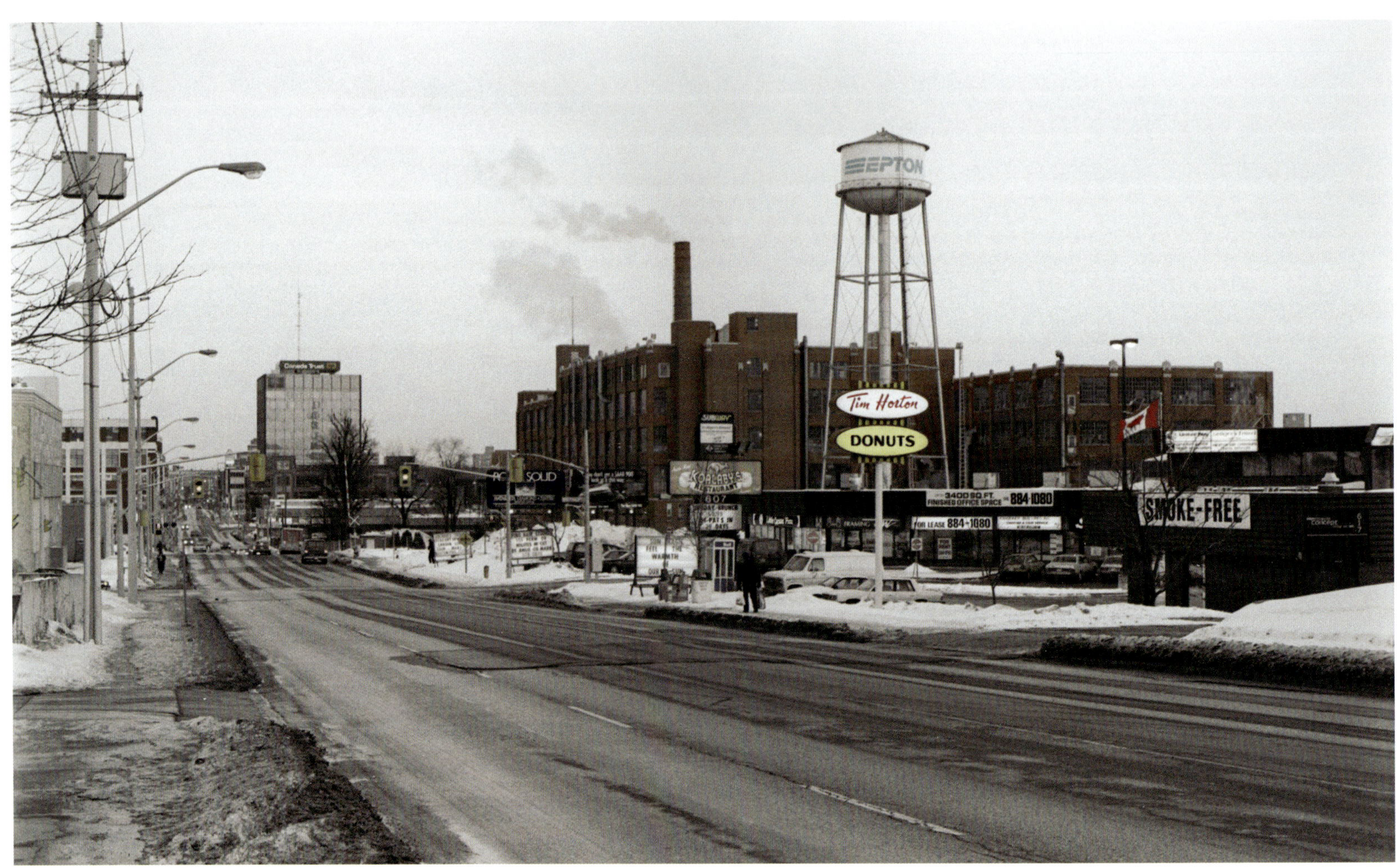
EPTON
Canada Trust
Tim Horton
DONUTS
3400 SQ FT.
FINISHED OFFICE SPACE
884-1080
FOR LEASE 884-1080
SMOKE-FREE
FEEL THE WARMTH

31 | **Epton** (*demolished*)

Epton was probably the largest factory in the central part of Kitchener. Originally founded as the Ames-Holden Tire Company in 1919, the company was purchased by B.F. Goodrich in 1922. In 1983 the plant was sold and became Epton Industries when employees purchased the failing company. The factory was demolished in 1997 after Epton Industries went bankrupt. Today King Street West goes underneath the railway tracks.

1992

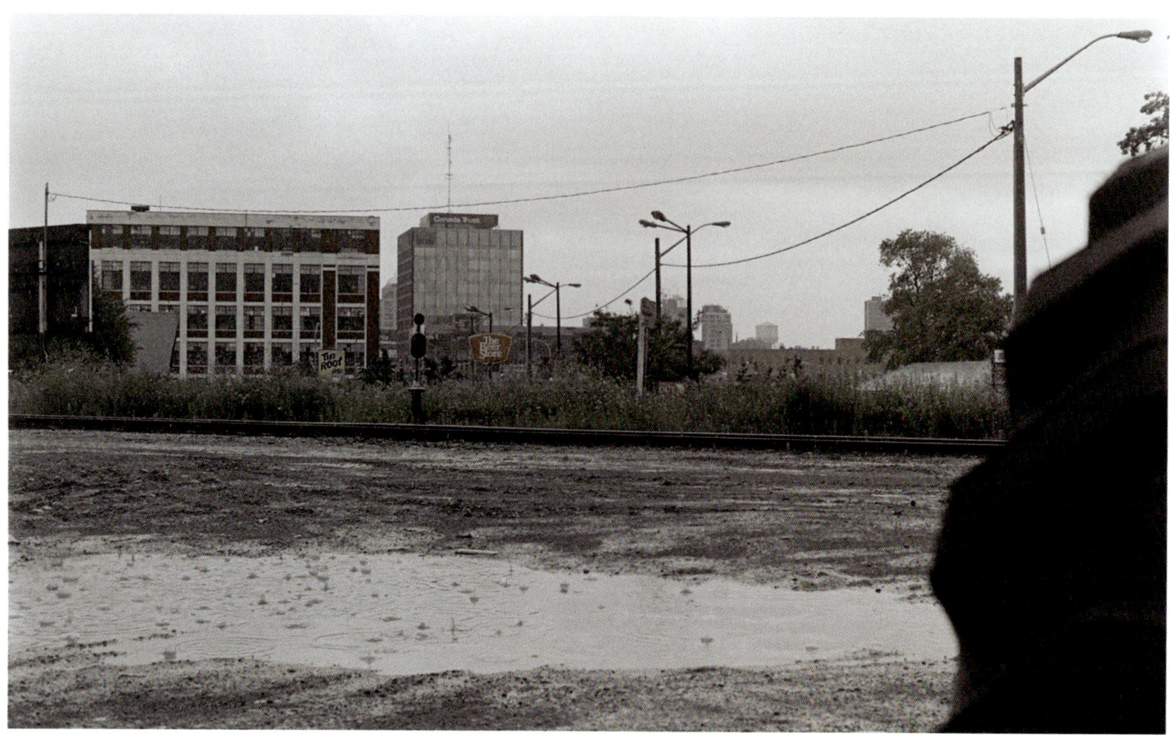

32 | By King Street West

On one of our usual Saturday walks to the Kitchener Market we sought a few minutes of refuge from the heavy rain behind the Breithaupt Block under the back of a huge earth-moving machine and contemplated the view for ten minutes until the rain abated. Prominent in the view were the Kaufman Rubber Company (now the Kaufman Lofts condominiums), built between 1908 and 1925 by American architect Albert Kahn; and the Canada Trust building at 305 King Street West, built in 1964 by Webb Zerafa Menkes of Toronto for Waterloo Trust. Now that King Street goes underneath the railway tracks, one can shelter there.

2000

33 | Path to the Beer Store

This view looks west along the mainline track from Weber Street towards Duke and King. The Kitchener Button factory on the left was another unsuccessful attempt at rehabilitation and reuse following the common pattern of filling in the window openings. If it had survived another 15 years, it would find a new use today, as have many other brick-and-beam factories. There are a couple of guys taking a shortcut (desire line, in planning jargon) to return their empties back to the Beer Store located at 490 King Street West at that time.

1993

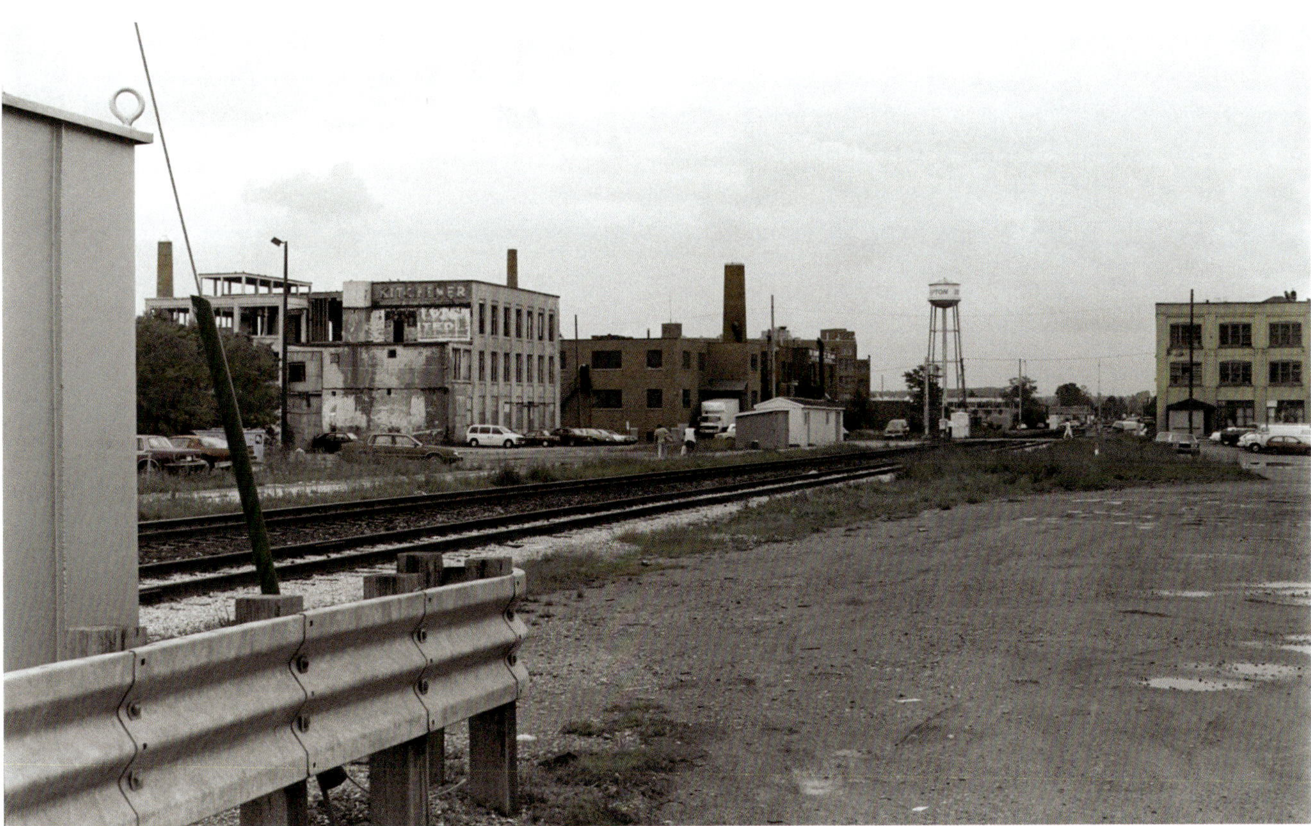

34 | Uniroyal, Strange Street

You can see west down the track if not all the way to Stratford, at least as far as Petersburg. Formerly the Dominion Tire Company, this factory was designed by the leading and influential American architect Albert Kahn and was constructed in 1912. Early photos show that the original building was much smaller, and that it was enlarged with several additions, including the majestic, towered section by the tracks.

c.1988

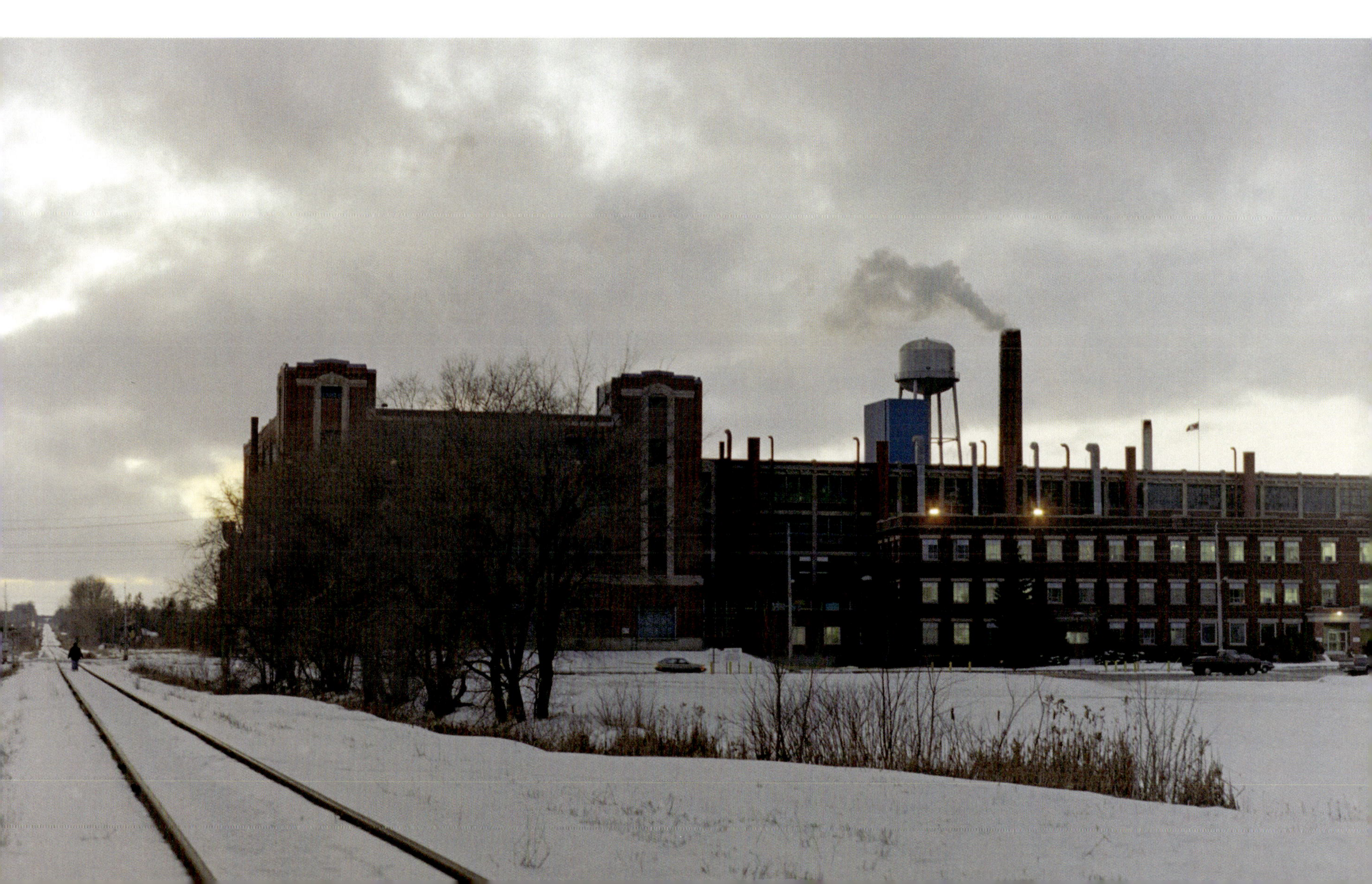

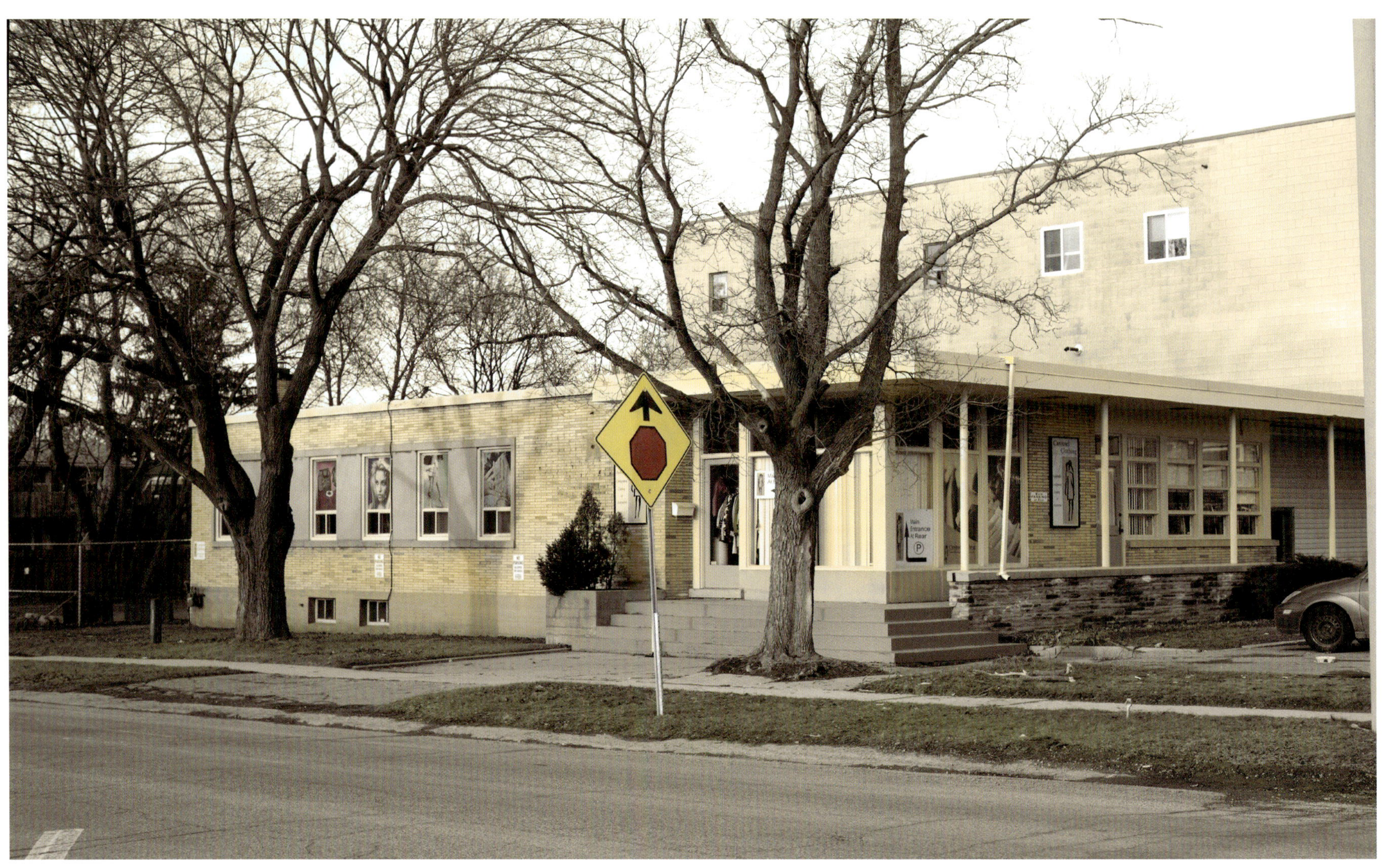
Main
Entrance
At Rear
P

35 | Breithaupt and St. Leger

A very Modern addition to an early 20th-century factory served as the office for the Greb Shoe factory on Breithaupt Street at St. Leger. This office or showroom addition has every feature of Mid-century Modern architecture: the beige roman brick, angelstone on the lower support wall, the large overhanging canopy with slender steel support columns, the high windows on both facades of the corner, the far-right window with multi panes and heavy subdividing bars, the series of windows on the St. Leger Street facade with the precast concrete frame and panels between. And a flat roof. I think they also made Bauer skates in the factory.

2017

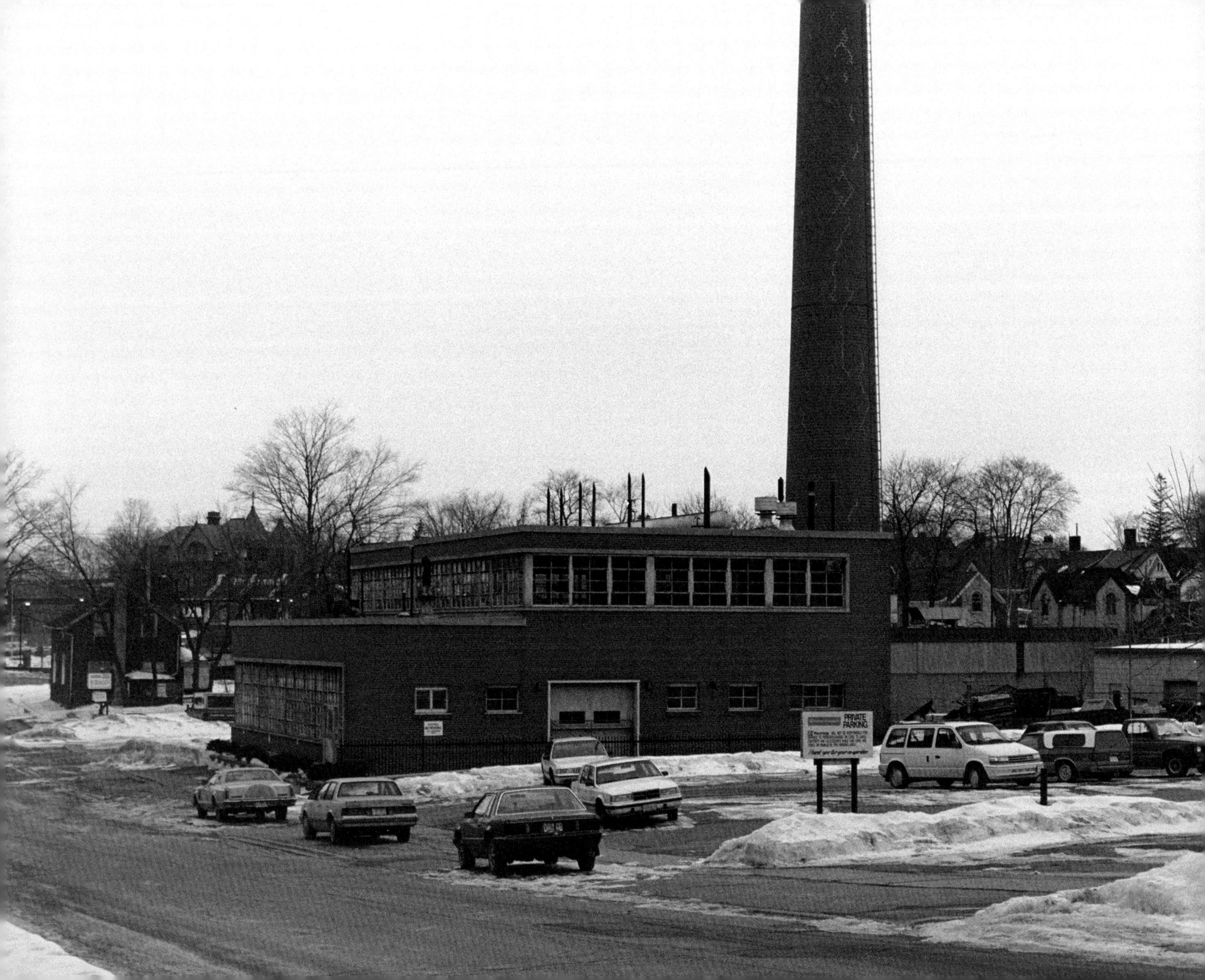
PRIVATE
PARKING

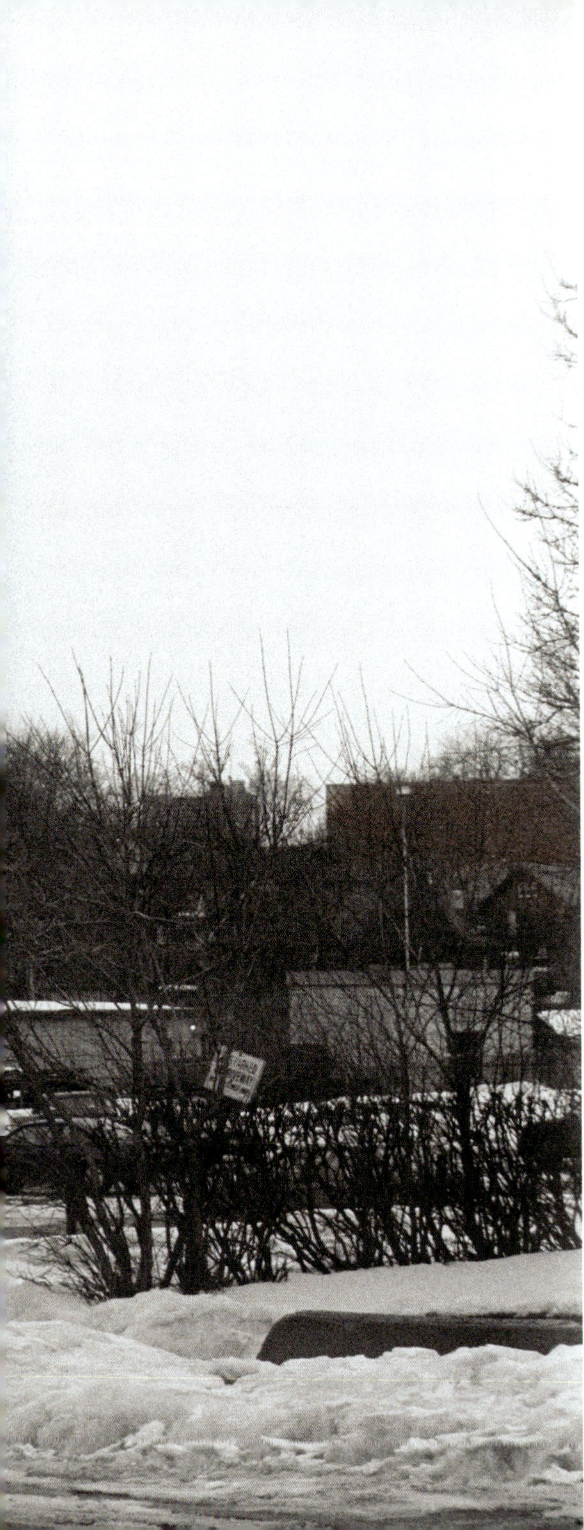

36 | Breithaupt Street Power Plant

(demolished)

This Modern building contained what I assume was heating and electrical equipment to support the former tire plant across the street. It exhibits some distinctive Modern features: the horizontal band of windows with the precast concrete surround on the upper level and likewise the large, glazed area on the front facade. In the distance is the Kaufman mansion, and the house on the left of the frame at the corner was clad in insulbrick over earlier board and batten.

1993

37 | King and Victoria *(demolished)*

In the background is the B.F. Goodrich factory which became Epton before its final demise. It is now the location of the University of Waterloo School of Pharmacy. Tin Roof Coffee and Donuts is in the foreground, located in an unusual "A" frame building. And at the corner of the major thoroughfares of King and Victoria stood one of the last phone booths.

1993

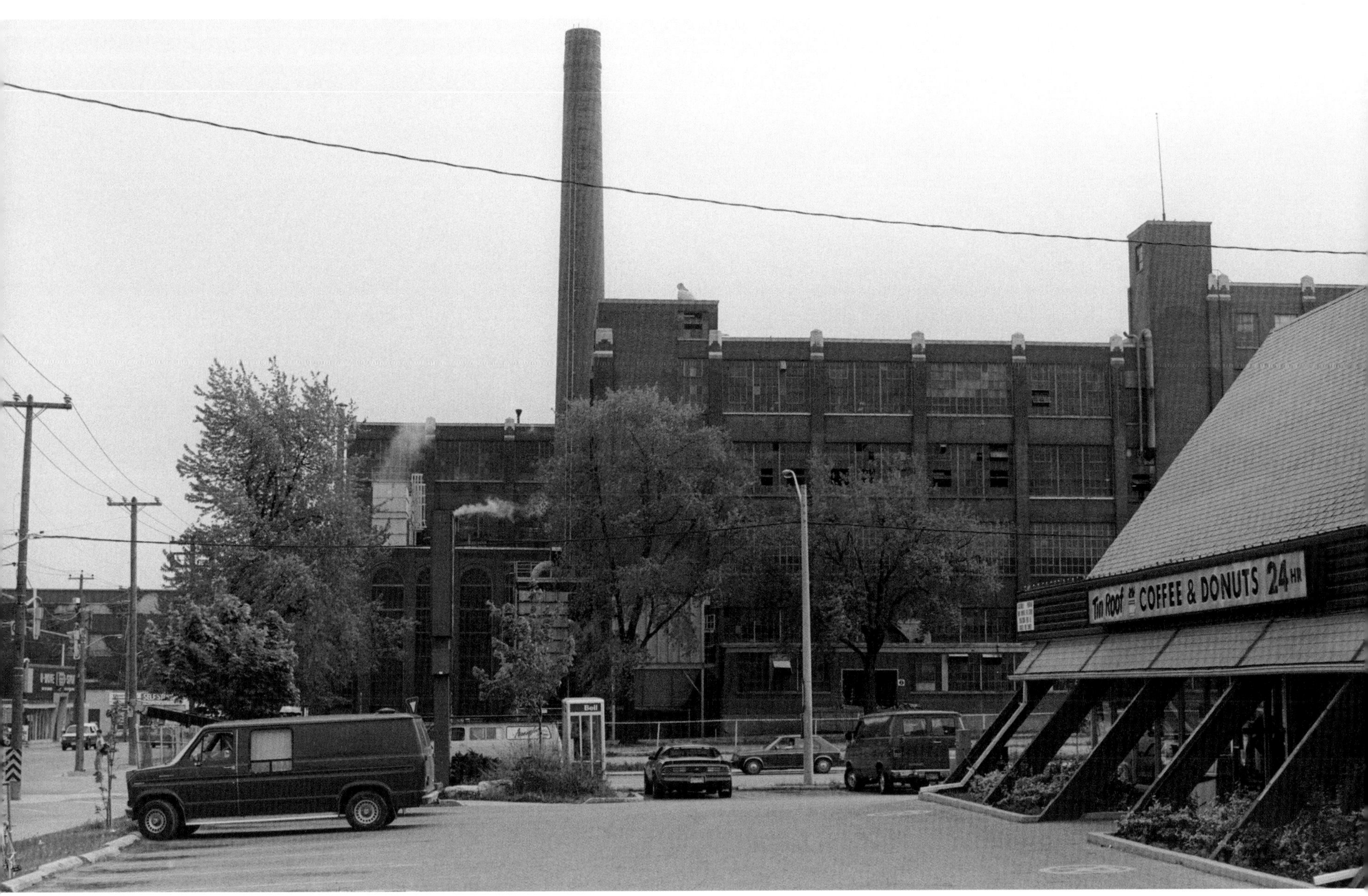
Tin Roof
COFFEE & DONUTS 24HR
Bell

38 | 97 Victoria Street North

Between the closing of the Mitchell Button Factory and its purchase by the Working Centre in 2006, this building was home to many small businesses. I worked there with my brother Richard in our cabinet shop for nineteen years. The front downstairs was always a second-hand shop: the Marion Centre, St. Vincent de Paul, and now the Working Centre's Worth a Second Look.

1993

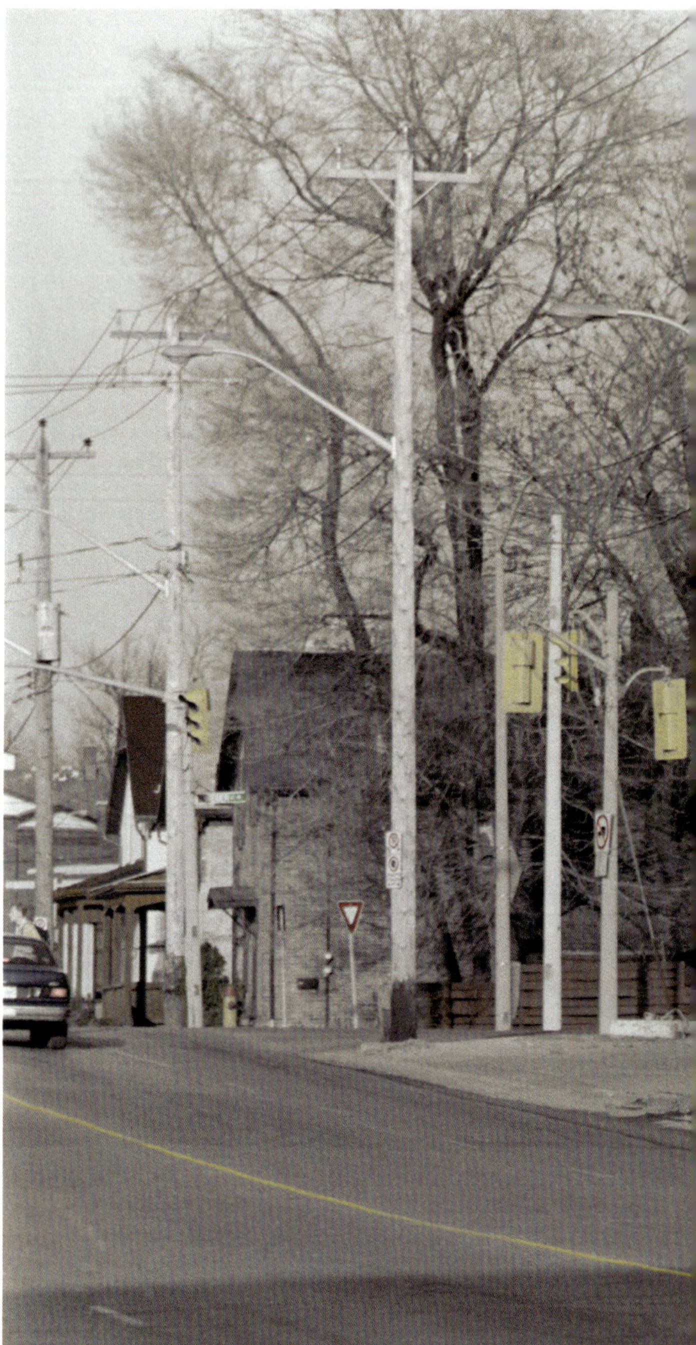

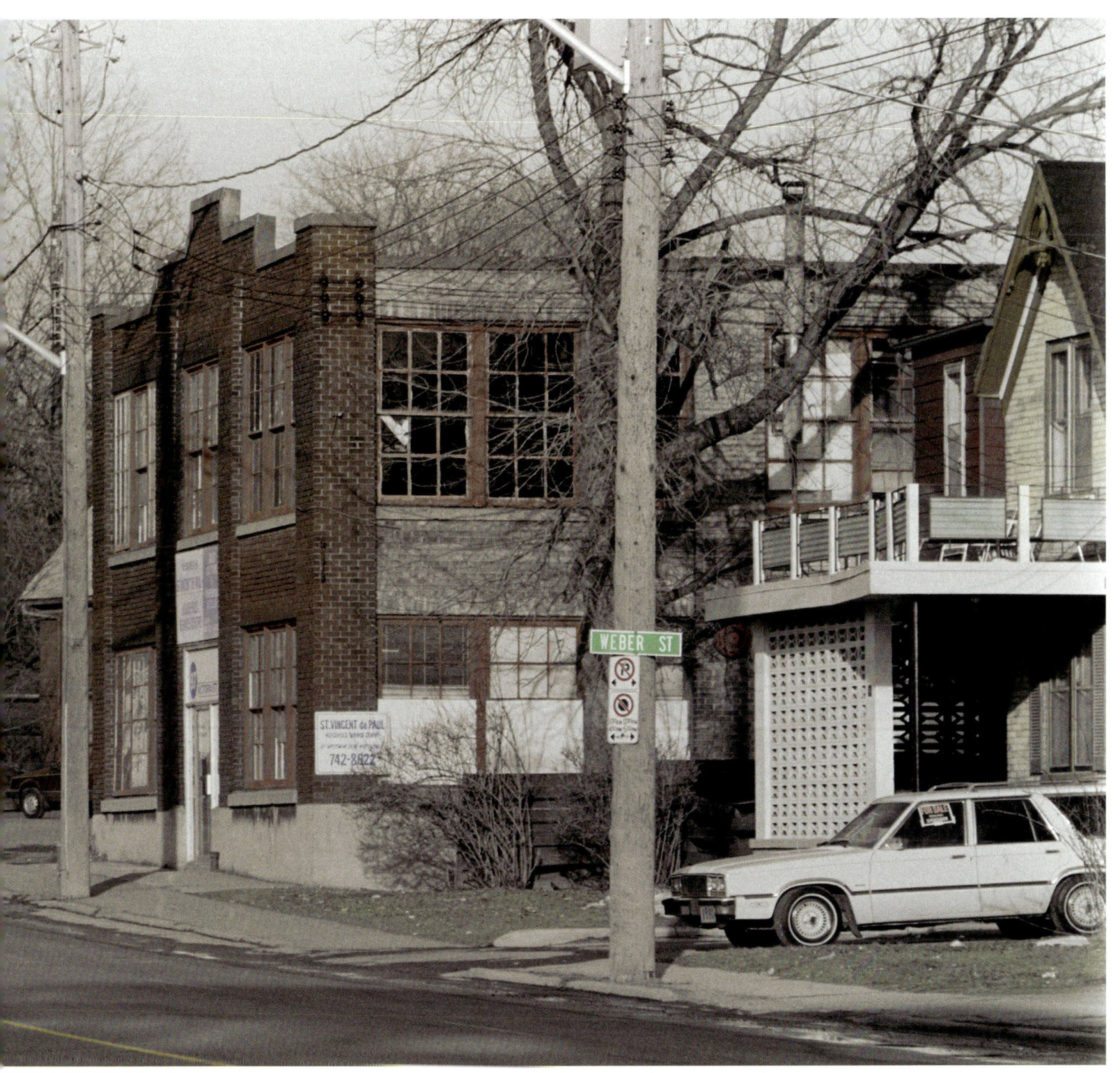
ST. VINCENT de PAUL
742-8822
WEBER ST

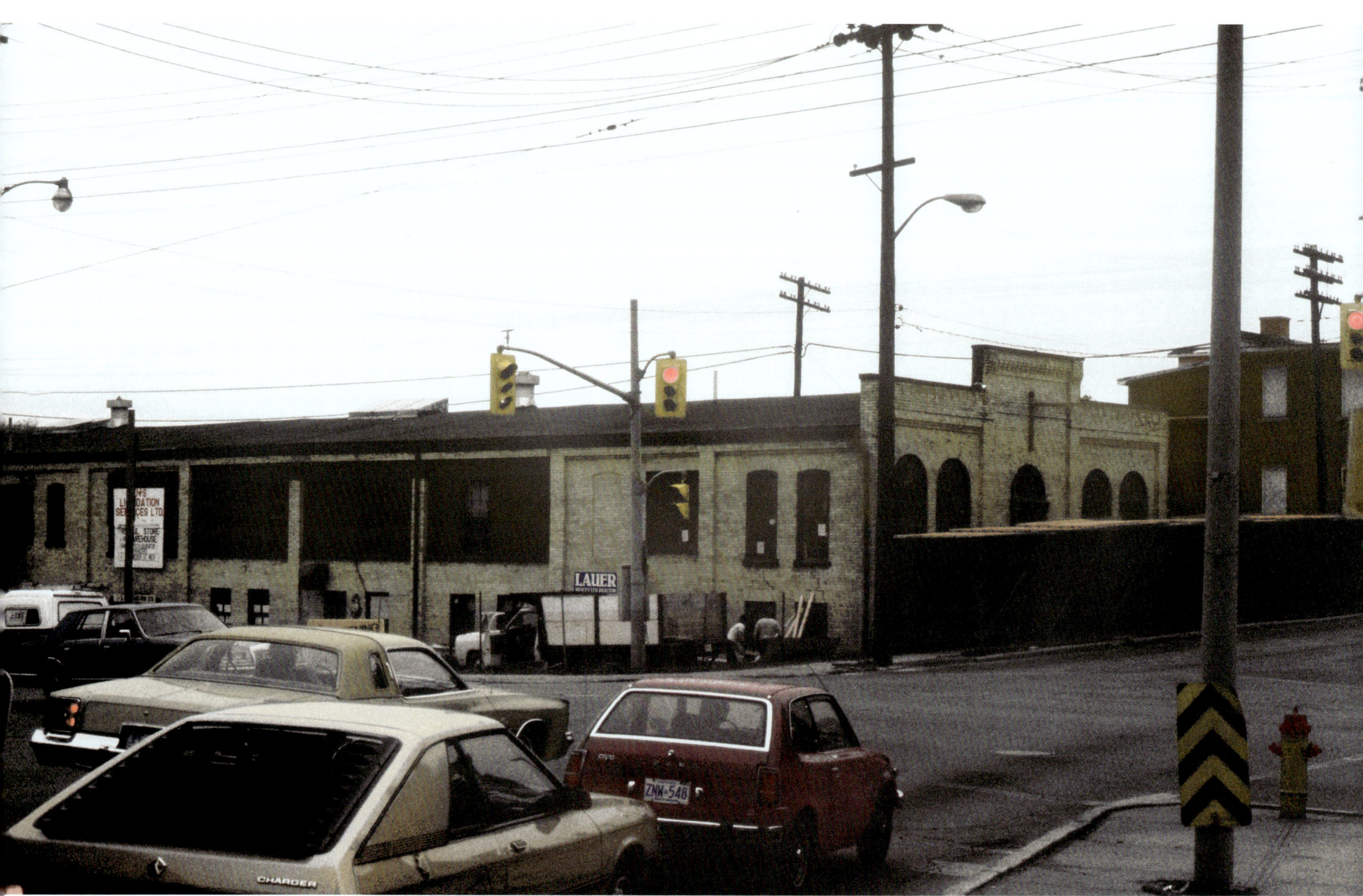
LAUER
ZNW-548
CHARGER

39 | Hydro City Shoe Company *(demolished)*

Built in 1893 by G. V. Oberholtzer, the company was renamed Hydro City Shoes during the Great War. Kitchener was referred to as the hydro city because it was first to receive electric power from Niagara Falls in 1910. When the company closed in the late 1960s, this building at the corner of Victoria and Weber became the home of numerous small businesses before it was demolished for a strip mall, now also demolished for the Weber Street underpass. One business which established itself there was Greenleaf Foods, a health food shop. The business became Full Circle Foods under new owners and still exists in downtown Kitchener.

c.1979

40 | Victoria and Weber, Station Hotel *(demolished)*

It was Friday afternoon, and the strip mall parking lot was full of hot cars and people hanging out just across the road from my old shop. The Station Hotel is in the background. According to the *Waterloo Region Record*, the hotel "traced its history back to 1867" and was destroyed by fire in 2001.

c.1990

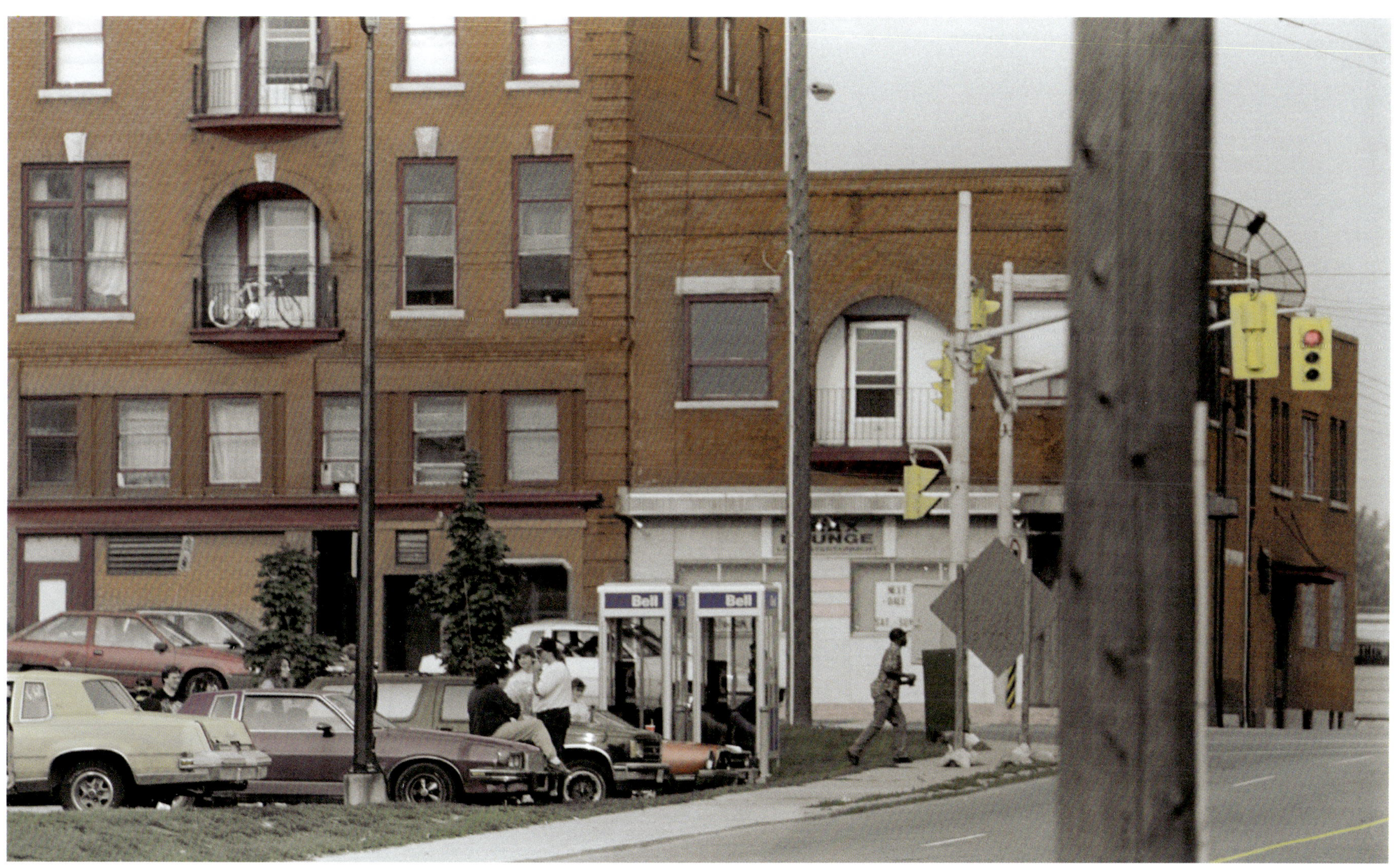
Bell
Bell

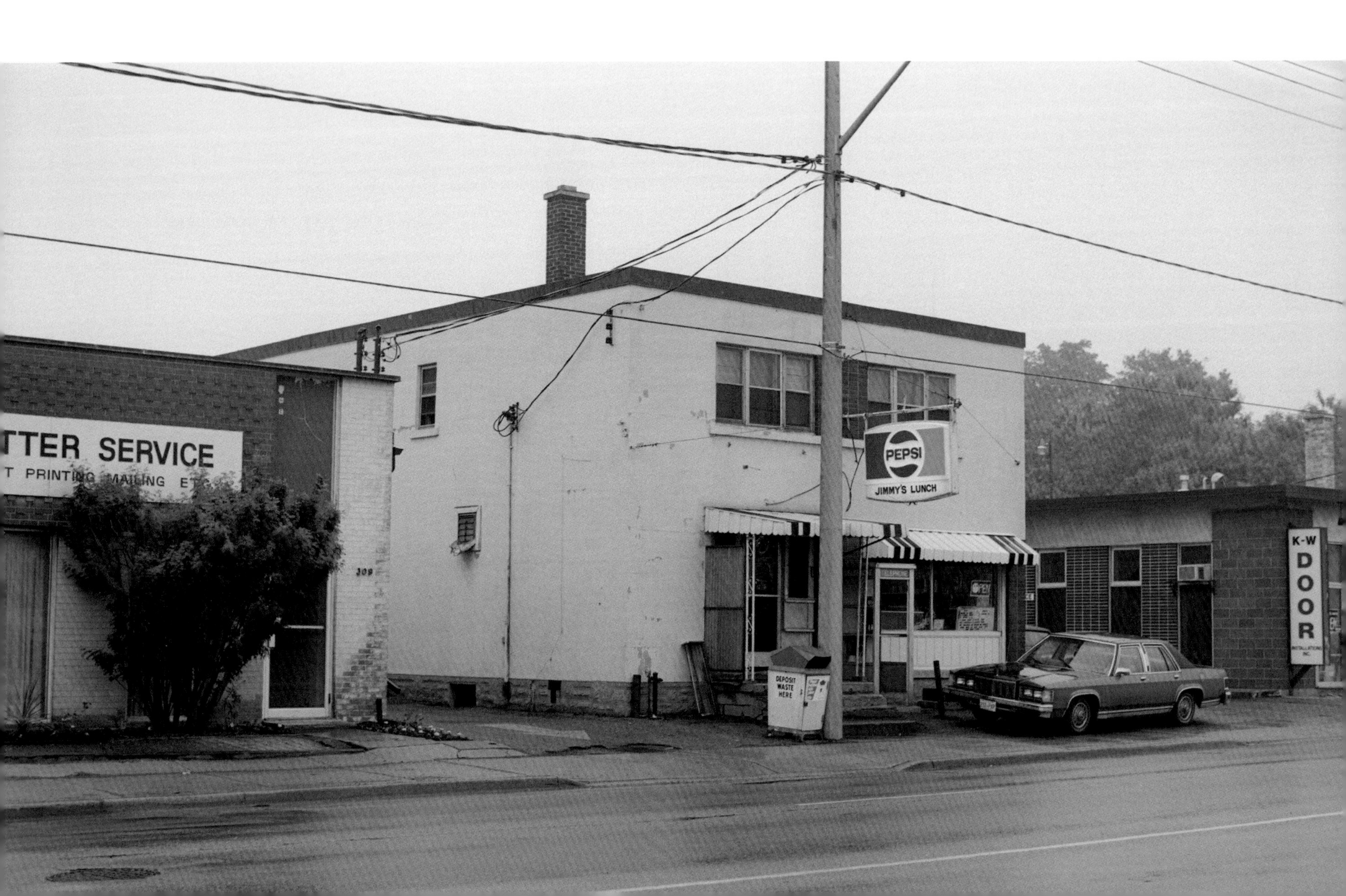
TTER SERVICE
T PRINTING MAILING ETC
309
PEPSI
JIMMY'S LUNCH
DEPOSIT
WASTE
HERE
K-W
DOOR

41 | Jimmy's Lunch

Jimmy's Lunch on Victoria Street North was famous as a 24-hour restaurant at a time when there were no others. Cab drivers I knew would stop in there late at night. While working with this photo, I realized there were stylish Modern buildings on either side.

1993

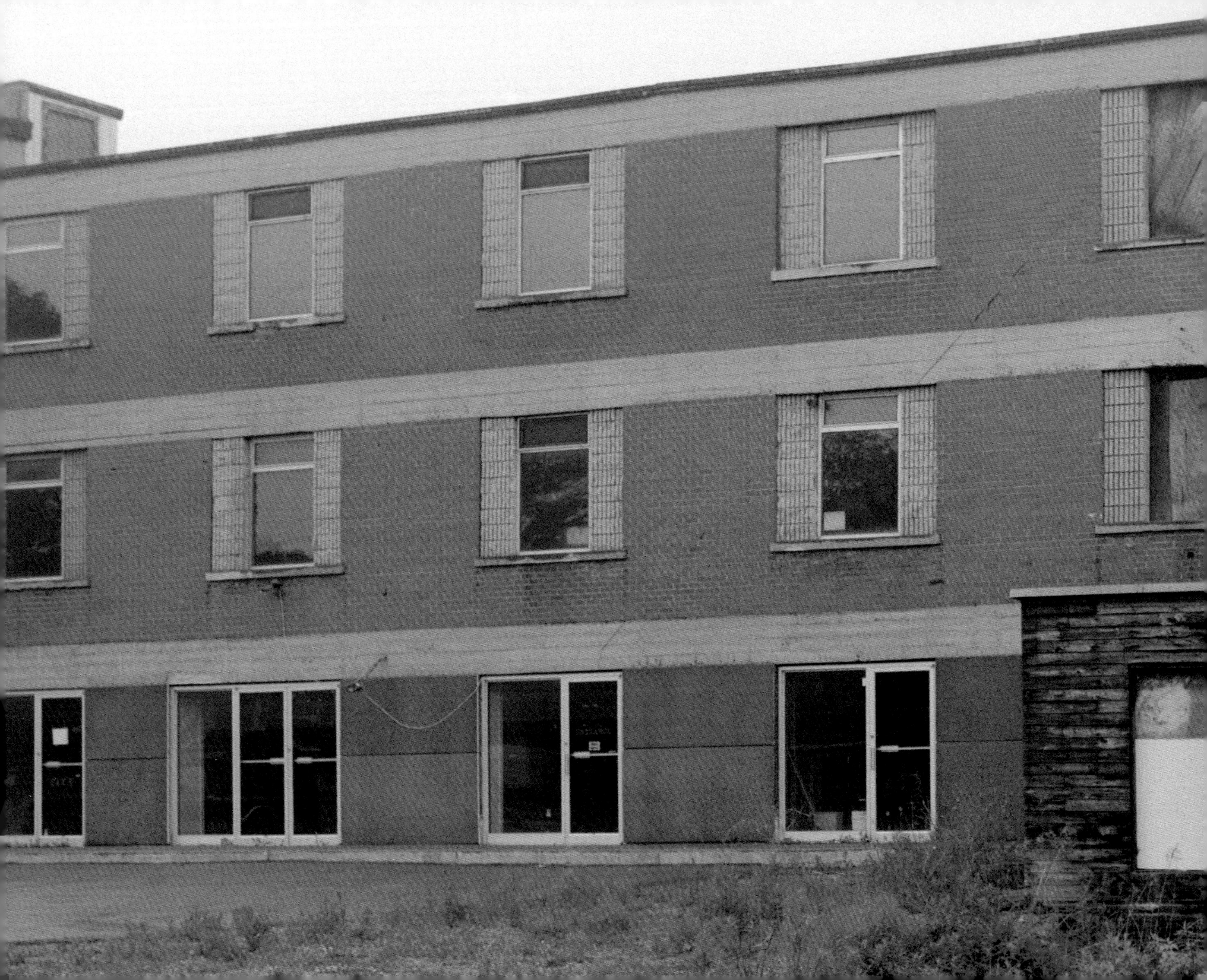

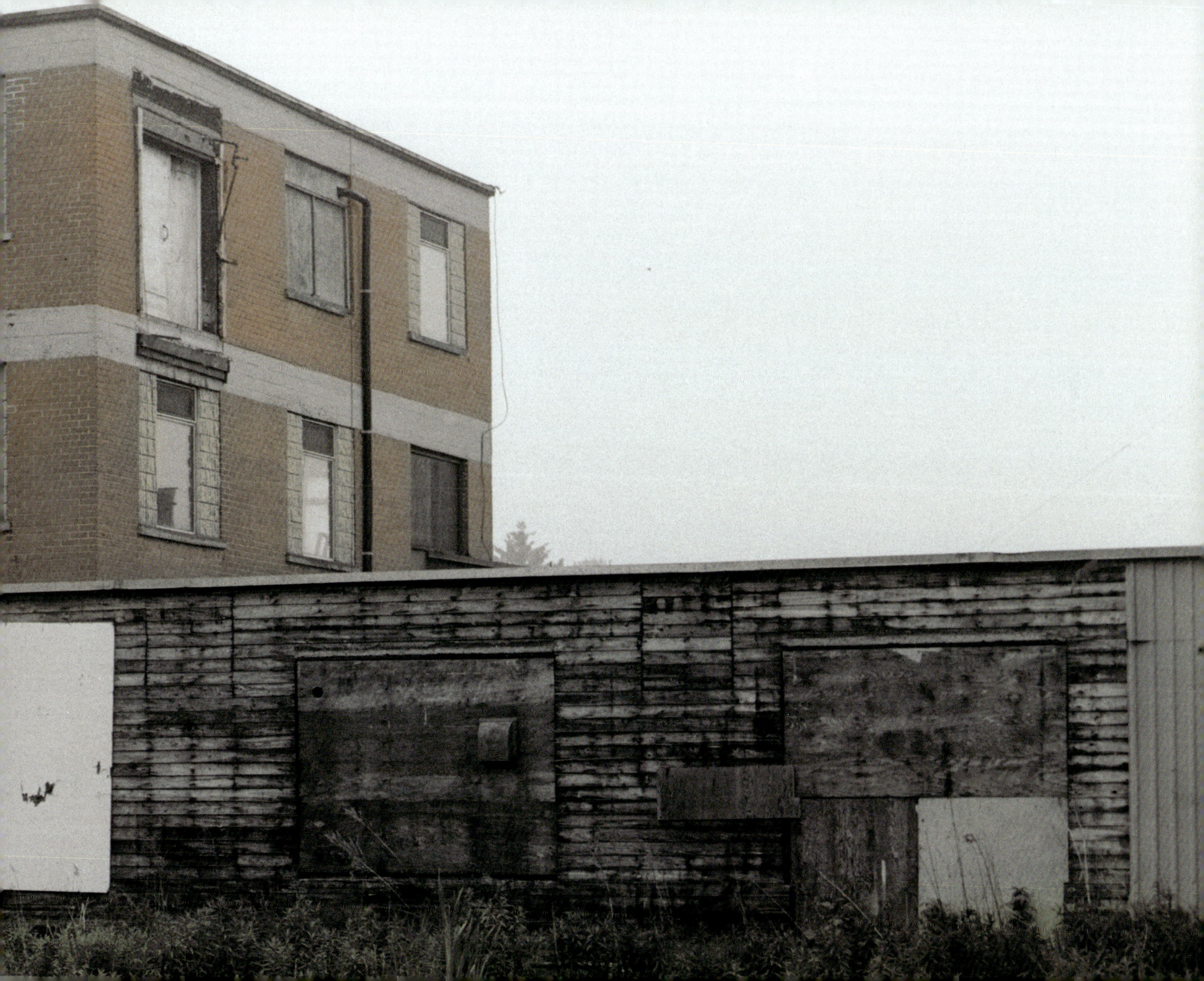

42 | Victoria Street North

This is 236 Victoria Street North, close to Margaret Avenue. Another factory building stood in the foreground (now demolished). There were a few buildings like this along the railway line in Kitchener where efforts at adaptation were made, before the high-tech boom. Rather than take advantage of the light from large windows, they were partially blocked in. The Western Shoe Company was located here. It was founded in 1927 by Ray Charles Bauer, who also started the Bauer Canadian Skate company, both purchased by Greb in 1965. In the 1990s, there were a number of brick-and-beam factories along this stretch of Victoria Street North that could have extended the Innovation District of recent years.

1993

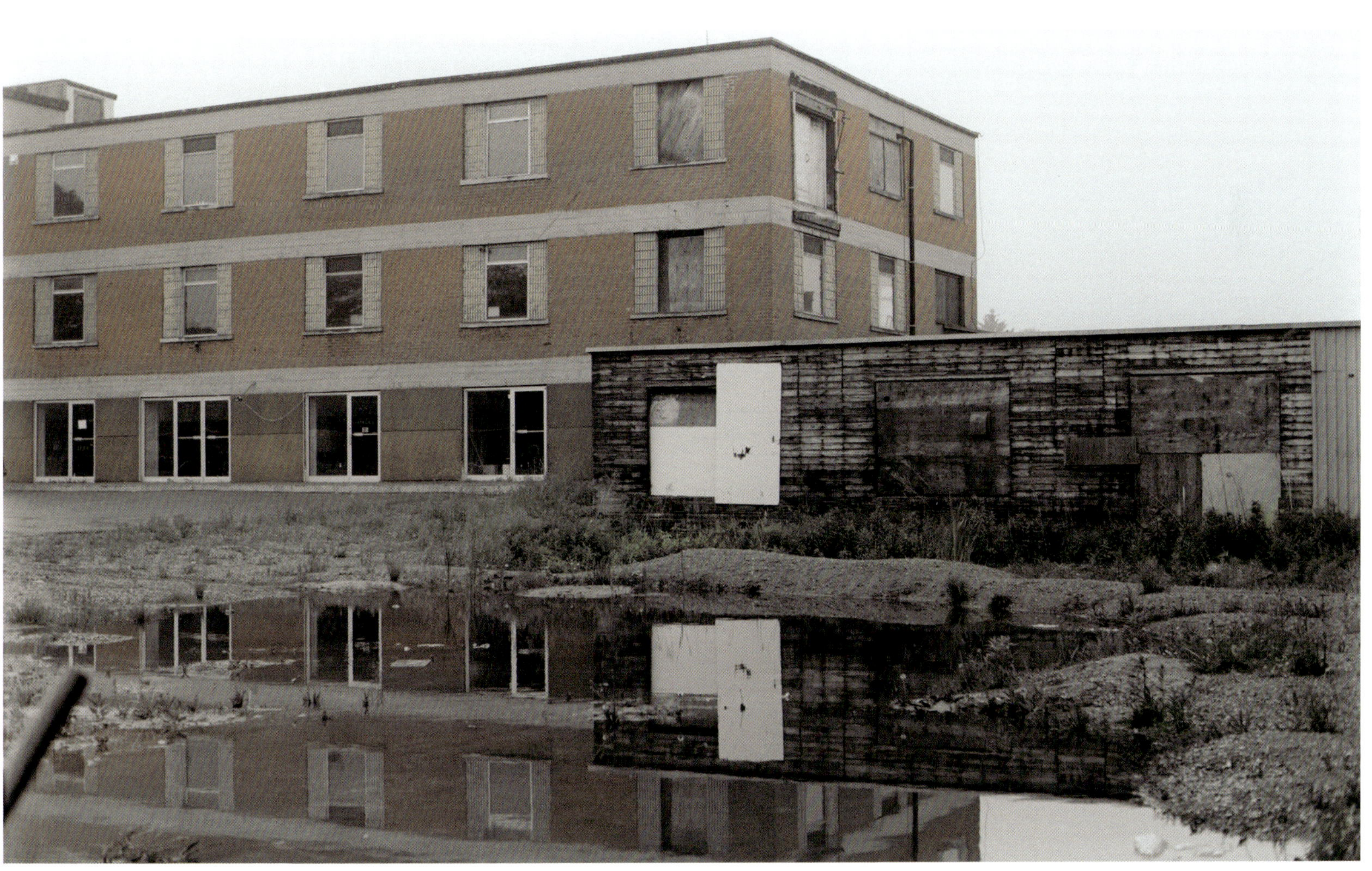

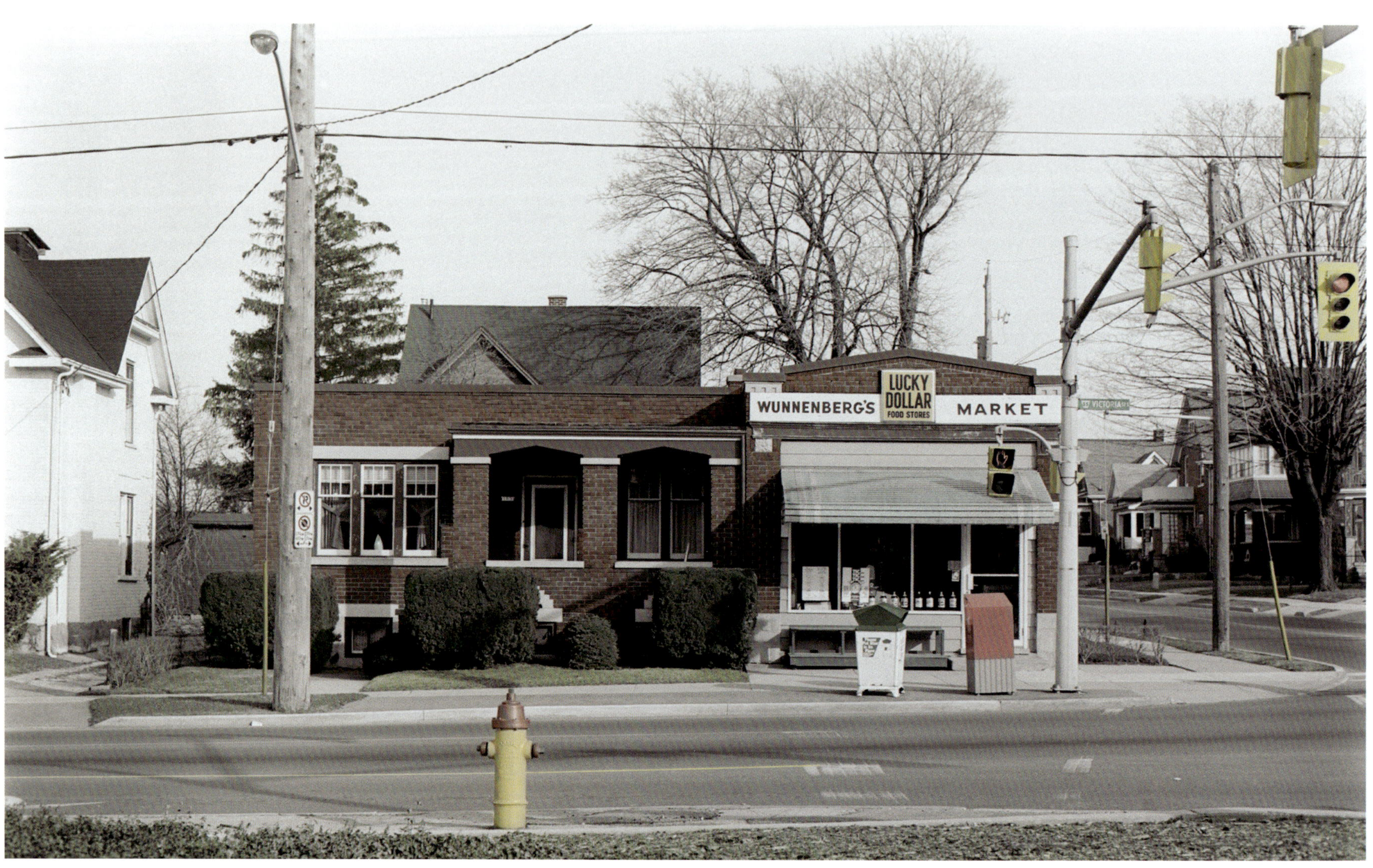
WUNNENBERG'S
LUCKY
DOLLAR
FOOD STORES
MARKET

43 | Wunnenberg's, Victoria Street South and Park Street

I believe Lucky Dollar was a retailers' association, and many members still exist. Here is another version of a corner store on one floor with the residence on the side. A very modest Beaux Arts style building, it is now occupied by the Guitar Corner.

1993

44 | Mario's Milk *(demolished)*

A double corner store at College and Weber has a stone identifying the Manz block. It was very close to my old shop, so I was a frequent customer of Mario's Milk and Variety when we needed more milk for coffee. After it was demolished, it became the parking lot for the Two Goblets restaurant. This building had two recessed balconies, which was not a rare feature on this type and age of building.

1993

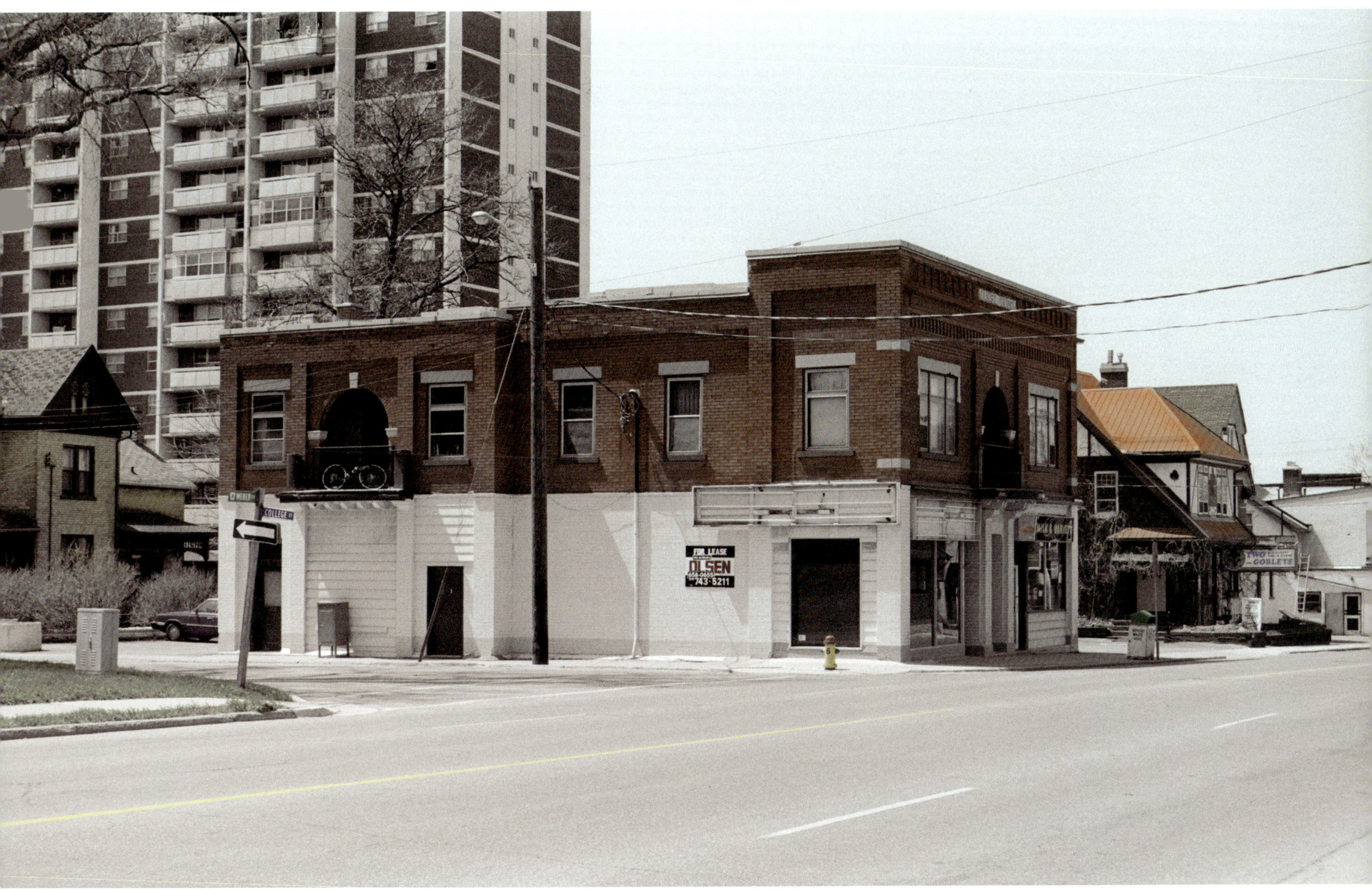
COLLEGE
FOR LEASE
OLSEN
743-5211
TWO
GOBLETS

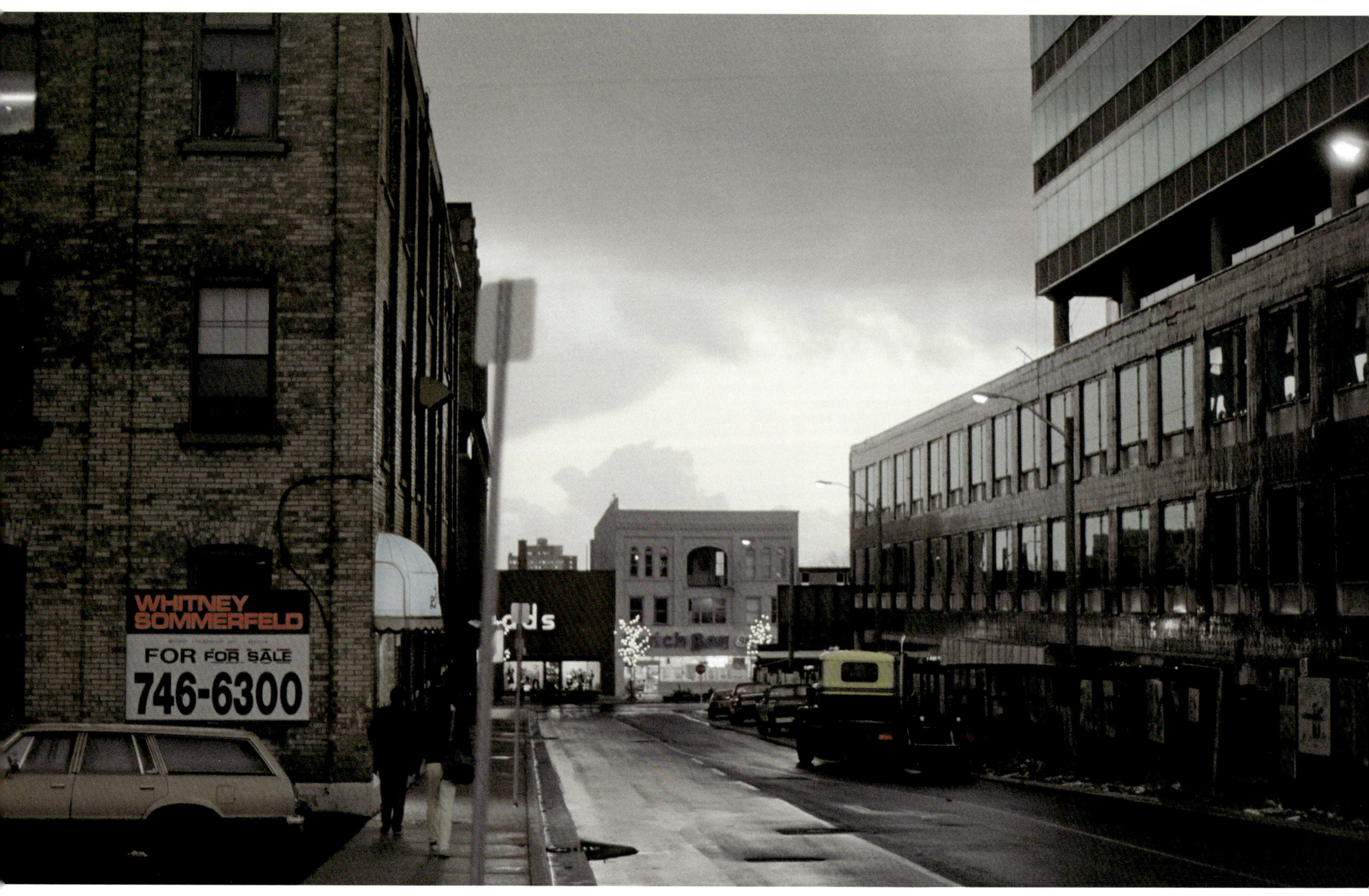
WHITNEY
SOMMERFELD
FOR FOR SALE
746-6300

45 | Young Street Kitchener *(east side demolished)*

This view looks south on Young Street. On the west side the new City Hall was under construction; and on the east side stood the Forsyth shirt factory (demolished 2006) and the Mayfair Hotel at the corner of King (demolished 2015). These frame a view of Budds clothing store and Dutch Boy grocery store, two quite old local businesses, both now gone. When Dutch Boy lost its store on the city hall lot, it opened in slightly smaller quarters next to Budds.

1992

46 | Money lenders, Water Street

It was lunchtime on a Friday, as I recall, on my regular walk downtown that I encountered this scene. A large crowd had gathered to avail themselves of the services offered by the payday lender. The two older gents in the middle ground seem to be strolling along without a care and oblivious to traffic.

1993

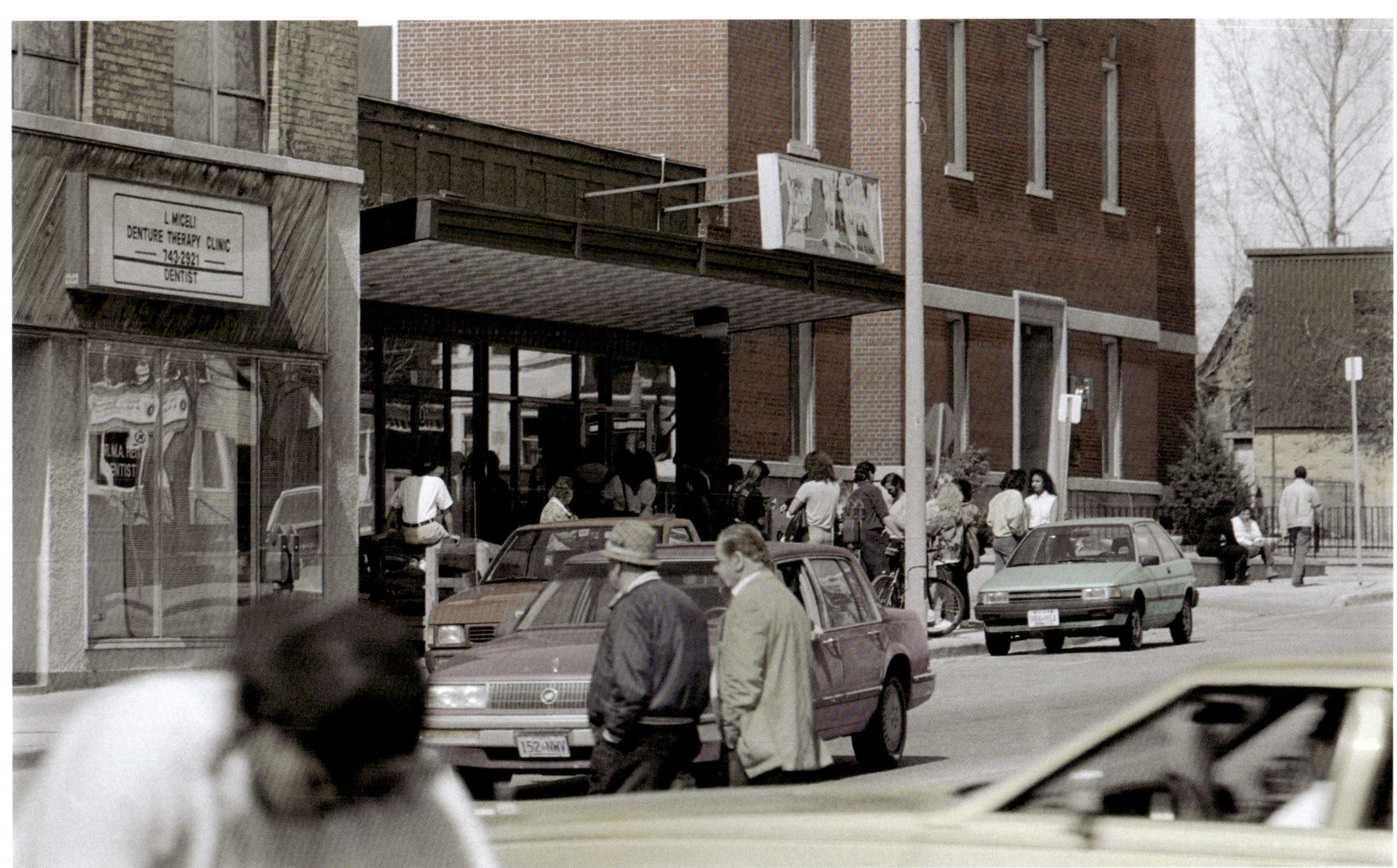
L. MICELI
DENTURE THERAPY CLINIC
743-2921
DENTIST

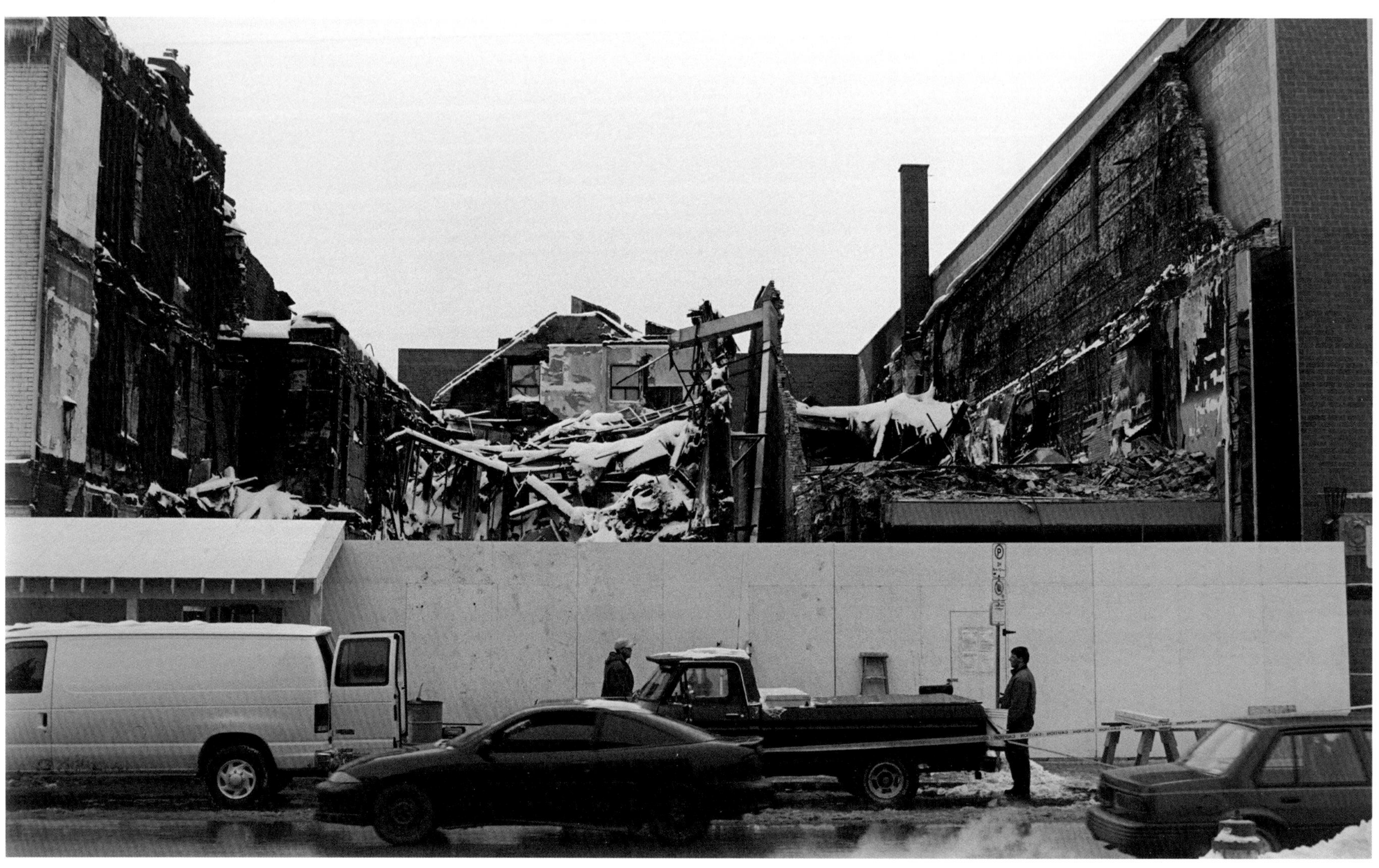

47 | Ackers Furniture (*destroyed by fire*)

This scene is at about 225 King Street West, Kitchener. Pretty well nothing remained of Ackers' fabulous vitrolite facade after the fire which began in the adjoining old wooden building. I had photographed the back of the adjoining building in 1970 for an article about slum housing in a Kitchener community paper called *On the Line*. The back wall was composed of horizontal planks incised to look like stone. The workmen in the foreground engaged in conversation were putting up the hoarding.

2001

48 | King Street West *(demolished)*

This view is looking west along King to the site of the current Kitchener City Hall which opened in 1993. According to reports there were 250 people living on the City Hall block before it was cleared. On the right side of the frame are the Mayfair Hotel and Hymmen Hardware, demolished in 2015 by order of the Chief Building Official for reasons of imminent public danger, a controversial decision which many thought unwarranted. The tall building with the facade mostly clad in dark brown metal was the Strand Bowl bowling alley in the late 1960s. It had large windows with horizontal pressed copper panels between them at that time.

c.1985

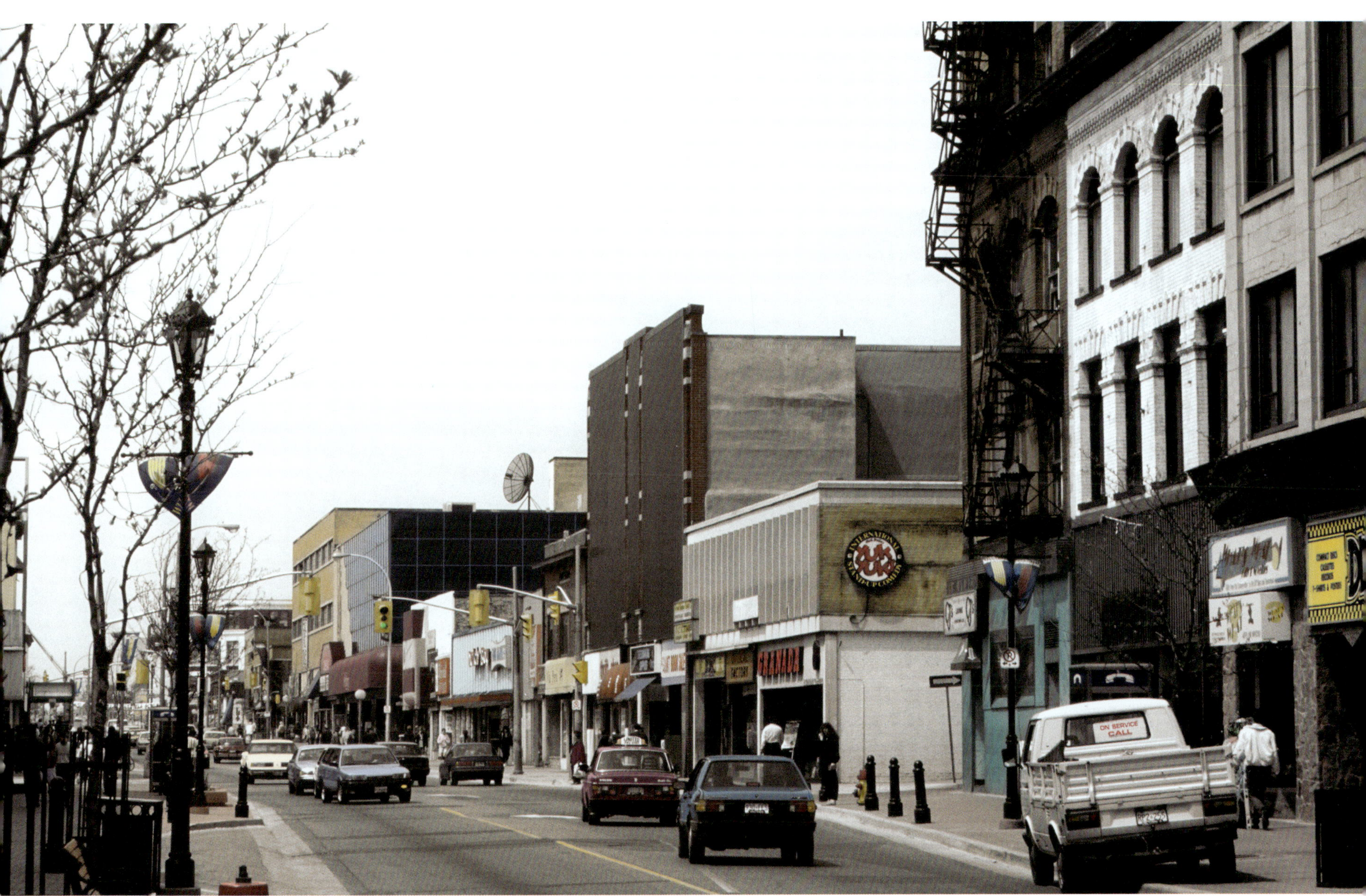

GRANADA
FACTORY
ON SERVICE
CALL

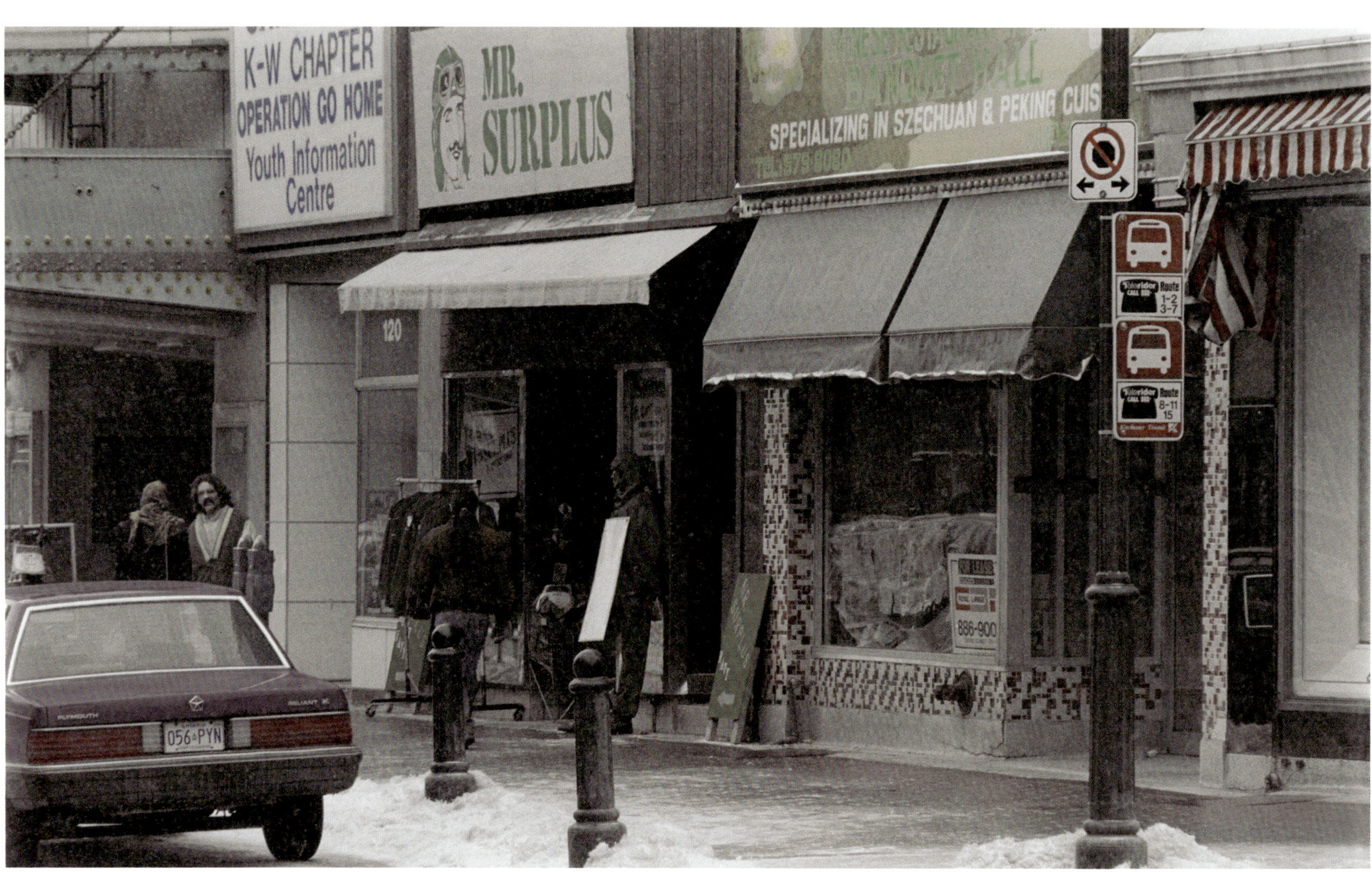

K-W CHAPTER
OPERATION GO HOME
Youth Information
Centre
MR.
SURPLUS
BANQUET HALL
SPECIALIZING IN SZECHUAN & PEKING CUIS
120
Route
1-2
3-7
Route
8-11
15
886-900
056 PYN

49 | Mr. Surplus *(demolished)*

These shops were on King Street West between Young and Ontario where the Young Condos apartment building is being constructed. The shop on the far right was Brodey Draimin Furs. Some of the buildings on this block were demolished by the City of Kitchener because of business it considered unwholesome being conducted in the downtown. The Lyric Theatre on the far left was demolished in 2002. The Chinese restaurant facade is clad in a random pattern tile which one sees here and there, but it is less common than it was sixty years ago.

1993

50 | King and Frederick

The Oktoberfest welcome tent was set up in the middle of Frederick Street next to a branch of the Toronto Dominion Bank, designed by Toronto architect Bruce A. Etherington in 1959. The Market Square had been updated from local architect John Lingwood's original design of 1974 with an overdue facelift in 1986 by an American firm, replacing the grand exterior staircase and second floor level plaza with a new green glass facade. The green glass is itself getting a bit dated.

1994

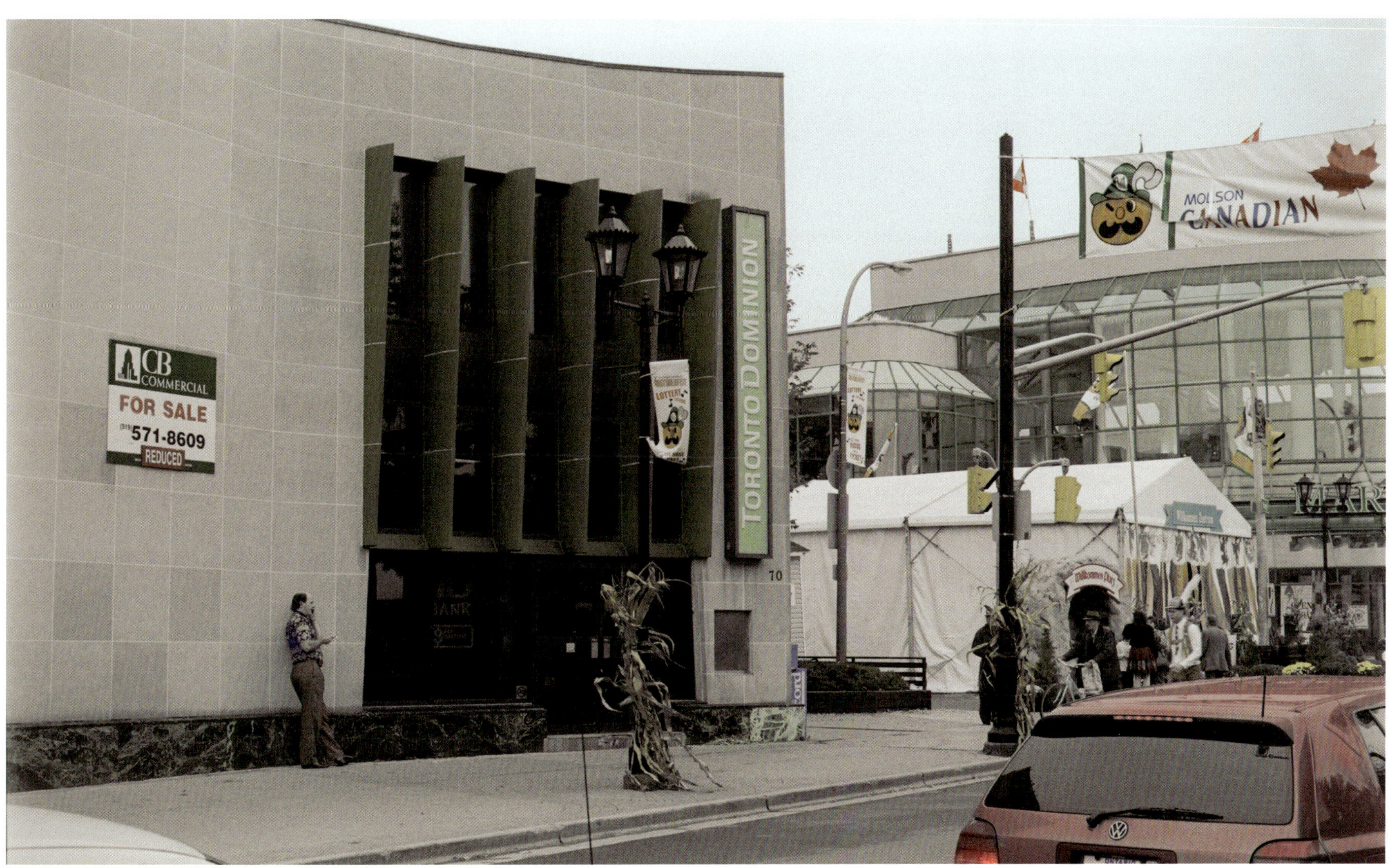
CB
COMMERCIAL
FOR SALE
571-8609
REDUCED
TORONTO DOMINION
70
MOLSON
CANADIAN

51 | David Street *(demolished)*

This house was in the middle of the block between David and Queen. It was quite old and may have faced Queen Street at one time. It became notorious for drug use and prostitution. Before it was finally demolished it became an art installation and was painted white as part of KAFKA 2014. The house on the left was painted black. I didn't realize until I started working on the image that there were three guys with a ladder at the back. They all turned their gaze to me as I took the photo, but they were too far away to do anything. They might have been cleaning the eavestroughs, but I doubt it.

1993

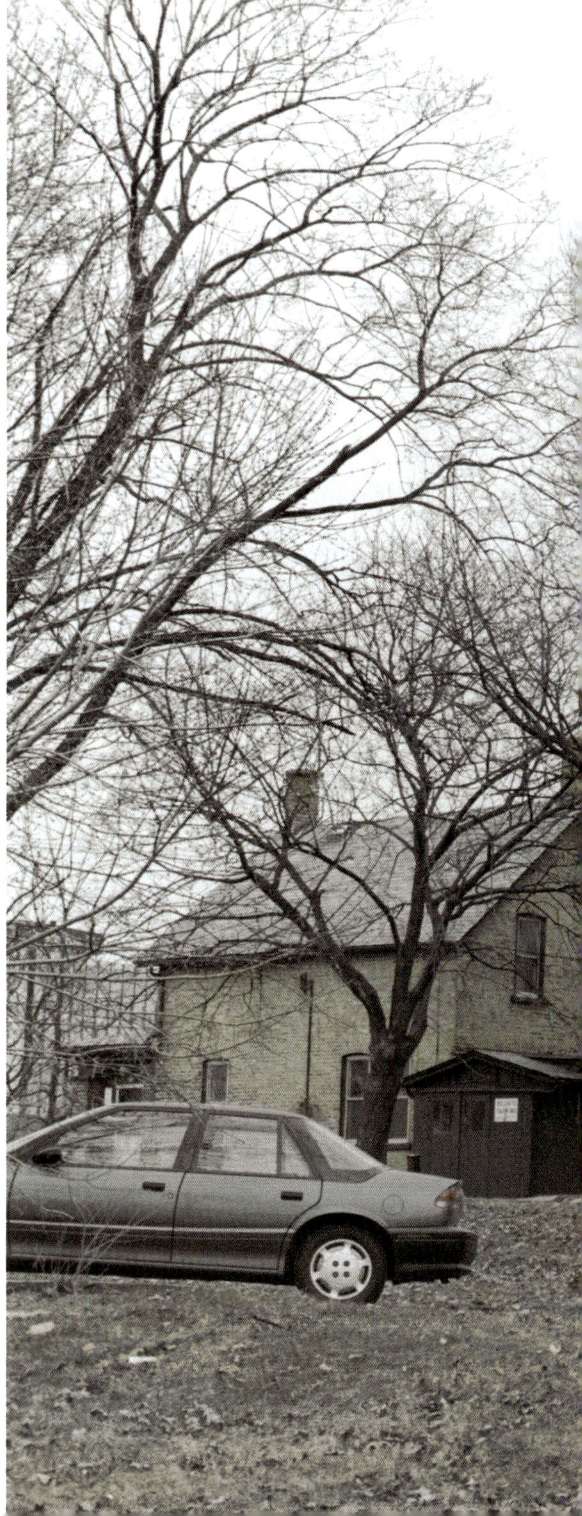

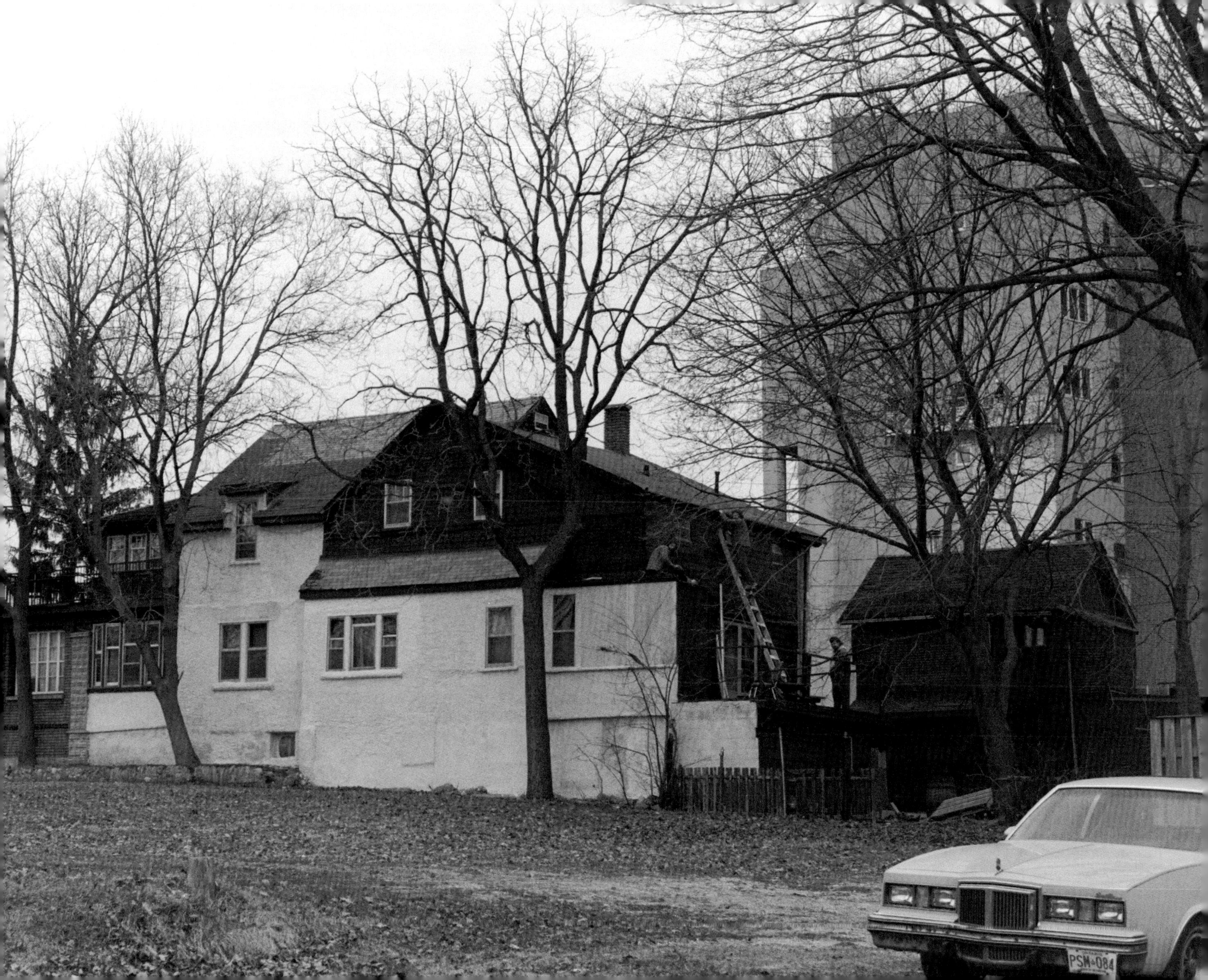
PSM 084

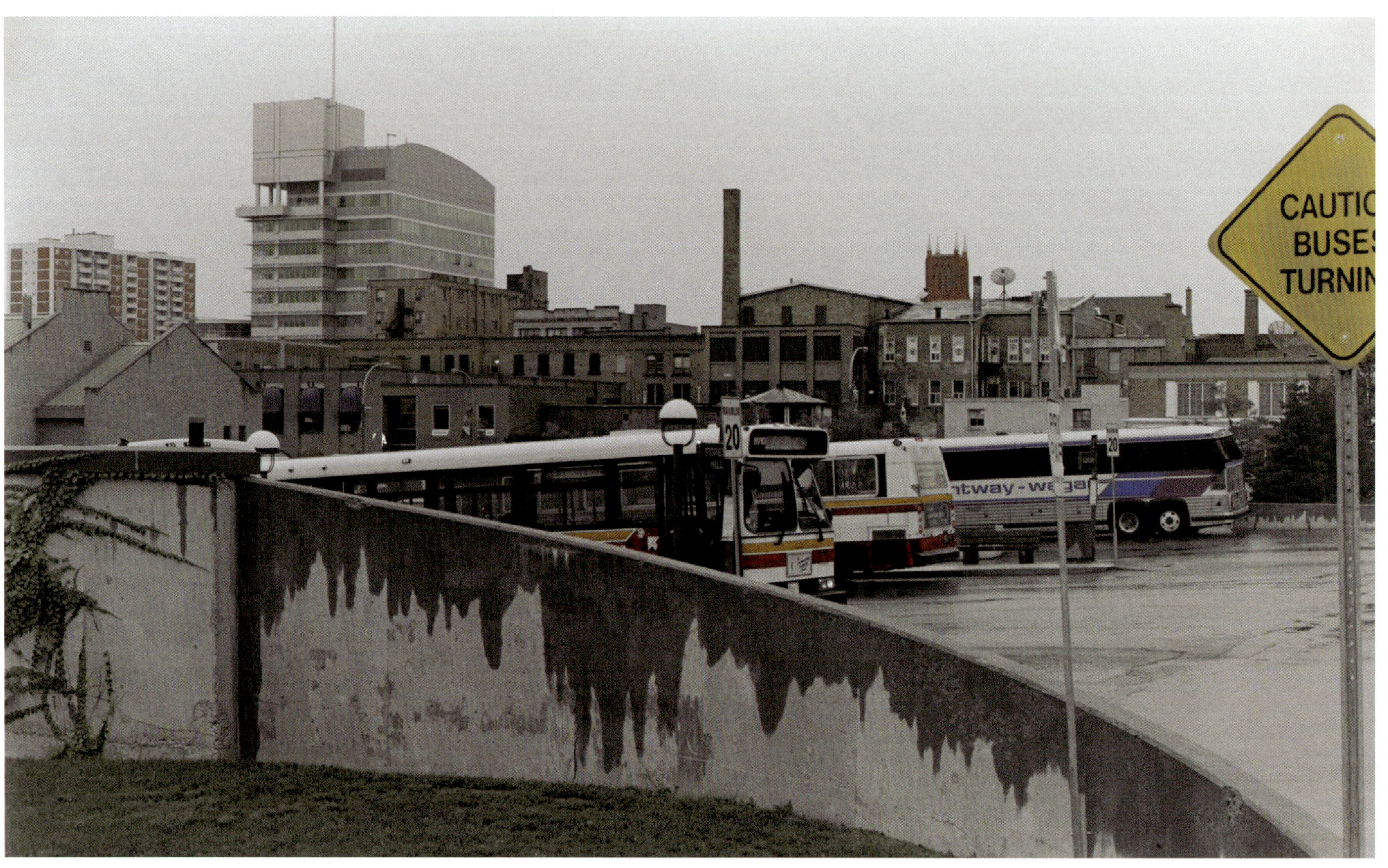
CAUTIO
BUSES
TURNIN
20

52 | Bus Depot, Charles Street

A section of Kitchener's skyline and part of Charles Street are the background of the bus depot viewed from the west. Designed by the celebrated Kitchener architect John Lingwood, the bus depot opened in 1988. The buses were operated by Kitchener Transit before the region took over public transportation. The Mayfair Hotel is seen partially in front of the City Hall and the tower in the distance is St. Mary's Roman Catholic Church.

1995

53 | Downtown Kitchener Parking Garage

As I was on my way to the Kitchener Market about 10:30 on a Saturday morning in April, I was struck by the absence of any life in this scene looking toward Frederick Street from King. It may have been the hostile urban environment, but I imagined the possibility of snipers on the corner tower of the garage.

2009

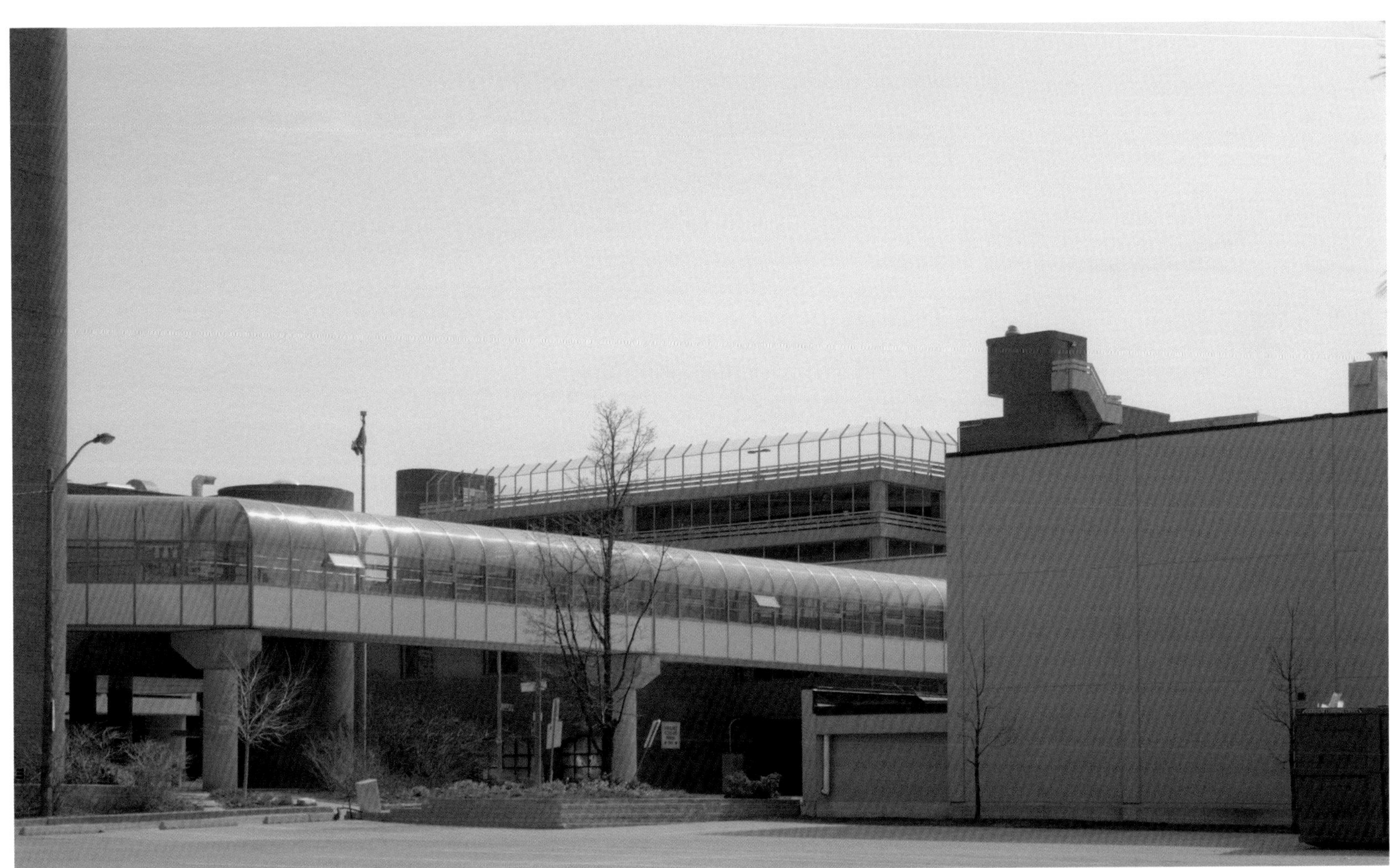

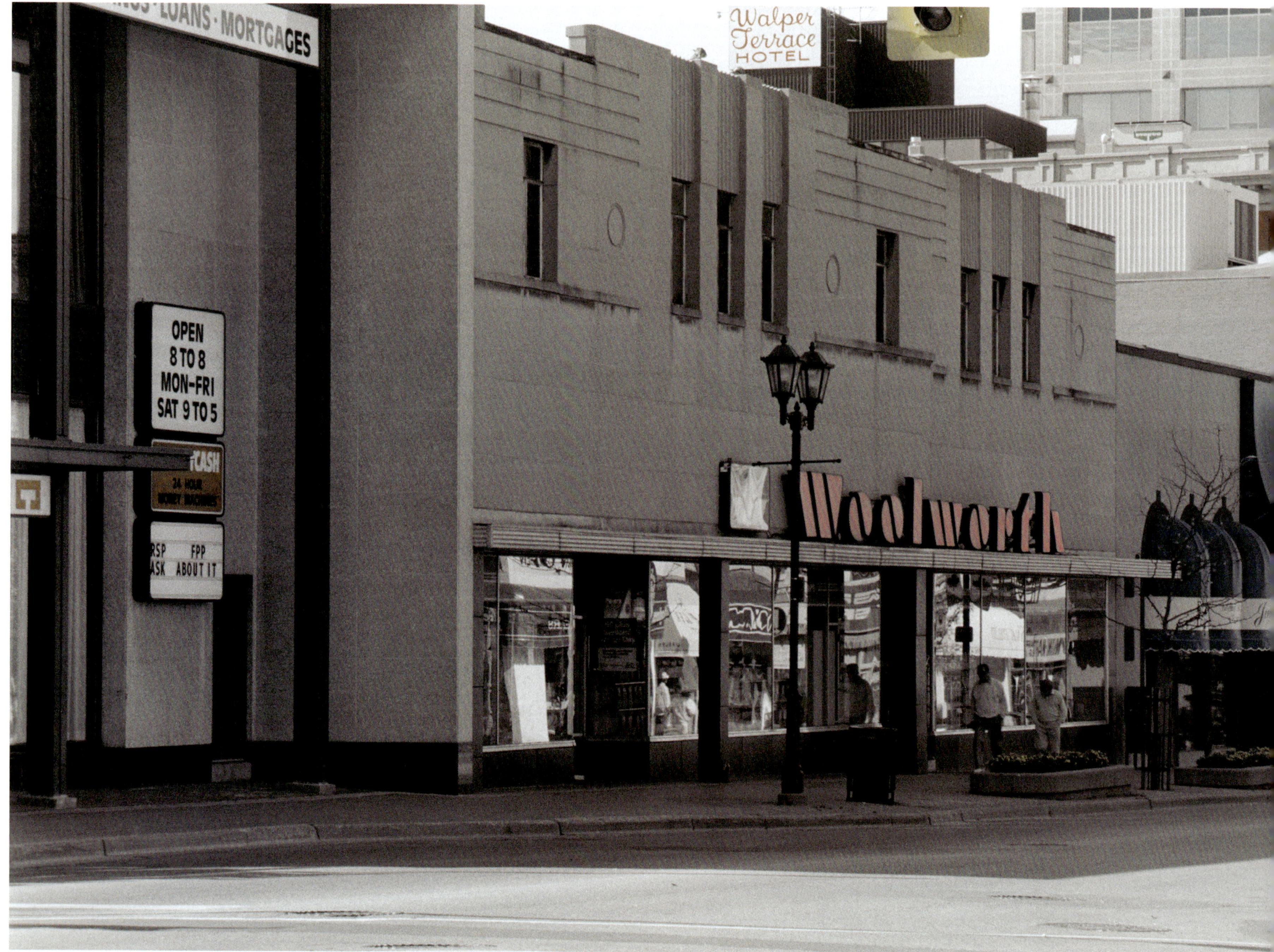
LOANS · MORTGAGES
Walper
Terrace
HOTEL
OPEN
8 TO 8
MON-FRI
SAT 9 TO 5
CASH
24 HOUR
MONEY MACHINES
RSP FPP
ASK ABOUT IT
Woolworth

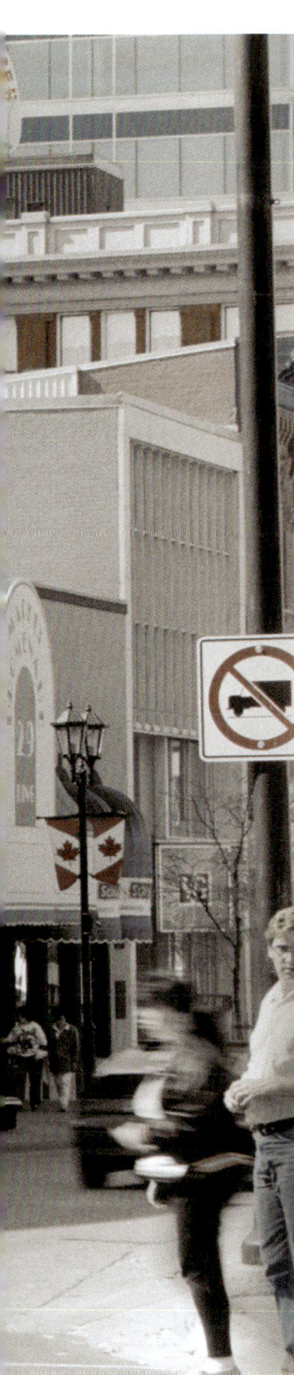

54 | Woolworth

Woolworth's, at 53 King Street East in downtown Kitchener, is one of a very few Art Deco buildings in the Region of Waterloo. It's interesting to speculate why not much happened architecturally in Kitchener and Waterloo in the 1930s, and why there was a huge explosion of building after the war. This building is fairly plain compared to some of the over-the-top examples in the world's major cities, but the inspiration is obvious.

c.1991

55 | The YWCA and Trinity United Church

The YWCA on Frederick Street has a datestone of 1937. If there were no datestone, the glass block window with the letters applied on the outside would be a good clue. In the 1970s it was the site of a popular local coffee house in the basement called The Tunnel Inn, which one entered by a sort of porte-cochère. I saw many local musicians there and played there a number of times myself. Barely visible is the now demolished Trinity United Church.

1996

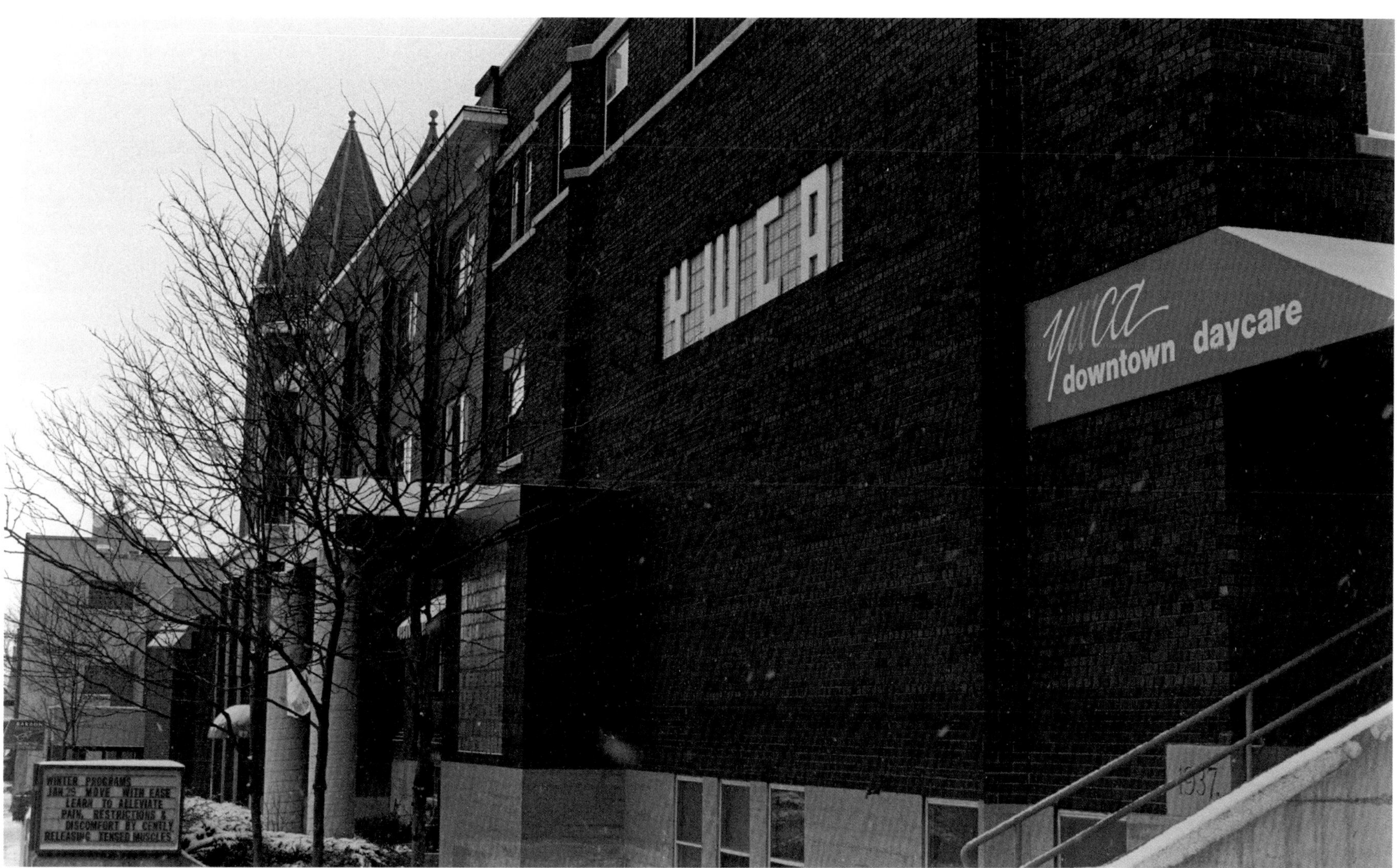
YWCA
ywca
downtown daycare
1937
WINTER PROGRAMS
JAN 29 MOVE WITH EASE
LEARN TO ALLEVIATE
PAIN, RESTRICTIONS &
DISCOMFORT BY GENTLY
RELEASING TENSED MUSCLES

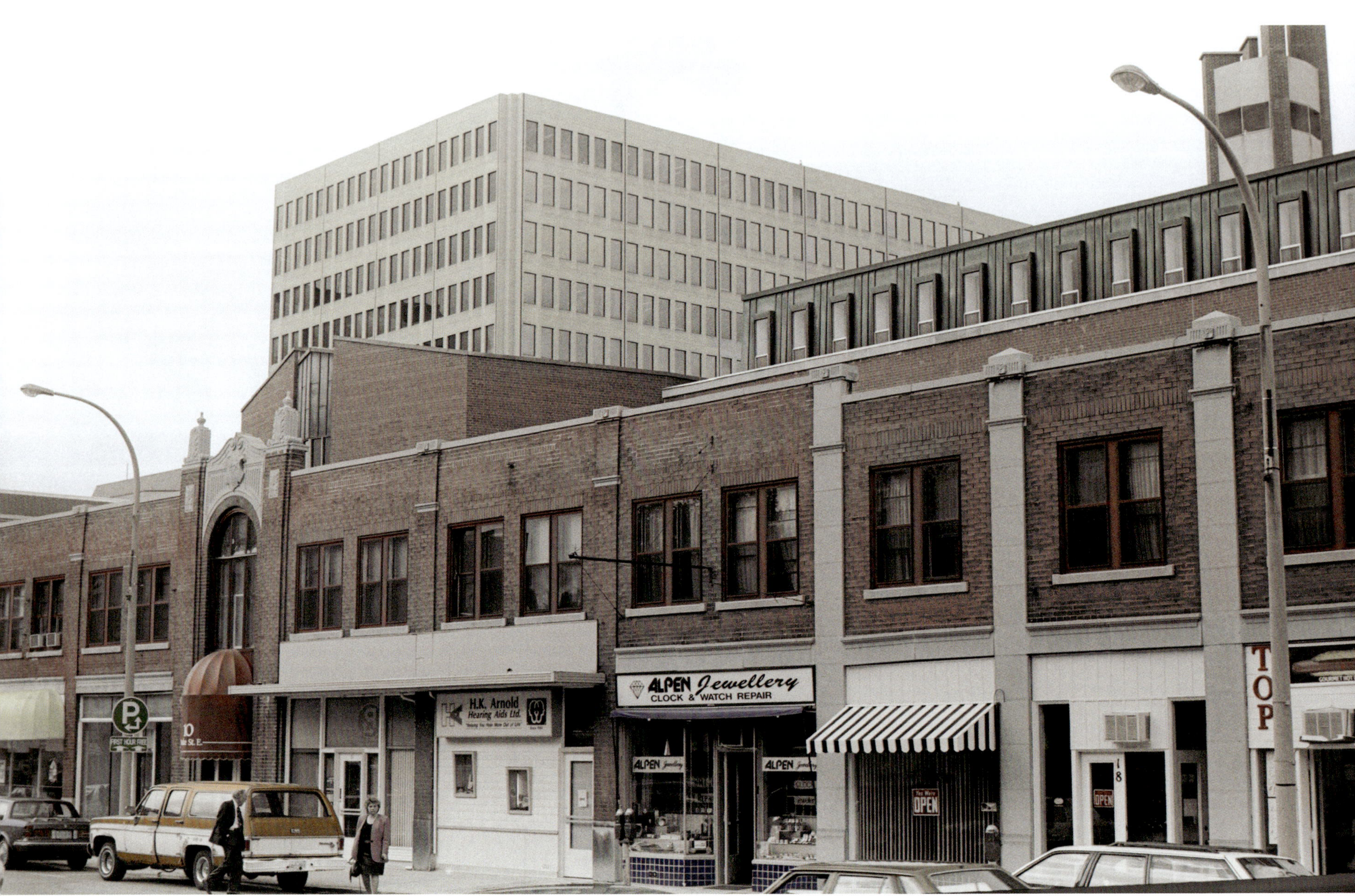
FIRST HOUR FREE
H.K. Arnold
Hearing Aids Ltd.
ALPEN Jewellery
CLOCK & WATCH REPAIR
ALPEN Jewellery
ALPEN Jewellery
OPEN
OPEN
18
TOP

56 | Duke Street

This Beaux Arts commercial block on Duke Street is very shallow in depth. It was recently known as the Duke Street Food Block when it was populated with restaurants and a bakery. Behind is St. Paul's Lutheran Church and the Commerce Court office building. The couple getting out of the old panel truck were perhaps going to the Federal Building across Duke Street.

1993

57 | Frederick and Weber

I was at the corner of Frederick and Weber, looking east. It was a bitterly cold winter's morning, I think in early January, and the air was thick with condensation from cars and heating systems. There was enough haze in the air that I could shoot right into the sun. The corner is high enough that one could see far to the east. The corner house still stands, but the rest of the block is the site of the Waterloo Region Courthouse.

1994

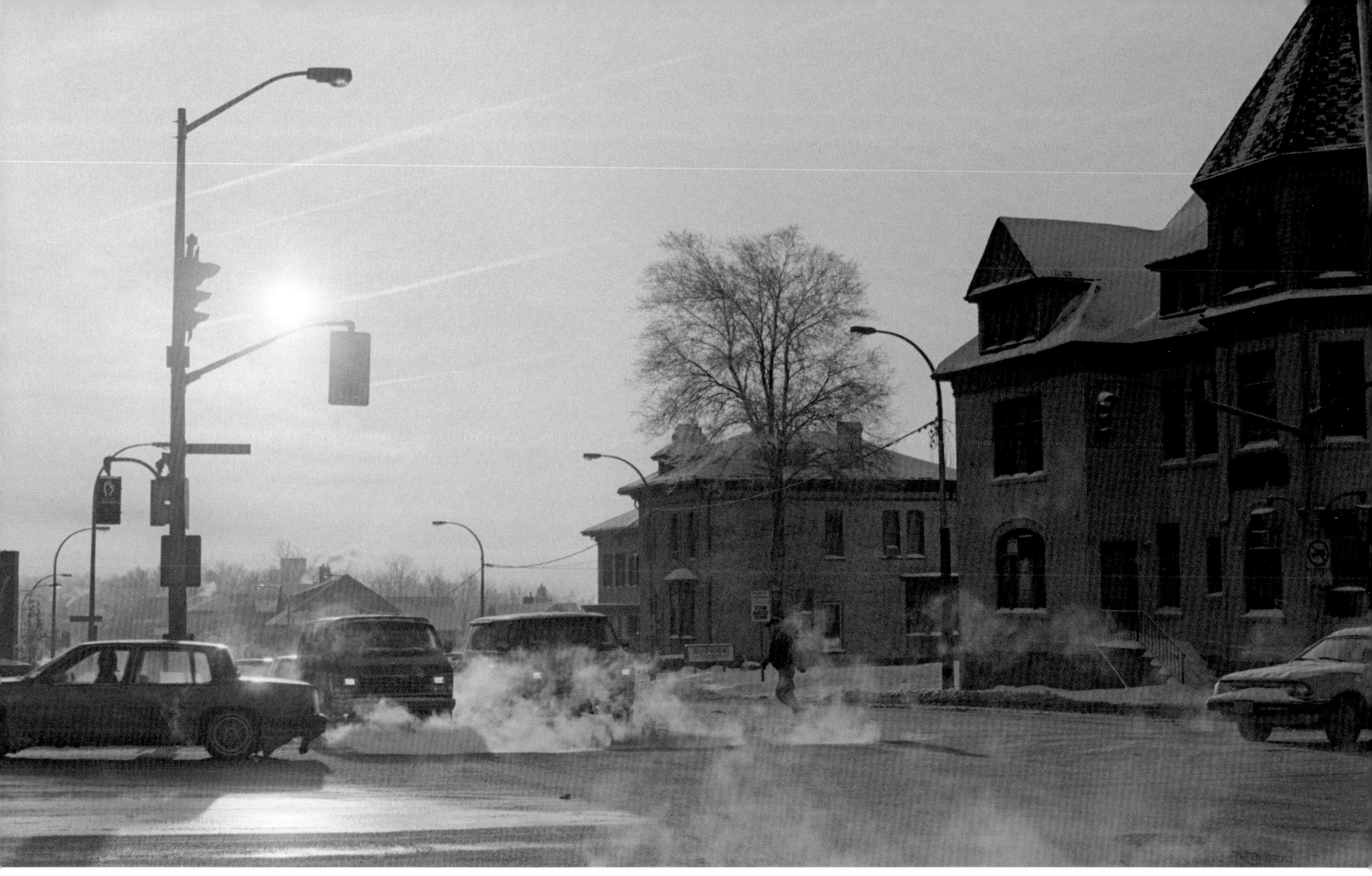

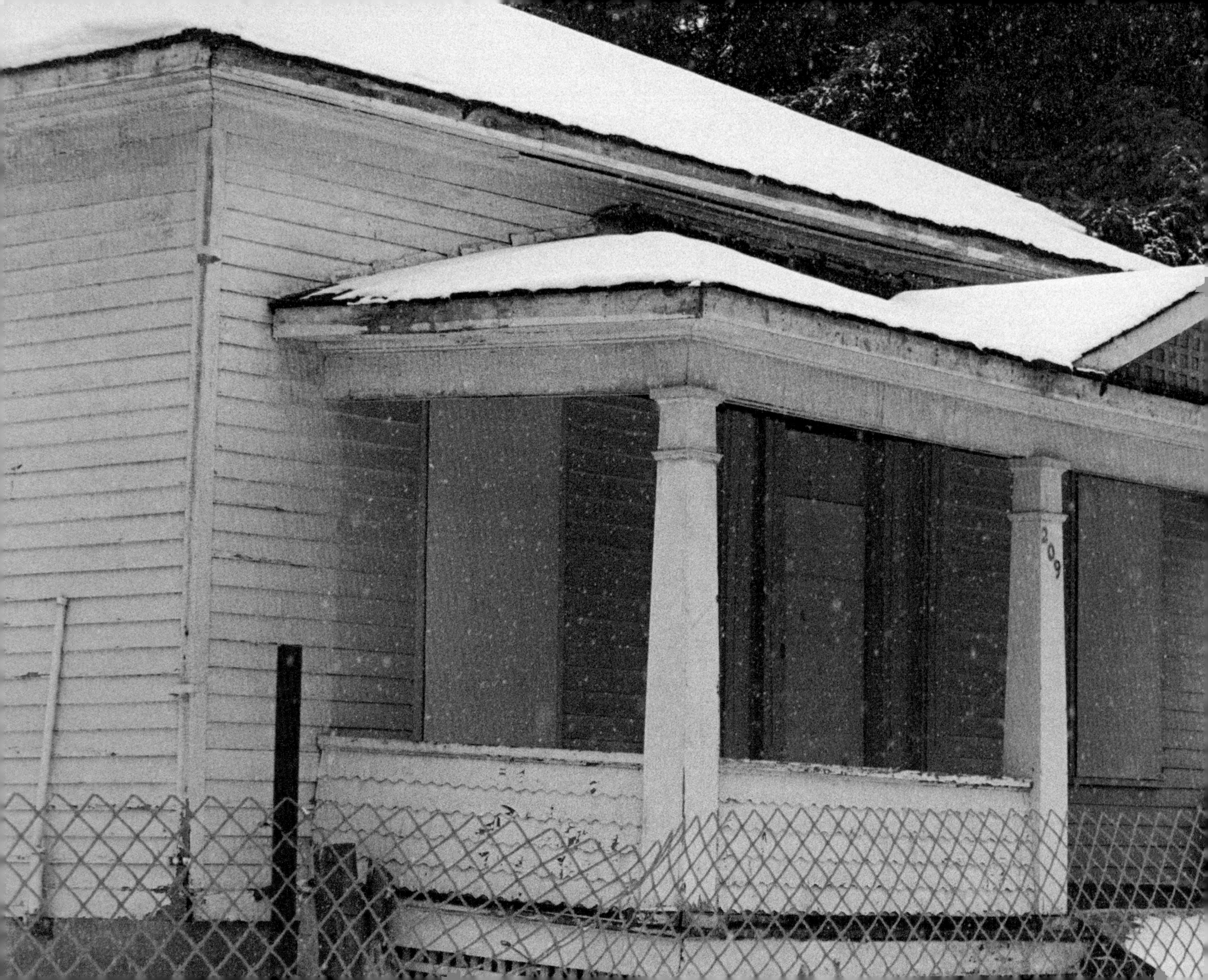
209

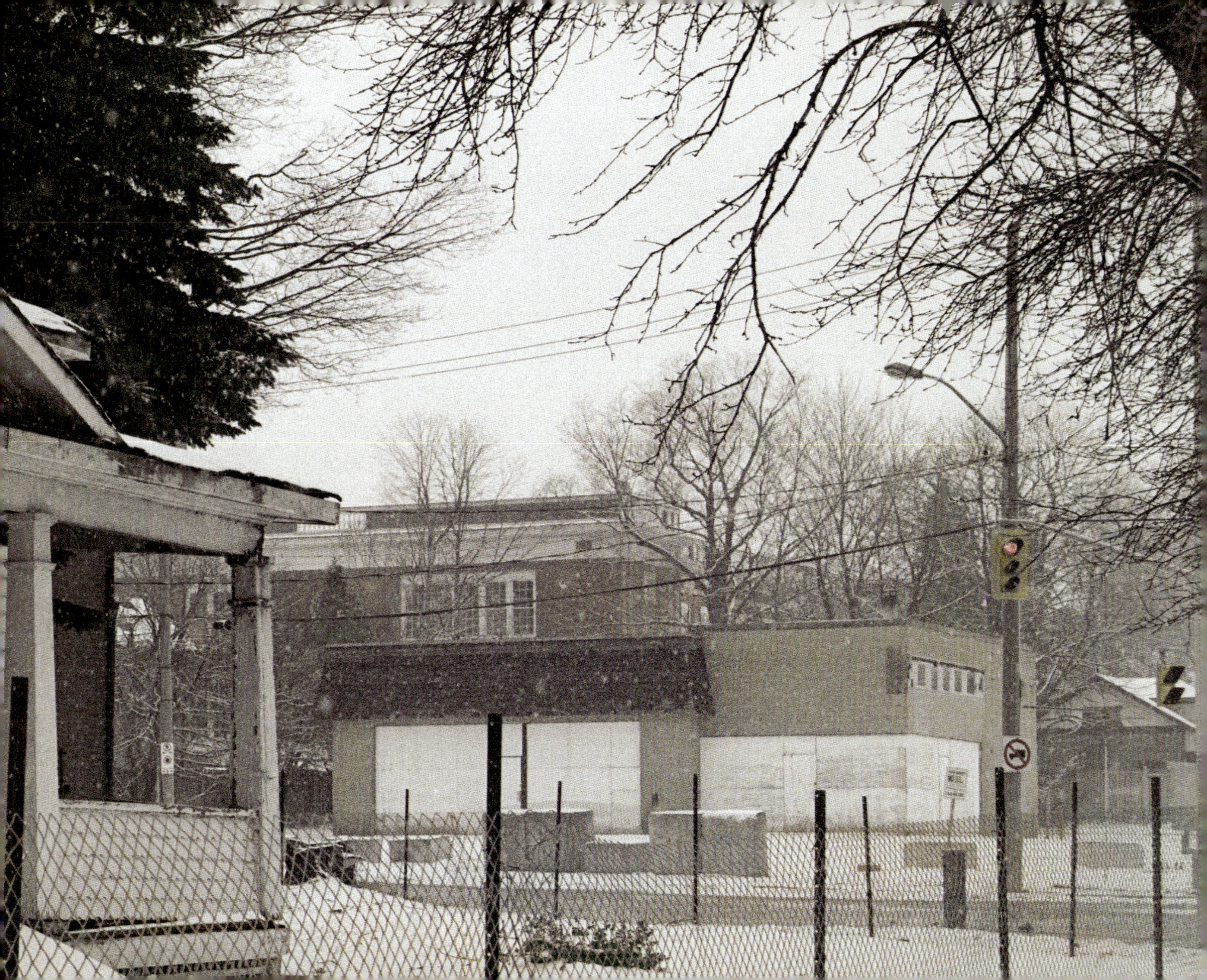

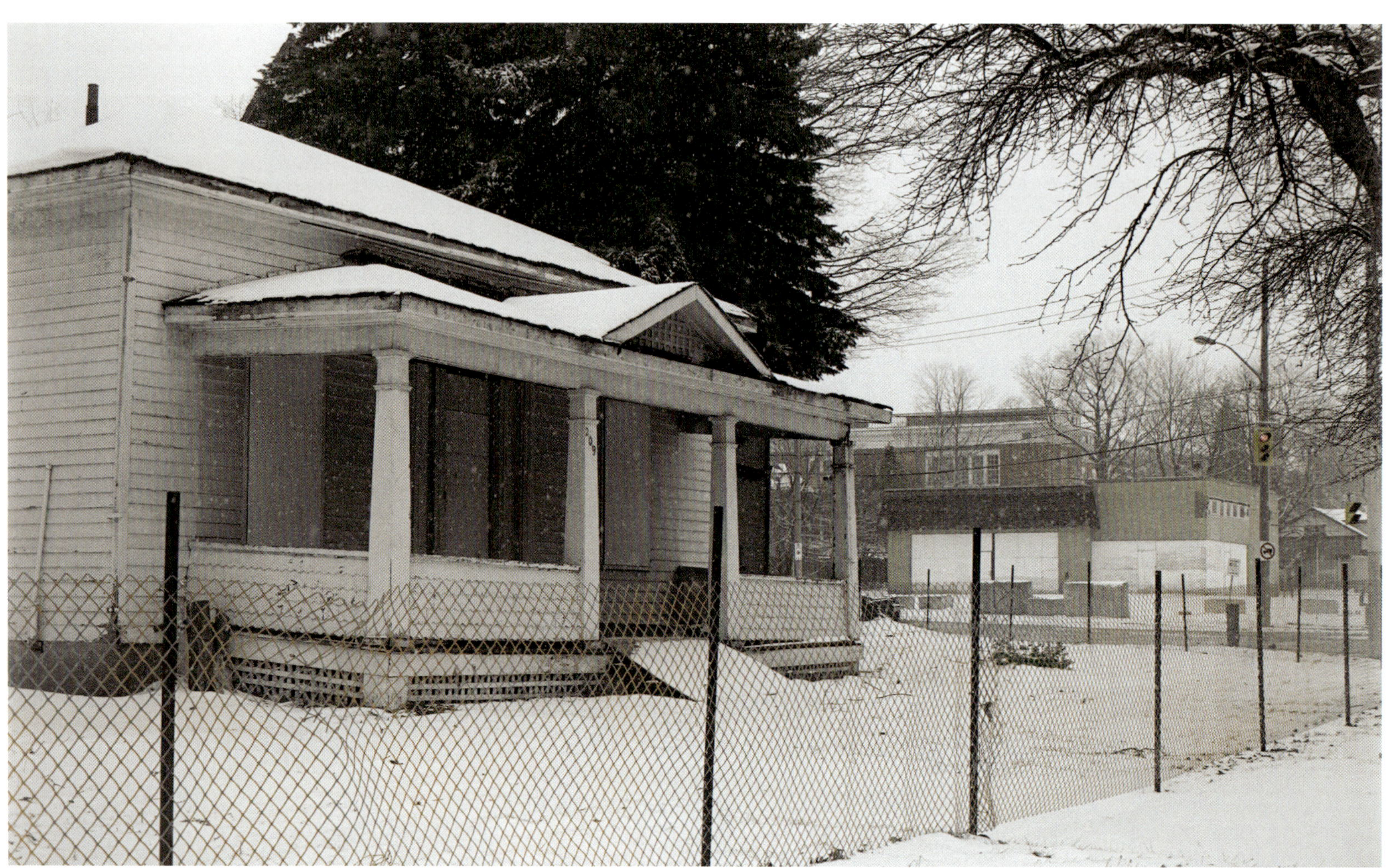

58 | Frederick and Lancaster *(demolished)*

Located at the corner of two of the oldest streets in Kitchener, this Regency cottage was built on the Samuel Brubacher farm in 1866. It had an elaborate front door surround, as well as the general form befitting the style. The only other Regency cottage that I can think of in the Region is the home of William Dickson in Galt known as Kirkmichael. The gas station across Lancaster Street was replaced by a Tim Hortons and is now to be replaced again by a larger residential building. In the background is Suddaby Public School.

2002

59 | Mill Street

Another very old road, Mill Street, looking east from Queen, was doubtless so named because it connected Joseph Schneider's sawmill (which once stood behind the Joseph Schneider Haus historic site) with Bliehm's (also spelled Bleam) mills and the mills at Doon, all built on Schneider Creek. At one time the road led past the farm of "Indian Sam" Eby directly down to Doon and Blair, but now sections of the road have been closed and altered. Samuel Eby was among the first Mennonites to come to Block 2 of The Haldimand Tract in 1804 and was so nicknamed because of his association with the local Indigenous population. When I used to drive up to Waterloo from Galt in 1966, I often took Mill Street. I liked the light reflecting here off the damp road.

1993

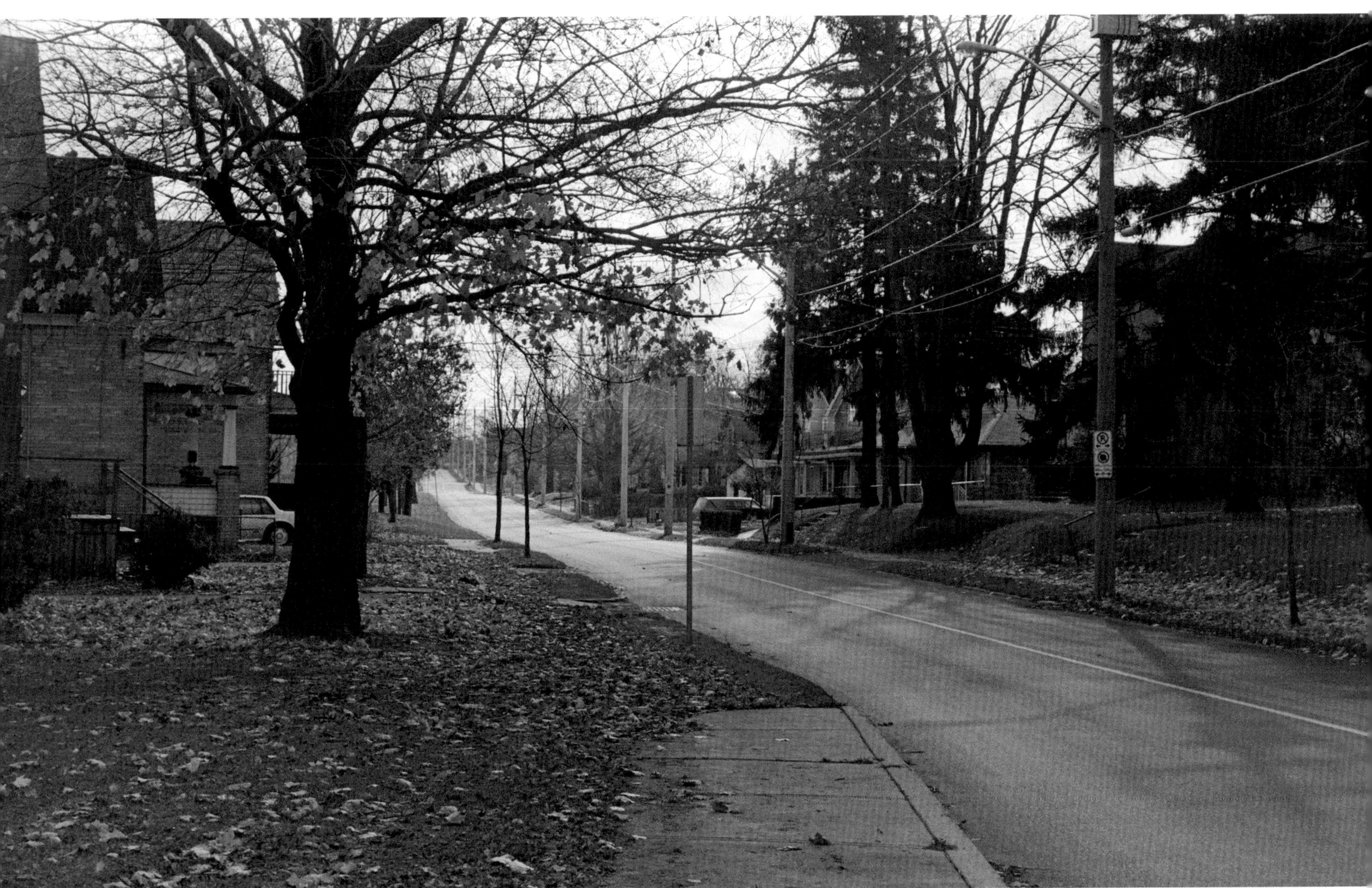

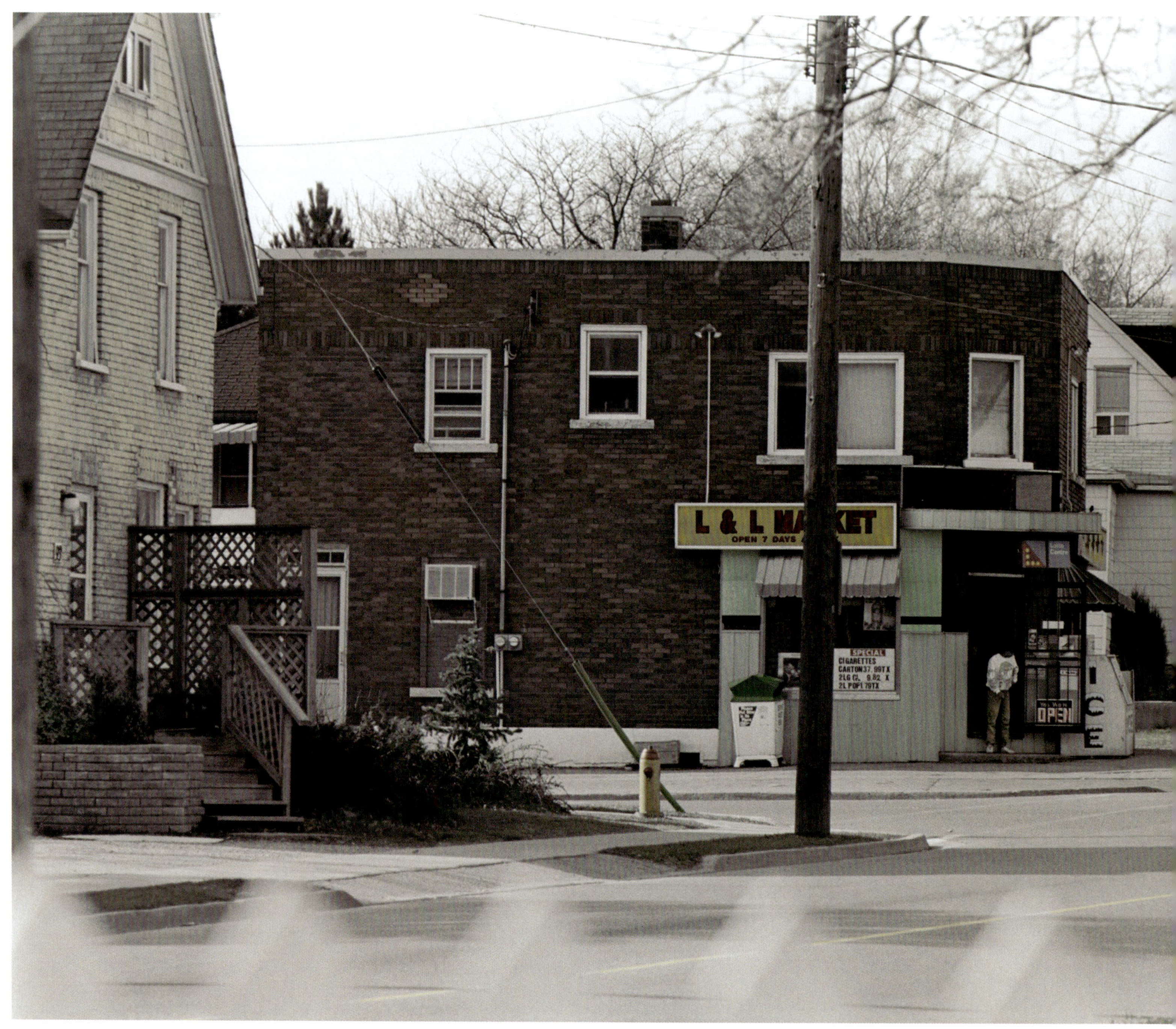
L & L
OPEN 7 DAYS
SPECIAL
CIGARETTES
CARTON 37.99 TX
OPEN

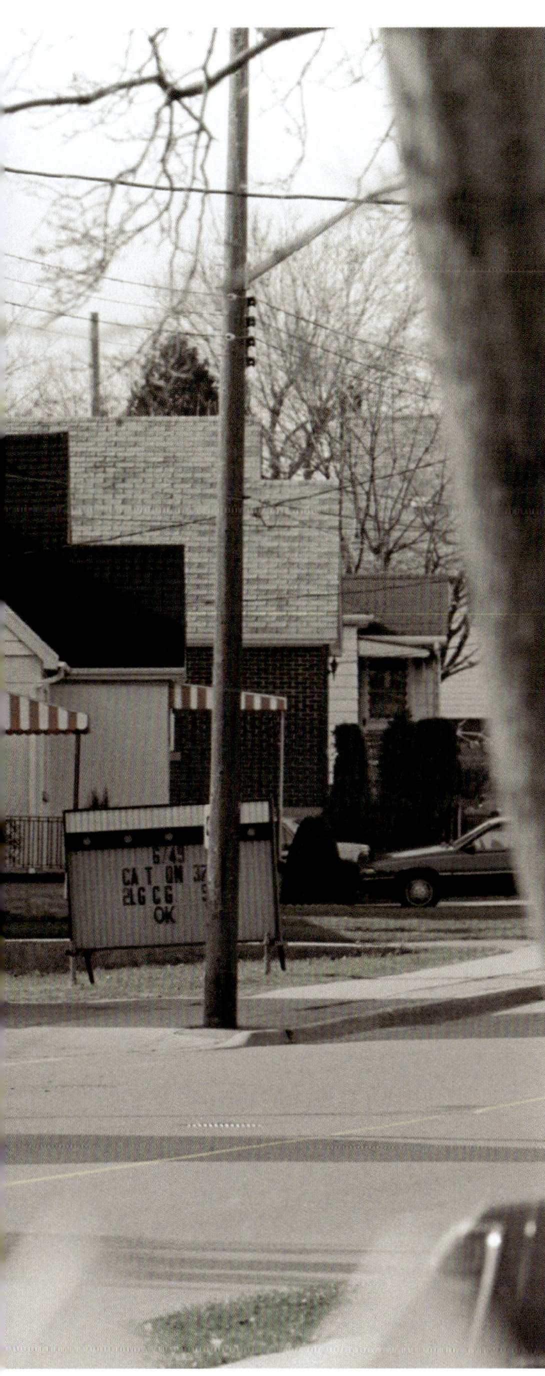

60 | Louisa and Lancaster

This corner store, cleverly named L&L after the streets that intersect there, still had some green and black vitrolite on it, which indicates that it is contemporary with many of the other corner stores. Vitrolite is a trade name for pigmented structural glass manufactured in the United States from the early 1900s to the 1960s. It became popular in Art Deco and Streamline Moderne buildings and could be found at one time on numerous shops in the region. Louisa and Lancaster Market is now a plant and garden shop.

1993

61 | Pandora Corner Store

This store at Pandora and Samuel may have had a row of windows right across the front of the second floor. It has a datestone of 1932. It has since been converted to a residence. When the flat roof was replaced with a hip roof, the pediment above the datestone was shaved off, but the date remains. It intrigues me that so many such shops were built in not much more than a decade, and now practically none exist as shops.

1993

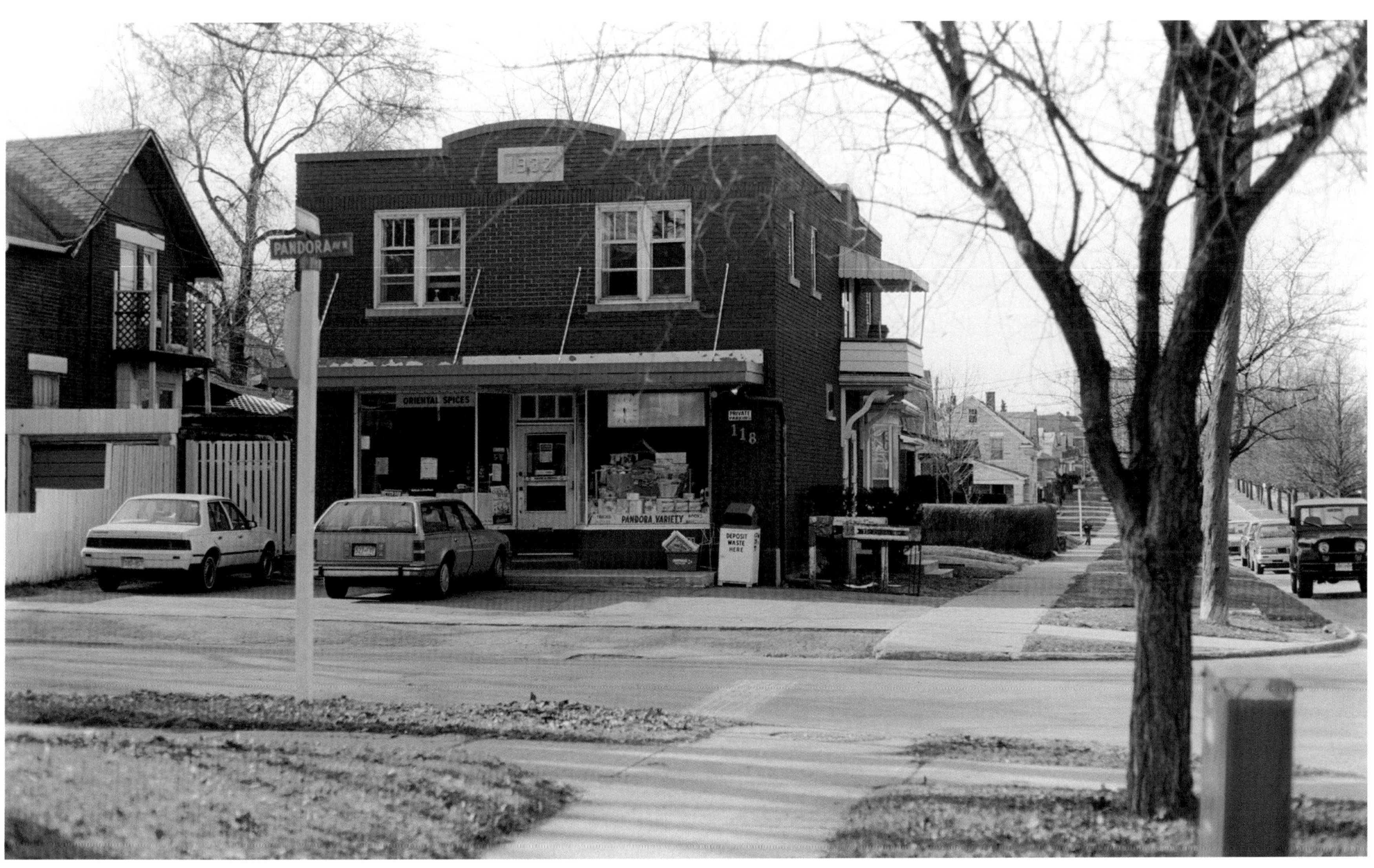
1932
PANDORA
ORIENTAL SPICES
PRIVATE PARKING
118
PANDORA VARIETY
DEPOSIT
WASTE
HERE

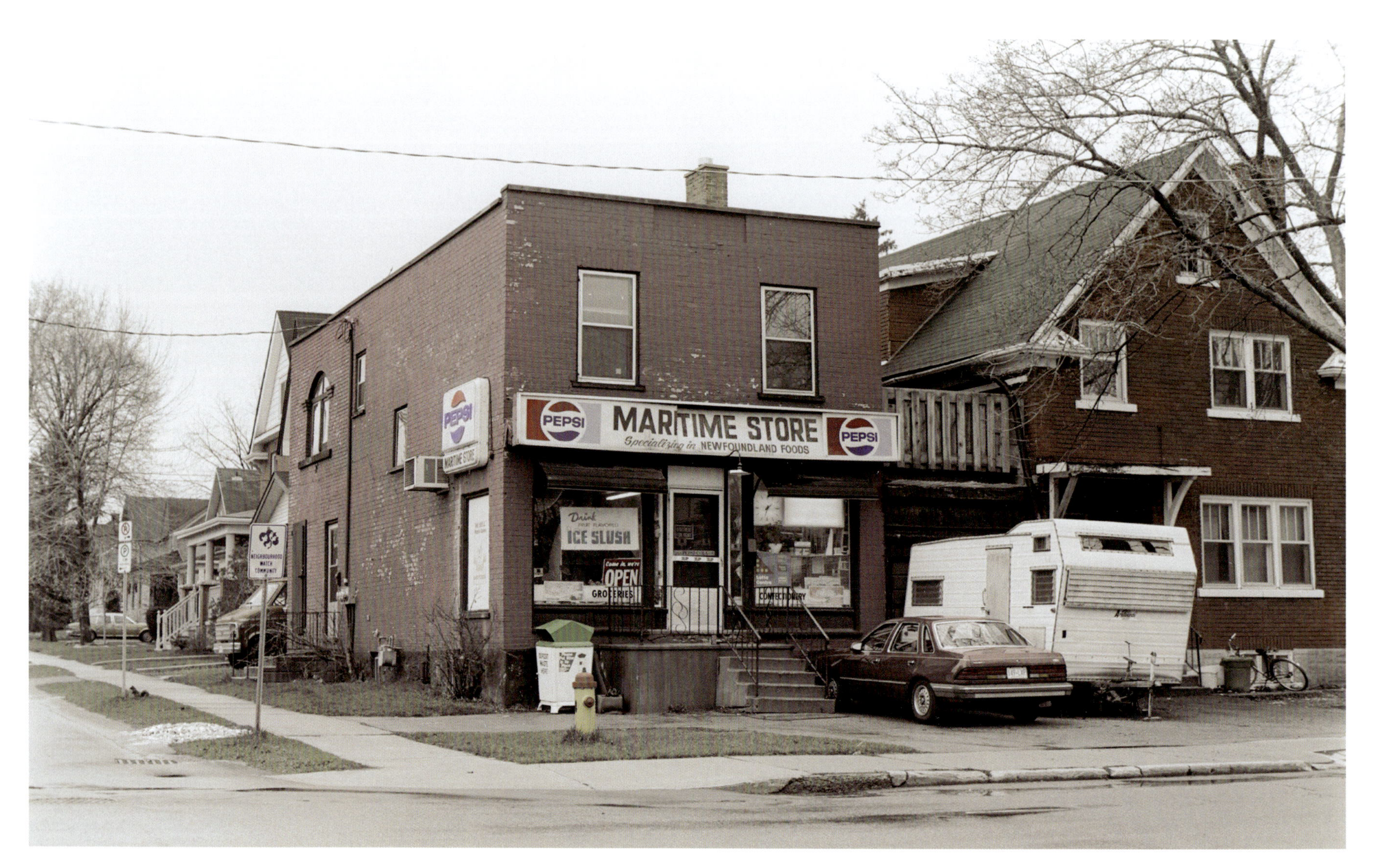
PEPSI
MARITIME STORE
PEPSI
MARITIME STORE
Specializing in NEWFOUNDLAND FOODS
PEPSI
Drink
ICE SLUSH
OPEN
GROCERIES
CONFECTIONERY
NEIGHBOURHOOD WATCH COMMUNITY

62 | Maritime Store (*demolished*)

This was in my old Kitchener neighbourhood at Samuel and Brubacher. Apparently, this building and the adjoining house, built about the same time, were at one time the location of a printing business. After the store closed, they stood vacant for many years and became an eyesore and an annoyance to the surrounding neighbourhood. Eventually the City of Kitchener ordered them demolished. I made a point of photographing as many of these corner stores as I came across. When I look back, I think I had a sense they were on their last legs.

1993

63 | 110 Madison *(demolished)*

I didn't go back to see if I could discover the type of construction of this house at 110 Madison Avenue, Kitchener while it was being demolished. It was a very old and typical Pennsylvania-German building with the paired square attic windows, return eaves, and asymmetrical facade, but it was unusual because of the door placement so far to the side. It could have been log. It had a very late style of insulbrick in a fake angelstone pattern, and asbestos panel siding in the gable.

1999

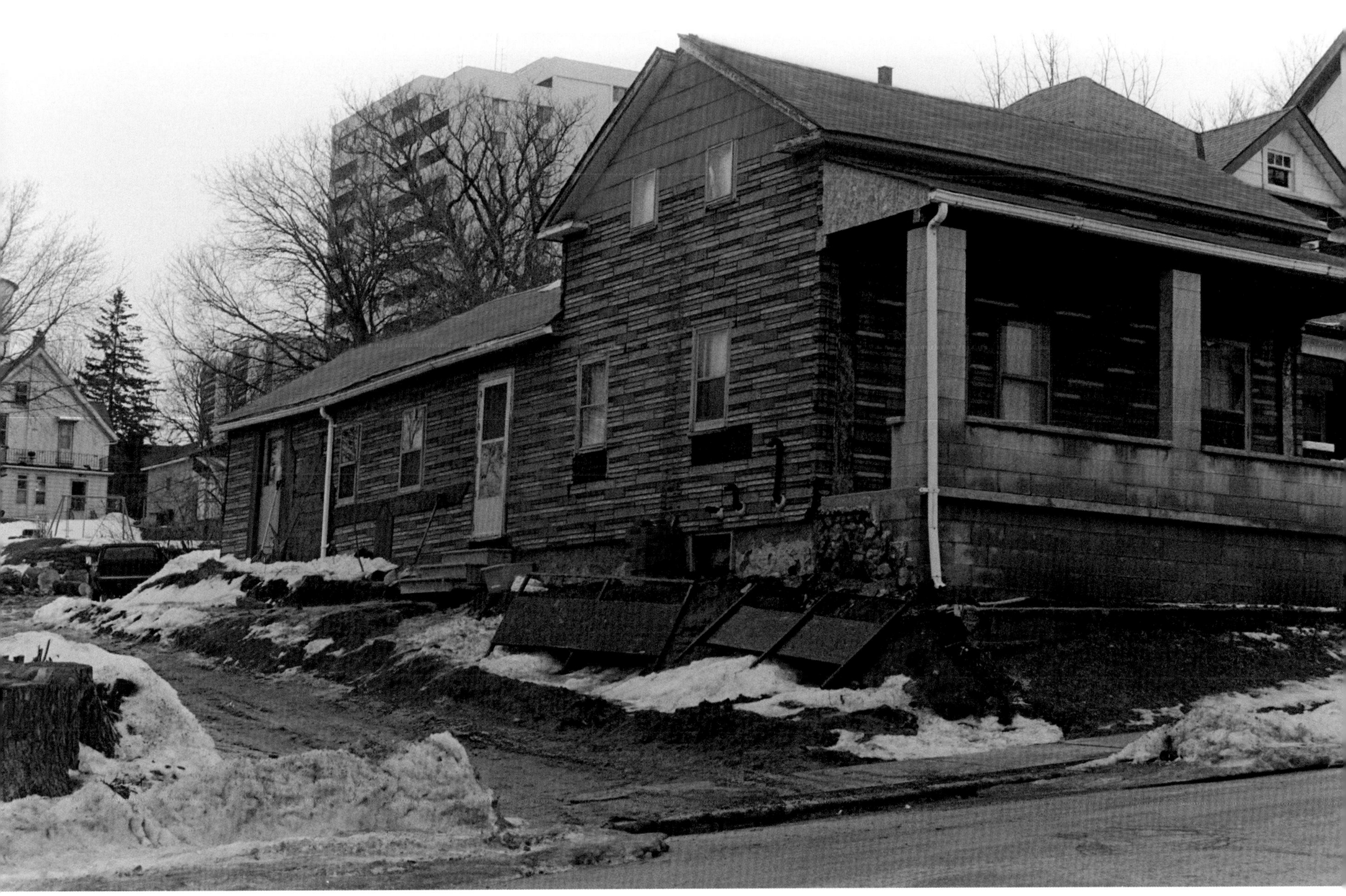

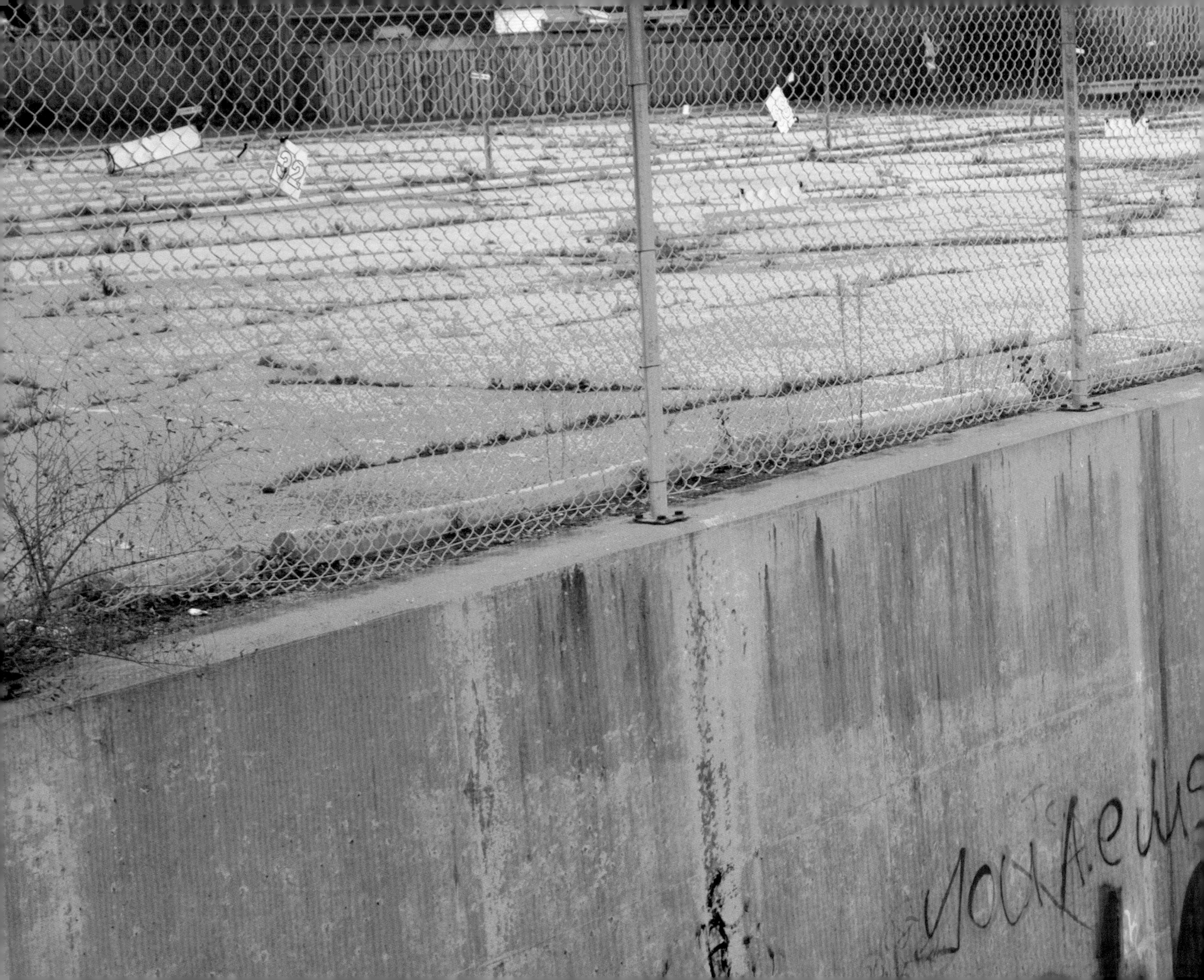
32

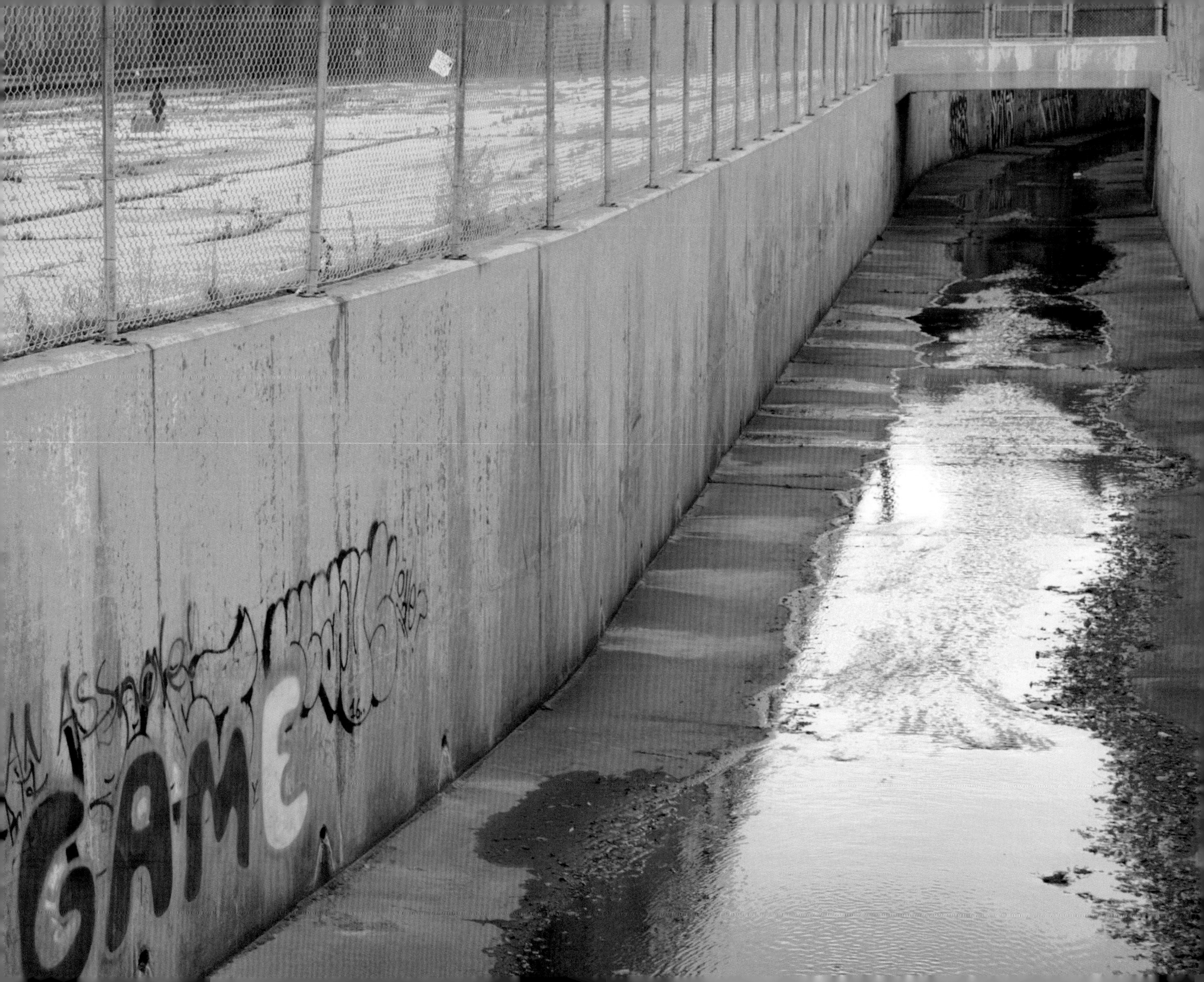
GAME

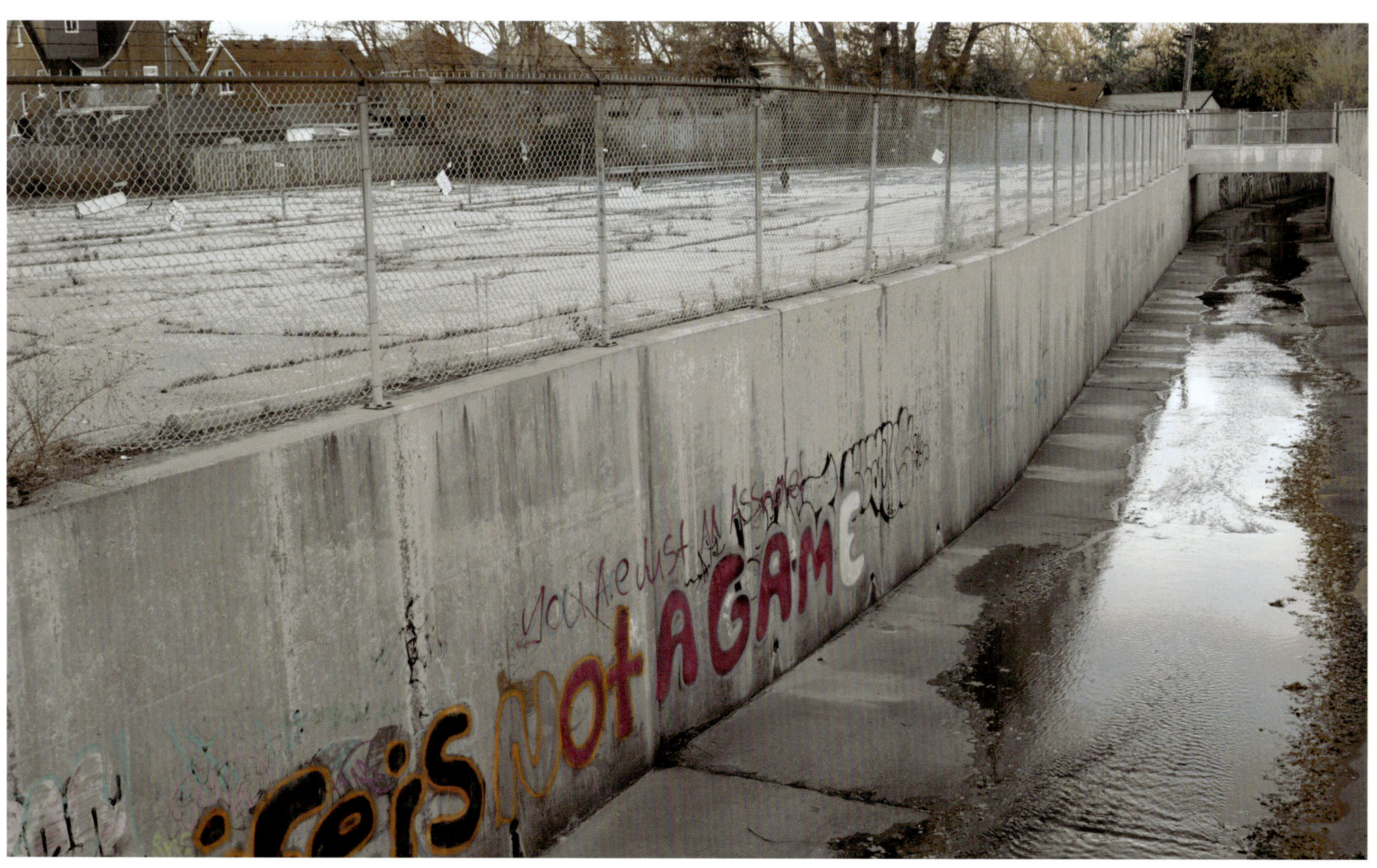
You Are just AN
is Not A GAME

64 | Shoemaker Creek

Shoemaker Creek, running through parking lots just east of the J.M. Schneider Ltd. meat packing plant, has shared the fate of many municipal watercourses, that of being turned into concrete drains to carry water away rapidly without any possibility of infiltration. There is hope that open culverts such as this will be renaturalized or "daylighted." The creek runs underneath the former plant, and perhaps at one time the water was useful to the business. Here is another opportunity that has been taken for public discourse through graffiti art.

2017

65 | 1027 King Street East

Viewed from Onward Avenue, 1027 King Street East was the location of the Onward Manufacturing Company for many decades. Founded in 1904 as the RiteAway Pen Co. by T. A. Witzel, the company began manufacturing Onward and Triumph electric vacuum cleaners in 1906. They also made and distributed Eureka vacuums in Canada. The company moved to this location in 1914 and after World War II greatly expanded its manufacturing facilities, branching out into many new products, including barbecues. The central tower is inspired by the Art Deco style.

1996

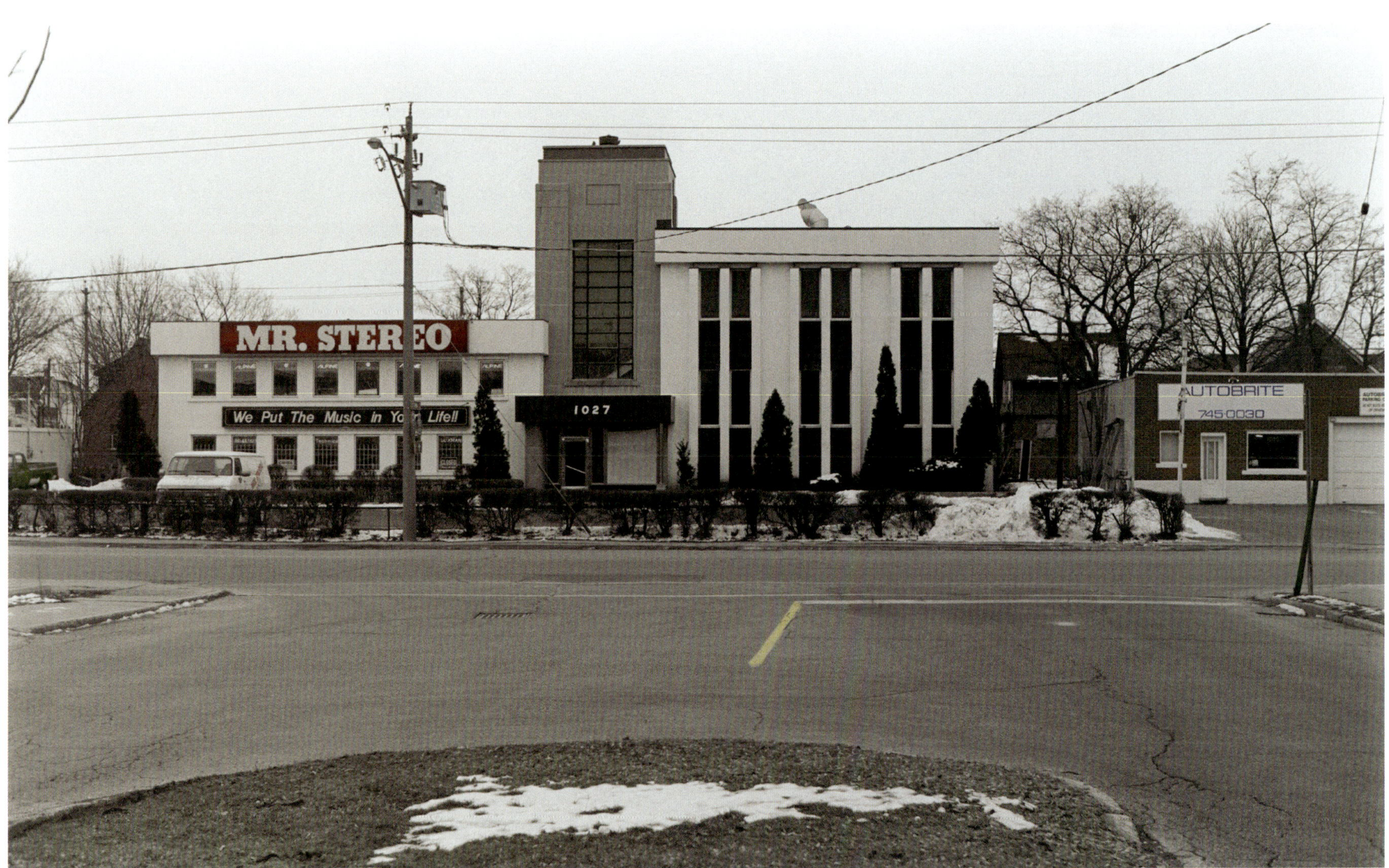
MR. STEREO
We Put The Music in
1027
AUTOBRITE
745-0030

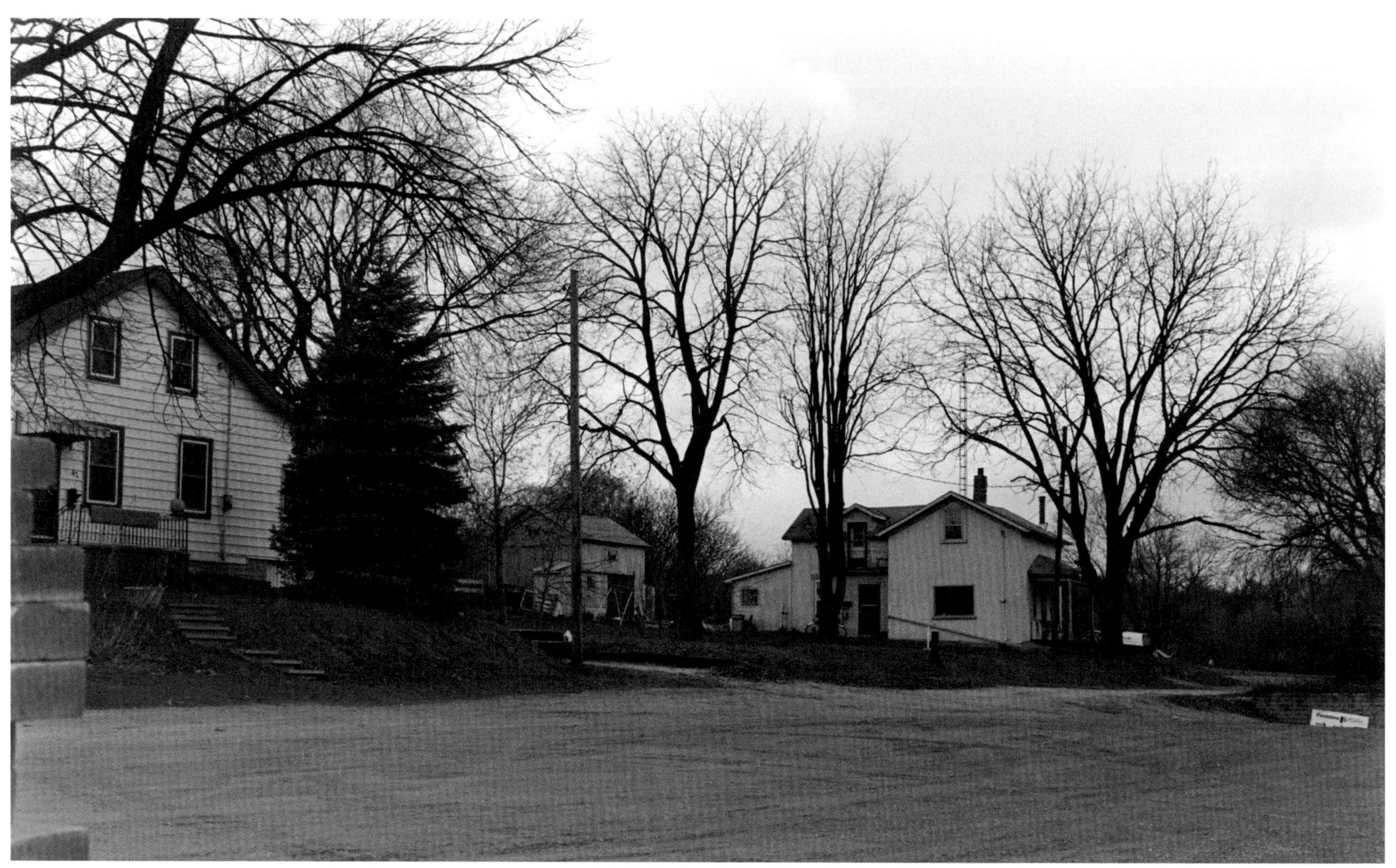

66 | German Mills

There are still some of the remnants of the community of German Mills. It was located around the mill founded by Philip Bliehm (Bleam) on Schneider Creek, alongside what is now Manitou Drive in Kitchener. A sawmill on Schneider Creek existed on the site from 1812, and a grist mill from 1825. When the mill complex was purchased by Samuel Leibschuetz in 1835, he laid out village lots which became known as the village of Jewsburg. The mill did not prosper, and it was taken over by Elias Snider in 1860.

1993

67 | Preston

Viewed from King Street, Laurel Street in Preston has a mixed 19th- and early-20th-century building stock. Preston was the first community to thrive in Waterloo County but has been superseded by Kitchener and Waterloo. Due to a diminution of its fortunes, and by chance, it contains many early heritage buildings which have not yet been redeveloped.

1993

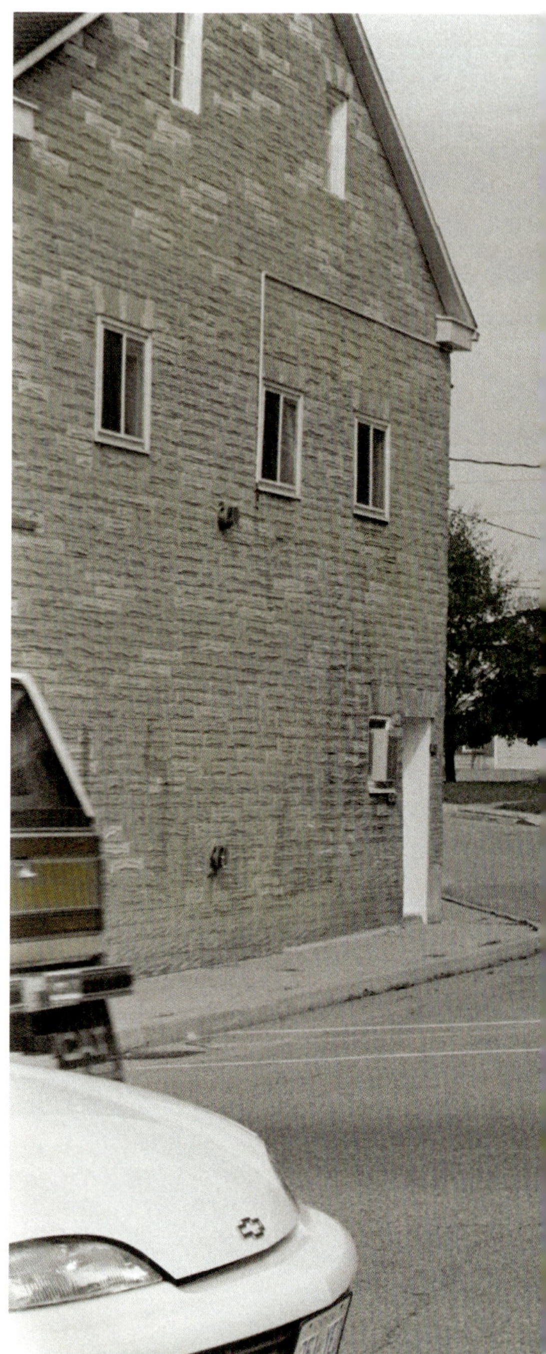

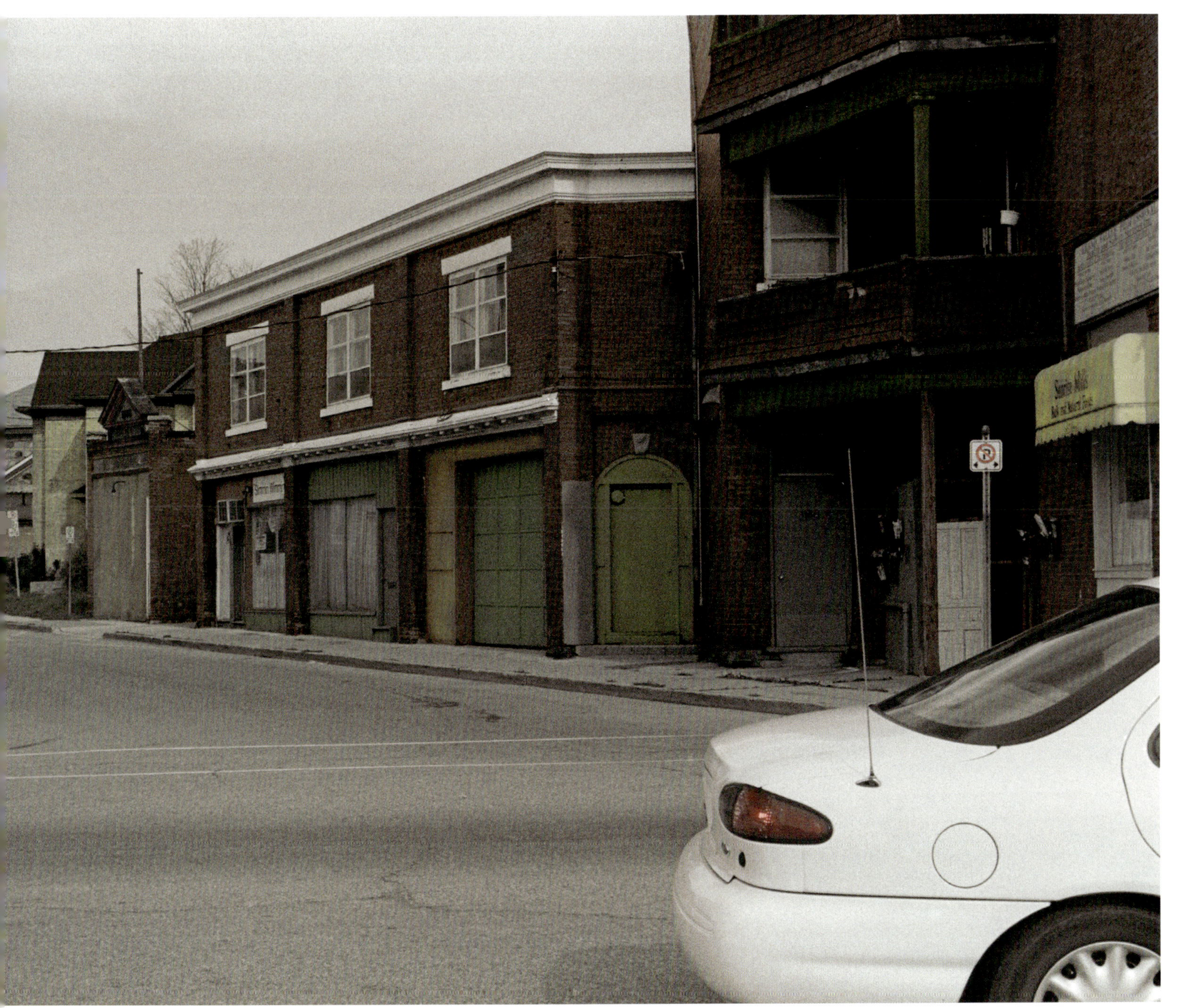

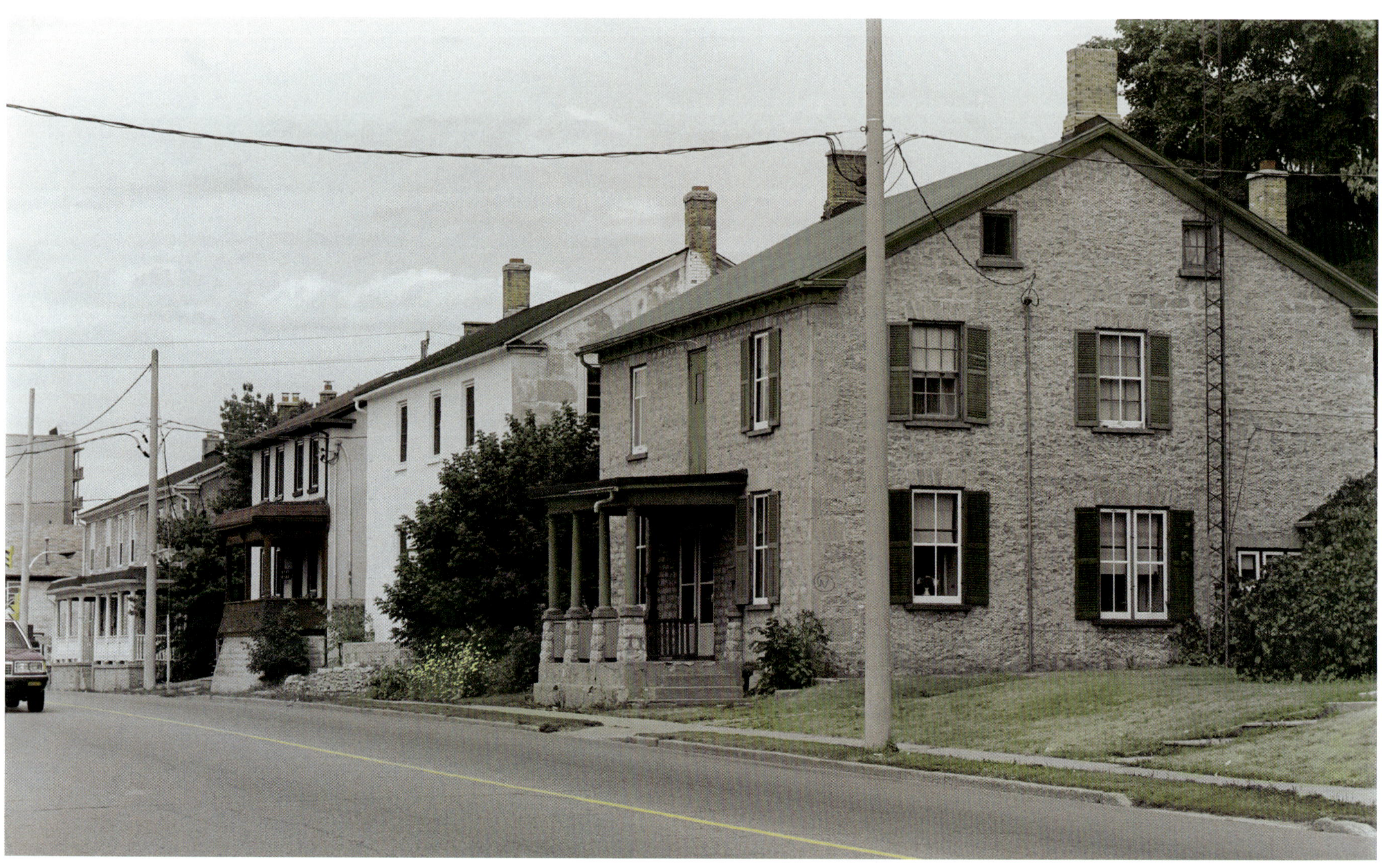

68 | King Street, Preston

A remarkable grouping of four grand Georgian houses on King Street in Preston, just east of Montrose Street North, provides some evidence to show what an important industrial centre Preston was in the mid-19th century. The east end of King Street still provides a visual link to Preston's German and Mennonite heritage.

1997

69 | Ward Bros.

Ward Bros. Hardware at Cedar and Glenmorris in Galt is an interesting conversion of a house to a store. It survived the competition of chains and big box stores for many decades. The loss of these local shops and corner grocers is a subtle change in the urban landscape. The show windows and the random pattern tile have now been removed, and the building is now a restaurant.

1994

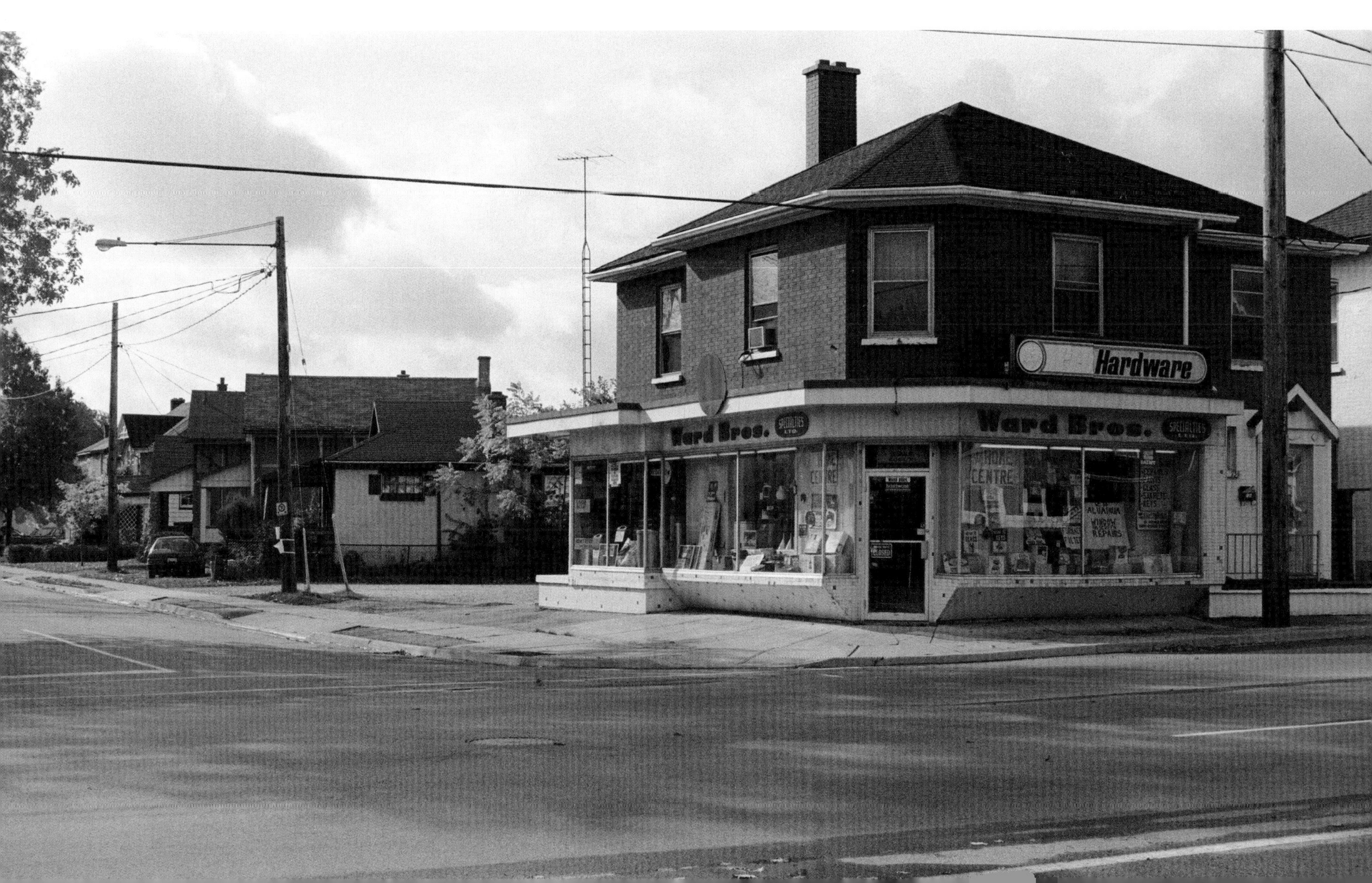
Hardware
Ward Bros.
Ward Bros.
SPECIALTIES LTD.

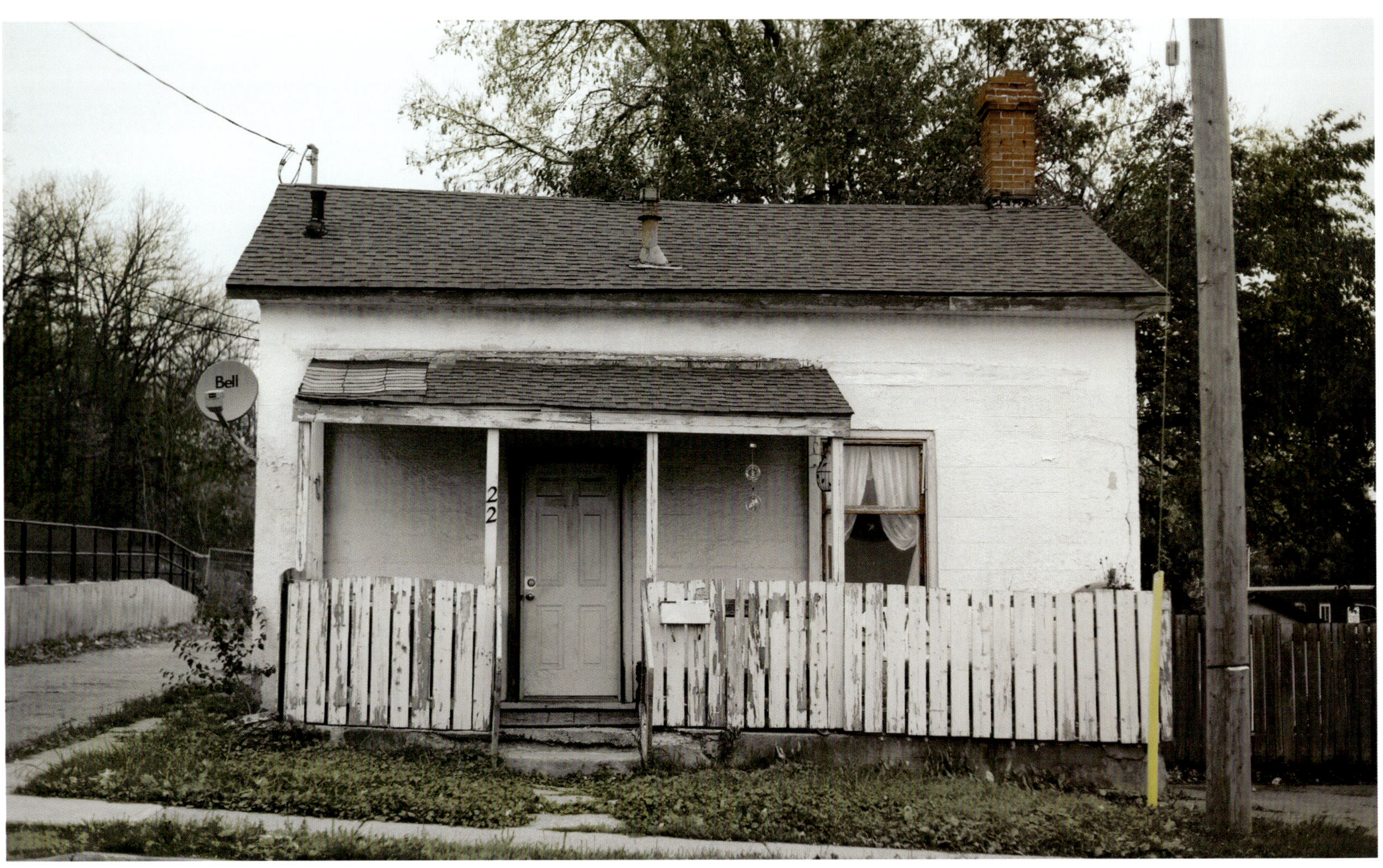
Bell
22

70 | St. Andrews Street, Galt *(demolished)*

Twenty-two St. Andrews Street, Galt, was a modest worker's cottage, one of many not far from the Goldie McCulloch foundry and safeworks, where steam engines and other heavy machinery were made, and just across St. Andrews Street from the Shurley & Dietrich Company saw works. Unless places like this are remembered or preserved, in two hundred years people will think that everyone in 2014 lived in mansions.

2014

71 | Grand River, Galt

I was looking north along the Grand River in Galt to the Main Street bridge. The double bowstring or concrete truss bridge was built in 1931. The former Silknit factory at the left end of the bridge is now the University of Waterloo School of Architecture. To the left of the frame is Goldie McCulloch's safeworks, which at one time was accessed by an electric railway. A pier remains in the river and is now used for a pedestrian bridge crossing the Grand. In 1995 I would stay with my parents in Galt when I was visiting the region on business.

1995

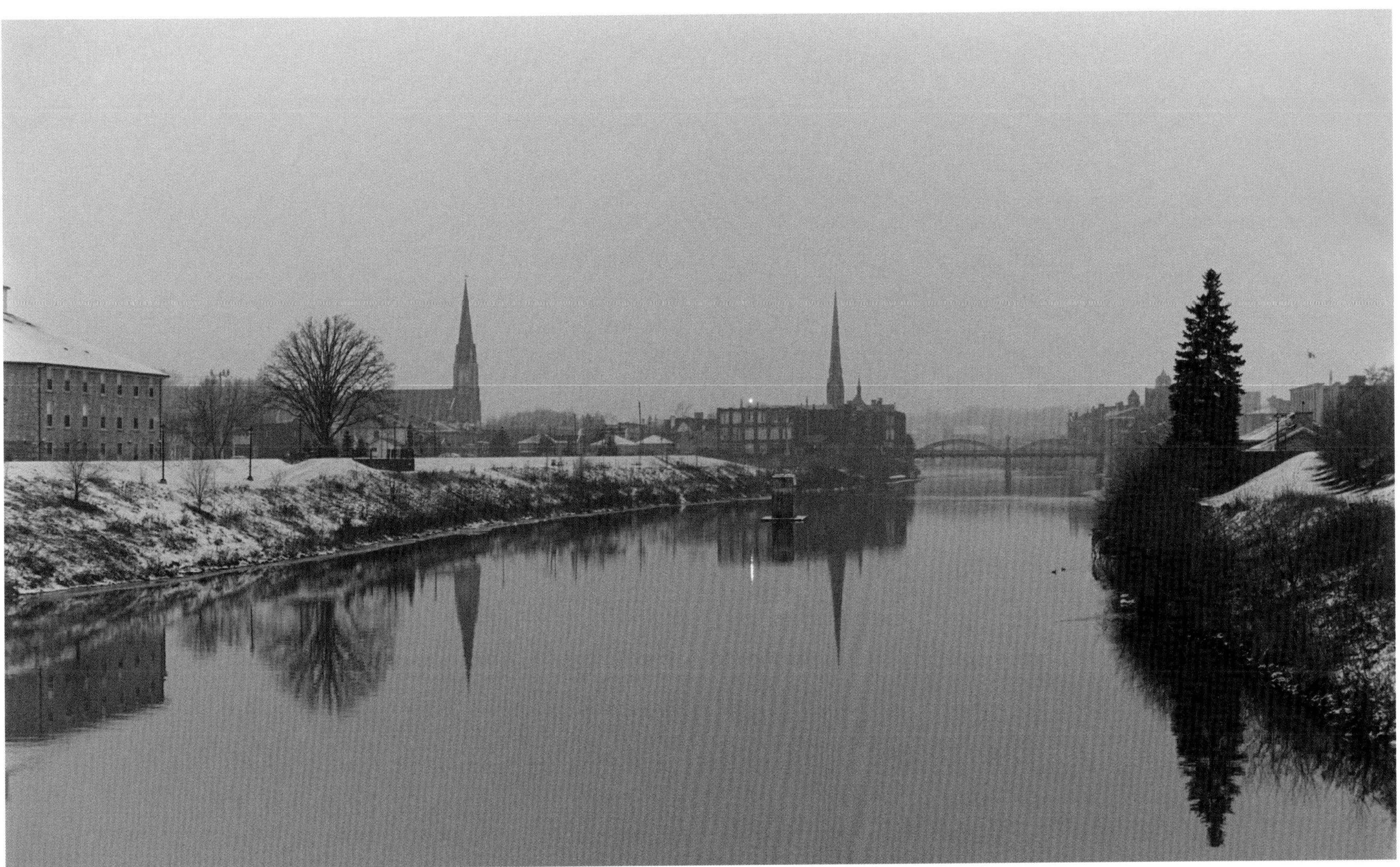

72 | Wellington Street, Galt

The David Durward Centre, the former PUC building at Dickson and Wellington in Galt, is now a multi-use community centre. I find it an interesting and not really jarring juxtaposition of a fine Beaux Arts institutional building with a modest stuccoed building in the foreground across Dickson Street, which might be timber frame or log, and two minuscule shops jammed into what must have been a laneway.

1994

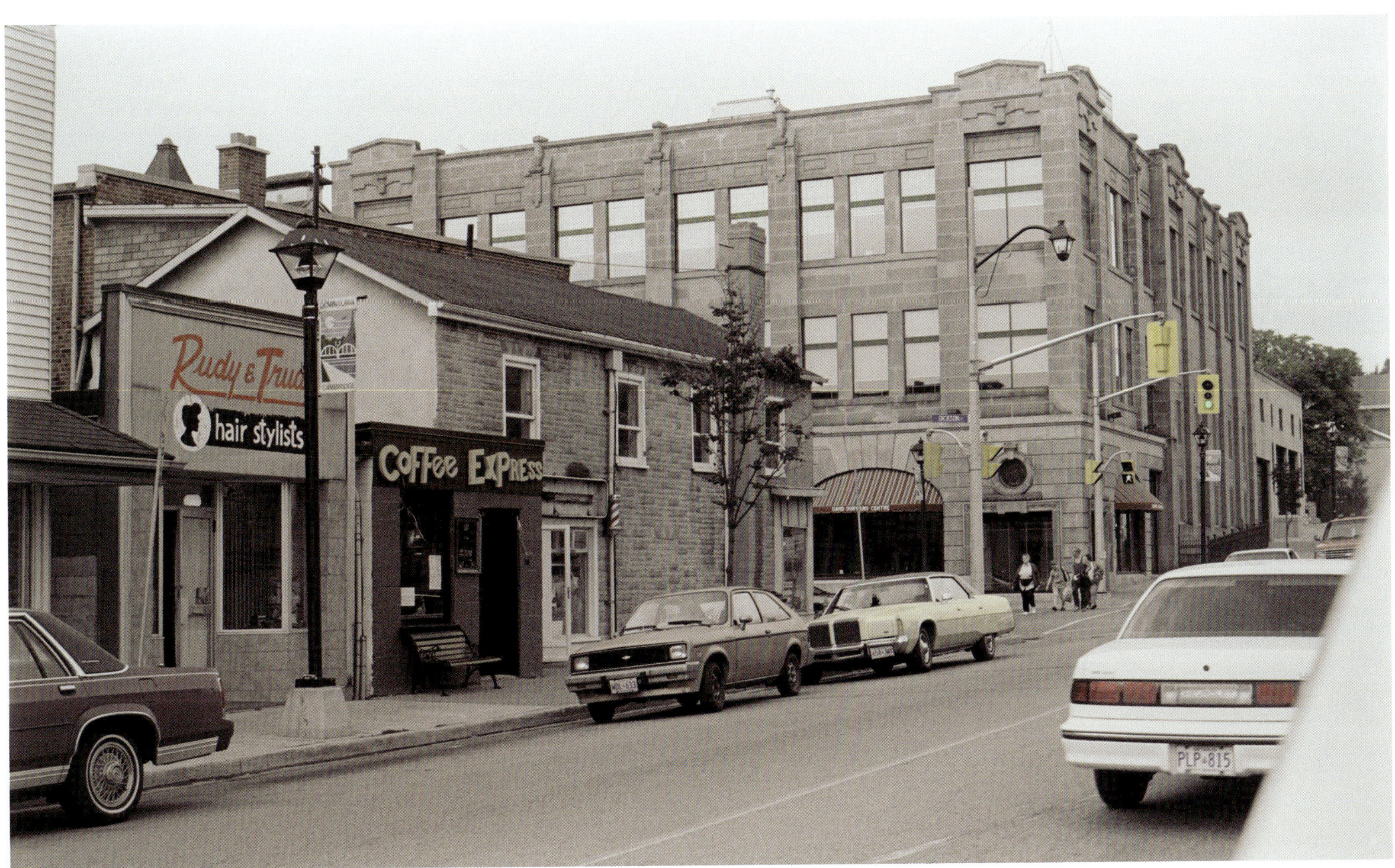
Rudy & Trud
hair stylists
COFFEE EXPRESS
PLP•815

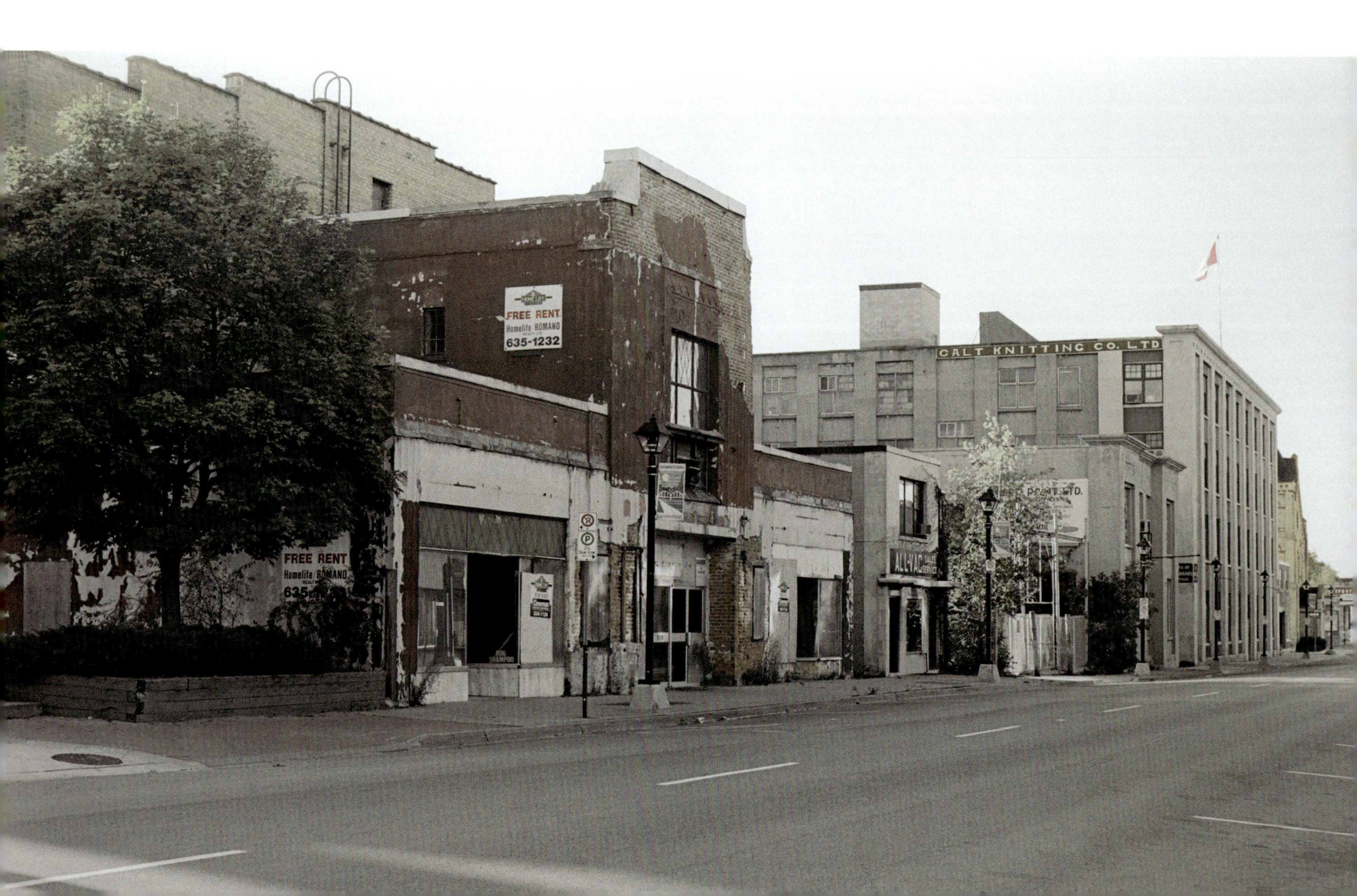
FREE RENT
Homelife ROMANO
635-1232
GALT KNITTING CO. LTD
FREE RENT
ALL-VAC

73 | Capitol Theatre, Galt *(demolished)*

The Capitol Theatre on Water Street in Galt had hit rock bottom when free rent was being offered. In its day it must have been stunning. There were still remnants of elaborate Art Deco designs worked into the plaster facade. Rather than the sad state of ruin, I see the magnificence and the beauty of what was once there. According to historian rych mills, it cost $200,000 to build at the beginning of the Great Depression and closed in 1977. It became a parking lot in 1995.

1994

74 | Dickson Street

This is Dickson Street in Galt, showing the historic Town Hall and the Farmers' Market building. I was on one of my regular visits to the region from Cornwall, Ontario, where I was living at the time. It's evident from the wiper blade that I was driving with a camera in my hand. I pulled over and took a few more photos in the pouring rain but I liked this one best.

1994

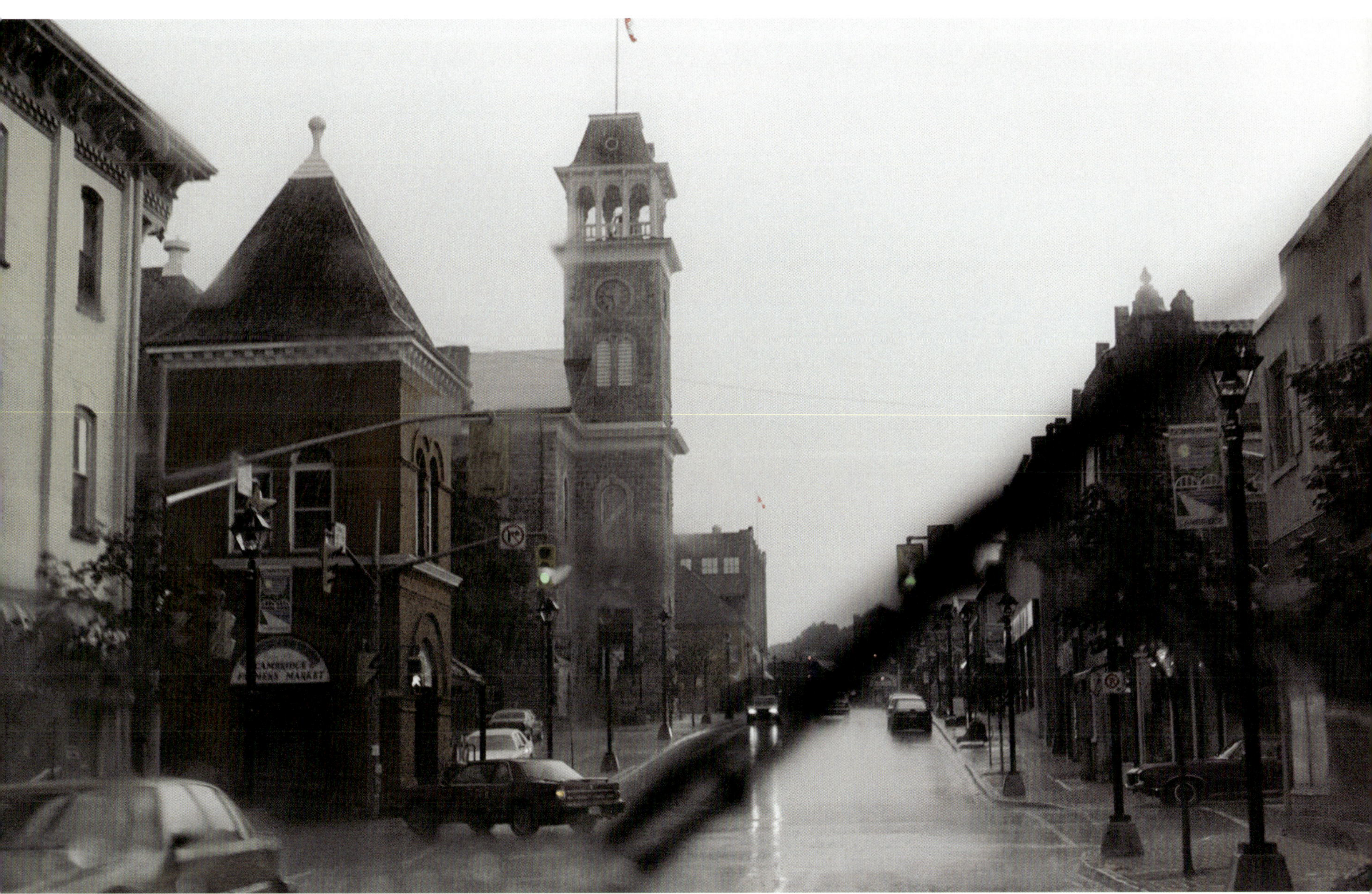

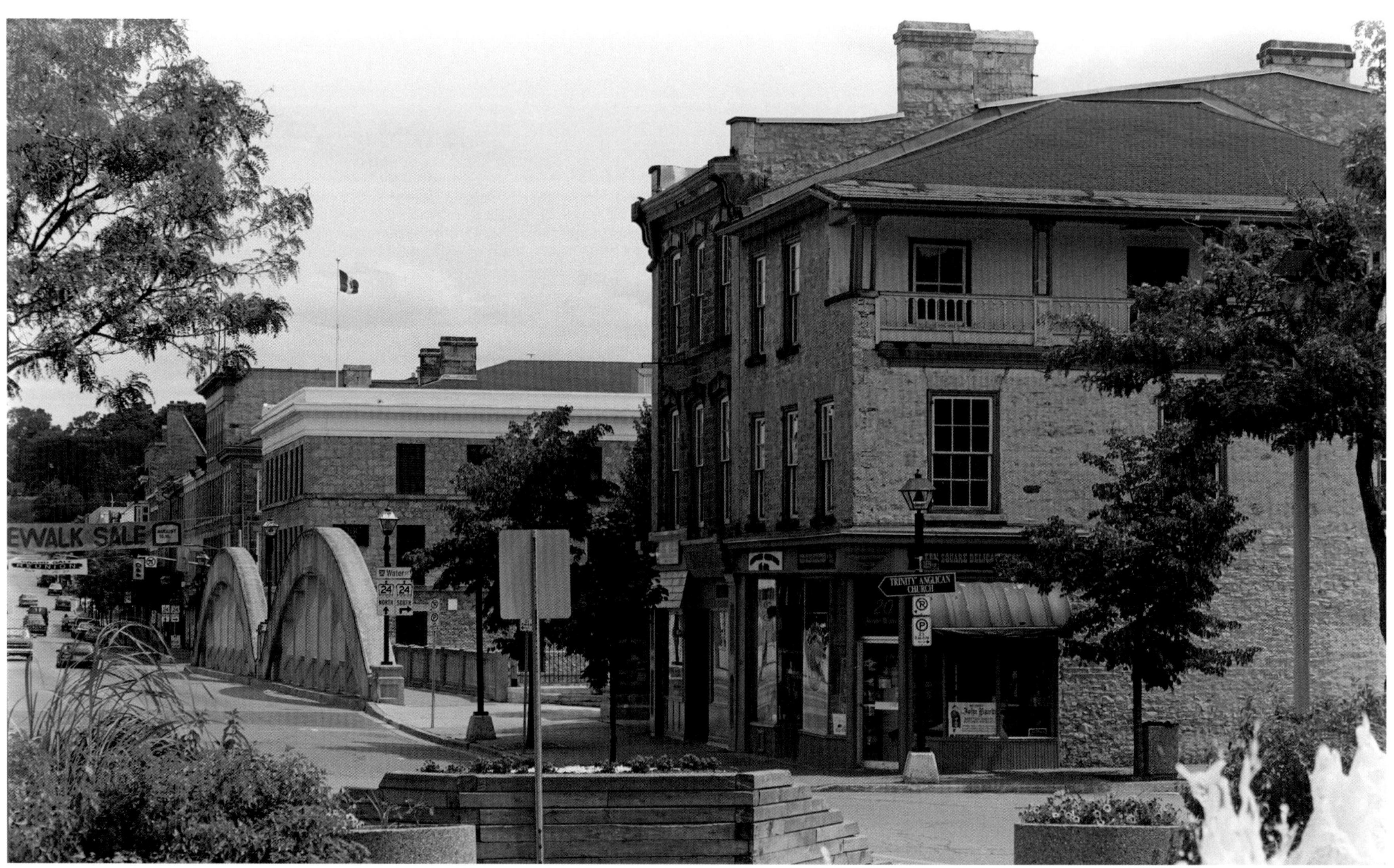
EWALK SALE
24 NORTH
24 SOUTH
TRINITY ANGLICAN CHURCH

75 | Main Street, Galt

The Main Street bridge in Galt from the west side of the Grand River looking east is one of my favourite places in Waterloo Region. The two prominent buildings in the foreground are said to be the oldest commercial buildings in the region. Built in 1856 for Gavin Hume and used originally as a grocery and hardware store, the corner building was a pharmacy for eighty years. Some will remember it as Dalton's. Although there is only a plume of water in the bottom right corner of the frame, I was looking across the City of Galt's Centennial project—the fountain in Queen's Square. This scene has been used in numerous films, and I have photographed it many times.

1997

INTERVIEW

Philippe Elsworthy and Adam Crerar

ADAM CRERAR: You've been taking pictures of the area since before Waterloo was a Region and Cambridge was Cambridge. When exactly did you start, and what led you to do so?

PHILIPPE ELSWORTHY: I think I began to get serious about photography and its use for documentation when I started work at the *Chevron*, the student newspaper at the University of Waterloo, in 1968. I was a news and features photographer. There I got comfortable using the *Chevron's* Pentax Spotmatic and consequently bought my own in the fall of 1969.

AC: How did this work at the *Chevron* lead to your interest in buildings and public spaces?

PE: The paper covered many social issues, an important one of which in 1967 and 1968 was student housing, so that led me to look at housing around Waterloo, and of course the factories amidst which the housing was built. There was no plan for the large influx of baby boomers, as they are now called, and Waterloo was a modest industrial town in those days with a fairly run-down housing stock in the central area. So an appeal was made to residents to take in student boarders, but it was insufficient.

AC: Not all university students are interested in housing and factory buildings! What do you think was the source of your interest?

PE: Good question. There are factors in my early life which inclined me to take an interest. I grew up near the centre of an old English town, Horsham, Sussex. One street I walked along to school had many 16th century buildings, then I walked through the churchyard of a Norman church to my school, which I think had been a religious cloister. My mother was a big influence, too. She was keenly interested in history and grew up in a very old French town, within sight of a fortification built by Richard Coeur de Lion.

AC: Some people having grown up surrounded by such historically significant architecture might have been disappointed by its absence in Kitchener-Waterloo. Why was this not the case for you?

PE: The house that I live in now is not greatly different from the Victorian house I grew up in, and I have some mementos from England to remind me. Apart from that, though, after being in Canada and homesick for England for a number of years (without realizing it), and after moving eventually to Waterloo, I adopted Waterloo as my new home. At that point, I plunged into learning as much as I could about Waterloo's history. It doesn't take long to see that Waterloo Region has a different history and character from the rest of Ontario and Canada.

AC: I'll return to that distinctive history and character later, but for now—how did that interest in Waterloo history affect your approach to photography in the years after the *Chevron*?

PE: This was concurrent with my woodworking, where I became interested in old Waterloo County furniture. My brother Richard and I had established a custom woodworking shop in 1975. I wanted to document the buildings, especially houses, for my own information, rather than for any other purpose. And, I photographed quite a lot of furniture of various styles, too. Furniture making is closely related to architecture, so in expanding my horizons as a cabinetmaker I studied architecture also. I felt it necessary to learn about design from ancient times to the present, pretty much. For instance, Frank Lloyd Wright and Charles Rennie Mackintosh designed from the setting to the building to the furniture, draperies, etc. I developed an affection for Art Nouveau and Art Deco, and although I rarely built anything related to these styles, I became familiar with them. Up until roughly the mid-17th century, furniture and building were very closely related, using the same techniques of joinery. These crafts began to diverge, but up until the mid-19th century, timber frame buildings were being put up in Waterloo County using the same techniques and methods as in the previous five hundred years and more.

I suppose what most intrigued me in older Waterloo houses was their finer parts—the windows, doors, and trim that were probably made by the same people as made furniture in the early 19th century, and then later when sash mills and small furniture factories began, they would use the same mouldings. I looked at my surroundings as a folk artist. A major motivation is simple curiosity.

And in looking at the buildings, I could see that the Pennsylvania-German Mennonites brought with them a simple but distinctive style of building, which was English Georgian but with liberties taken.

Everything was built to last. Thinking about furniture, for instance, I believe they thought that a chest of drawers or dish cupboard would last at least 500 years, and houses and other buildings would last as long as possible too. These are values that I find agreement with.

I also read quite a bit about the technique and history of photography in order to document my own work. Having come across the work of Eugène Atget, for whom in North America the photographer Berenice Abbott was such an important advocate, I fell in love with it—and realized that photography could be "art" as well as documentary. It was always a thin line anyway.

AC: What do you love about Atget, and how has his work influenced yours?

PE: This is a complicated question. The influence is in spirit rather than direct, although I am frequently tempted to consider working with a large plate camera and older materials. I think it is the tranquility of the scenes, the detail—and attention to it—and above all the lack of judgment. This is also what I try to do: to show the city as it is. So in a sense it is documentary. But, of course, there is always some judgment or choice in the vantage points, time of day, etc. Atget's choices of subject and his own placement, the time of day, everything was carefully thought out and had to be in view of his equipment. Someone said photography is painting with light, and it is the light in Atget's photos that is so appealing.

AC: And can you elaborate on your commitment to documenting craft?

PE: The idea of preserving craft skills has been important to me since I became involved with the Joseph Schneider Haus Museum in Kitchener, first as a volunteer, and then, in 1990, I was the first Folk Artist in Residence as cabinetmaker. Part of the activities and educational programming at the Joseph Schneider Haus was preserving craft skills, of which I both learned a great deal and contributed my skills and insights as Folk Artist. But it also comes from my family background. The notion of self-reliance has been important, due to my dad's influence. My dad grew up in a poorer part of London, England, where it was part of the culture to be self-reliant, imaginative, and inventive—to do more with less. Just for example, I was taught as a six-year-old how to straighten nails on a brick with a hammer. But generally, people of the early 19th century were very nearly completely self-reliant.

In the course of our business, although from time to time we did small production runs, my brother Richard and I realized that there was no point in trying to compete with large factories, so our business turned to more highly skilled hand work, both in building furniture and in antique restoration.

AC: Phil, your photos capture what Berenice Abbott called "the past jostling against the present"—the interaction of different times or eras in buildings, car models, even fashions and hair styles. What do you find important or interesting about this dynamic?

PE: It's really the present jostling with the past. I think of it as layers accumulating on top of each other. There are several good analogies. Planners speak of an urban fabric. This is useful in the sense that you can see discontinuities or holes, places that have worn out, others unsuccessfully patched. Time, though, is the critical factor where layers accumulate like paint, in waves rather than a steady fashion. One can learn to read the layers and understand better the place, starting with the landforms, mostly resulting from glaciation, and the earliest roads, which likely followed Indigenous trails. Many of the farms and hamlets, villages, and buildings from the earliest non-Indigenous settlement still remain today. And upon this, development from different eras and of different styles is superimposed, as well as decay and destruction.

I have puzzled for some time about how Abraham Erb, one of the first non-Indigenous settlers in Waterloo, knew where to make a mill pond and build his mill. I have come to theorize that the natural conditions he found made it obvious. There was high ground, which provided prospect and refuge, according to neuroscientist Colin Ellard's concept, and which was probably a former Indigenous site. And, since, in the earliest days and up until the 1950s, the creek was known as Beaver Creek, there was probably a beaver dam and pond, which indicated an advantageous site for a mill pond. Just thinking about layers, there are some places where every trace of the landforms, vegetation, and anything else have been removed for new housing subdivisions, so there is only one layer. These places are uninteresting, even sad.

AC: What does a "multi-layered" community bring to the self?

PE: The layers bring a richness to life. I think of my visits to France and trying to decipher the different eras piled on top of each other. But even here with a shorter period of (European) settlement, one can look back and imagine the environment that was occupied by Indigenous peoples, as well as two hundred years of subsequent development. All this to say that one can't simply look at architecture in isolation. It has a complex and central role in our lives. Layers give people multiple ways to connect to their environment, which can lead to *a sense of place*. This is an emotional attachment through which a place is valued.

AC: You're an award-winning heritage activist and a long-serving member of the City of Waterloo's Municipal Heritage Committee. What is "heritage" for you, and how do your ideas about it relate to your photography?

PE: Heritage is the temporal dimension of culture, both material and intangible culture. And culture is our interface with the world that enables us to survive. To quote from the United Nations Educational, Scientific and Cultural Organization, "Heritage is our legacy from the past, what we live with today, and what we pass on to future generations. Our cultural and natural heritage are both irreplaceable sources of life and inspiration." So heritage is the buildings, history, traditions, languages, and practices of the past which are still important. Importance is a question upon which opinions vary, but in my view the broader and richer our heritage is, in all its facets, the more robust and resilient our society will be.

One's heritage is the culture that one receives, and which helps a person deal with, and survive in, their environment and their society. Culture can be divided into two parts: material culture and spiritual or intangible culture. Material culture includes buildings (shelter), tools, food, and anything which leaves a physical trace, while intangible culture includes spiritual beliefs, language, and social practices (like shaking hands, for instance).

The history of the built landscape of our communities is a part of our cultural heritage. Conservation of built heritage is the process of saving physical traces of the past in order that people can continue to learn from it—a vital effort given that landscapes and buildings are, for most people, more immediate reminders of the past than written records. It's obvious that our physical environment is constantly changing in many small ways, so photography for me has become a method of conserving or at least capturing reminders of how things have changed. I think I'm more conscious of this now than I was 40 years ago.

AC: Can you elaborate on how your perspective on heritage has changed over the past 40 years?

PE: My perspective has changed greatly. As noted earlier, I had certain predispositions to being interested, but when I think back to when I was a young adult, as a university student I would walk around central Waterloo with absolutely no idea of what I was surrounded with, or any real idea of the history of the place. The appreciation of my earlier state of ignorance leads me to believe that many other people are in a similar state. It is really only my own effort to educate myself, plus my association with others who already had an appreciation of architecture and history, that has led me to where I am today. Additionally, I think that the appreciation of the value of heritage has increased over those years, both in scholarly work and among the interested public.

AC: Why, for you, *should* people have a general interest in the history of the built landscape of the communities in which they live?

PE: The built environment has a profound effect on people's stress levels and mental well-being. Also, the built environment can foster a sense of connection to a community, or it can form barriers, and exclude people. One can learn both from the mistakes and from the achievements of the past.

AC: What is the connection between appreciation of heritage and good mental health?

PE: It is not a matter of appreciation, but the unconscious reaction to one's surroundings. A link between heritage landscapes and mental health is something I and others feel intuitively, but recent research at the University of Waterloo by Colin Ellard has shown a clear link between different urban environments and physiological stress responses. I was also involved in a health studies project several years ago that involved urban environments, run by Amanda Johnson, part of the Healthy Communities Research Network at UW. She was looking at anecdotal evidence of how people related to different spaces, why they liked some and not others.

Ellard's book *Places of the Heart* is a good introduction to the subject. The book and his work explore how our brains and bodies respond to different types of space. Jane Jacobs' brilliant observations in *The Death and Life of Great American Cities* have certainly shaped my views in that she points out the value of heritage buildings for new businesses, and for supporting community life. Generally, she says that a diversity of buildings and spaces allows a diversity of life, which permits more casual contacts in the street, builds a web of public respect and trust, and in turn supports a more resilient community. Some quibble with points Jacobs has made, but to her defence she encourages readers to observe for themselves, and to test her ideas against their own observations. Her book still stands up as a landmark work sixty years later.

AC: What do you see as the value of heritage in giving one a sense of pride and ownership in a community? Some critics of heritage efforts have argued that they are conservative and filiopietistic and serve to reinforce in Kitchener-Waterloo the status of people of German, Mennonite, and British background at the expense of Indigenous peoples, newcomers, or perceived "newcomers." How would you respond? Of what value is Waterloo heritage to the recent immigrant or someone who doesn't identify with the groups traditionally seen as the Region's "founding peoples"?

PE: I would agree that some heritage efforts in the past have been motivated by a desire to support a dominant culture and a certain historical narrative. I try to take a broader view of culture and heritage, and nowadays I think others are adopting a more inclusive understanding. Our heritage in all its facets is the result of contributions of many groups and peoples. Indigenous people have left a mark on our physical surroundings, and in the early days of contact they taught European explorers and settlers a great deal about how to survive in this part of the world. I think there is still a lot to learn from Indigenous people of a spiritual nature regarding our relationship to the natural world, especially now in this era of climate change. The Mennonites, too, have left both physical traces and an enduring intangible impact on our notion of community. Without going through a cultural history of the region, I can say that many people from many parts of the world continue to contribute to our shared culture while maintaining aspects of their own culture, which they have brought with them.

Speaking as an immigrant myself, though not one who faced barriers of race, I found that I made many small adjustments to living in Canada and Waterloo Region, and I came after many years to embrace the heritage of Waterloo Region as my own. Mais comme j'ai dit à mes cousines en France, "je suis un petit garçon français dans le corps d'un vieux canadien."[1]

In the end, feeling part of a community is a strong human need, whether the community be smaller or larger.

AC: In terms of learning about the mistakes of the past: can you think of a particular example of how a greater public awareness of and commitment to heritage would have made a difference?

PE: My first thought is of natural heritage, and the present-day building of apartment buildings on springs and underground watercourses, or the corduroy road in uptown Waterloo, which was revealed during excavation for the light rail transit tracks in 2016.

Most of the clues as to why Waterloo was established in wetlands are now gone, but knowing why Waterloo is located where it is helps one appreciate the limitations of the site. For the first 50 years, the Pennsylvania Germans were able to deal with those limitations quite well, but it becomes more problematic now. I'm speaking of the City of Waterloo because I know it best, but the same more or less applies to Kitchener and Preston, not so much Galt. The land of Waterloo Region consists of glacial deposits of sand, gravel and stone laid over a limestone bedrock, which is visible and accessible to quarrying in the southern part of the region. Kitchener and Waterloo, as well as parts of the townships, are covered in huge quantities of sand, which obviously varies from place to place, but I recall the figure of nine metres being mentioned with regard to a particular site. According to Clayton Wells, writing in 1928, there were at one time more than 65 flowing or artesian wells in Waterloo, and it was thought the town lay over an underground river. The water table has dropped due to extraction, but it is still on average just several metres below grade. Many new apartment developers are still obliged to build several floors of above-ground parking, and to pump out ground water, sometimes for months, in order to put in a foundation.

AC: Certainly your interest in older architecture is not just limited to grand houses and public buildings—indeed there are relatively few of these in your pictures, and many more modest homes and

1 "But as I've said to my cousins in France, 'I'm a little French boy in an old Canadian body.'"

industrial structures featured. Can you talk a little more about what seems to be your demotic and even democratic approach to heritage?

PE: I have been greatly influenced by my friend Susan Burke, who spent much of her museum career as curator/manager of the Joseph Schneider Haus Museum in Kitchener, and her views of the role of museums and collecting for them. Her purpose was to show the everyday life of ordinary people. I think that in the 19th and early 20th centuries, museums collected the finest and richest examples. This leads to a false impression of the past through suggesting that everyone lived like the wealthy and literate. I think in the early days of heritage conservation in Ontario a similar approach was taken, where fine Victorian houses were recognized, and the more ordinary were forgotten (and demolished). I didn't start out with this understanding, but it has come to influence my choice of subjects.

AC: I suppose I'm also struck by the ways that your photos capture how buildings relate to one another. What have you been trying to catch in this regard?

PE: The relationship of buildings is something that interested me from the very earliest of my photos, and the photographers that inspire me have also often taken as subjects public spaces and the buildings that frame them. I was struck by how the residential and industrial mingled in central Waterloo, and this was the case in most communities before the automobile. The Ontario Planning Act, passed in 1946, expanded the powers and scope of earlier legislation, so after World War II it became the practice to segregate land uses. Before planners got interested in the relationship between public and private space, Jane Jacobs was the first observer (she was not a planner) to write about the huge importance of the relationship. The buildings which frame streets have an immense impact on the diversity of uses and people, and safety of the street. Even today, land use planning looks at each development or redevelopment in isolation, and the "public realm" is an afterthought. As I have looked around our urban areas, the older form of mixed use, though diminishing, is still apparent. Mixed use is being accepted by planners as important, but it's like a fire: you can mix the wood, paper, and matches together, but it won't necessarily light.

AC: Can you give an example of what you see as a particularly interesting relationship between or among buildings?

PE: Some relationships between buildings are very pleasing, and others jarring. And everything between. It's a question of how the space makes you feel. The scale, the safety, the comfort, and so on. I can cite what I think of as the best and worst in the City or the Region of Waterloo, but the variety is infinite—except in the vast tracts of suburbs.

AC: Some would see the relationship between older and "newer" buildings as inherently jarring. But my sense is that your definition of heritage is broader, temporally, than many people's. What is the value of being attentive to buildings and streetscapes beyond, say, the Edwardian era?

PE: It's not directly a matter of age, although in different eras, architects or builders have had different ideas about what they were creating. In recent years I have come to appreciate the many post-war "Modern" buildings in K-W, and they are mostly of such a modest scale that they don't stand out in a streetscape. I can recall Rick Haldenby, now retired director of the University of Waterloo School of Architecture, saying that in the mid-1970s architecture lost its way, and in that time some of the worst places were created. It's not simply a matter of age. Scale is important, level of detail, "rhythm" as some call it. I think my favourite place in Waterloo is by the big oak tree next to the library on Albert Street. There's a certain openness, but the space is framed by buildings built over the course of more than 100 years. I've taken many photos of the area, but the *genius loci* of the place is difficult to capture. There is something special about the place, being the brow of a hill overlooking a valley that must have appealed to Indigenous people as well as the first European settlers. Today I know a great deal about architecture and its history. Forty years ago, I knew practically nothing. So for me it has been a long process of learning about my environment, my home place.

AC: You've mentioned that Waterloo buildings and streets have a distinctive form. How so?

PE: The unusual form of streets and roads in Kitchener-Waterloo and Waterloo County generally was due to the fact that it was not surveyed by the British, who laid road allowances in a strict grid pattern, usually without any regard for topography. Likely, all of the early roads followed Indigenous trails, and generally roads were established where people wanted to go. The earliest buildings were clearly a continuation of building styles in Pennsylvania.

AC: Can you elaborate on the implications of this—how the "look" of the community even today is distinctive?

PE: The Mennonites from Pennsylvania had a distinct building style, which itself was an adaptation of English Georgian building. Most communities in the region have examples of this style, except, perhaps, Kitchener where they have almost all been demolished, with the notable exception of Joseph Schneider's home on Queen Street South, now a regional museum. It's interesting to think that if you were travelling around Ontario before the Second World War, you would have seen a huge difference between the various communities. One difference was the availability of building materials in the early days of settlement. There was limestone in Preston, Galt, Hespeler, and Guelph, but in this part of Waterloo County (Kitchener-Waterloo) there was wood and fieldstone.

AC: Was the Georgian style distinctive to Waterloo? Or was its prevalence distinctive?

PE: The Georgian style was named after King George I. It started in England and migrated to America and Canada. Just as with all styles, there were grand examples built by the rich, then imitated by everyone else. It was dominant in the 18th century, and then in the 19th, new ideas began to be introduced. But the Mennonites were very conservative, so they didn't keep up with new style. It was a very interesting culture that they brought here.

It's difficult talking about styles, especially before 1870, because there were common features but also considerable variation. The Georgian style was symmetrical. So there are early buildings that have symmetrical front facades, for example, the former Failte pub (image 8) and the Georgian houses on King Street in Preston (image 68). But generally, the Mennonites adapted this style by off-setting the front door, and using two windows on one side and one on the other. The gable end facades were still symmetrical, and the paired attic windows and return eaves are really distinctive clues. Proportions and roof slope are other indications (images 10, 27, 63, 68) of this style. The house next to the old post office that burned down, which was 37-41 on King Street in Waterloo (images 11), is another example. It was timber frame with no basement and minimal foundation. The facade was modified, but the proportions and form are there. The earliest houses were wood construction, since it was a few decades before brick was made locally, and then brick was later imported by rail.

There were many new styles or fashions of building of which there are no examples at all in Kitchener-Waterloo. For instance, the French Second Empire Revival style: there are only three examples I can think of. It was far more common elsewhere in Ontario. This is not surprising in a strongly Germanic community at a time when there was considerable antagonism between France and Germany. Also, Regency cottages were uncommon: there were farmhouses of the style that I have encountered in Kent County, but I know of only one locally, at Frederick and Lancaster (image 58), aside from Kirkmichael, the home of William Dickson Jr., in Galt.

AC: Do you see your photography as having a particular politics? If so, how do you see your politics as being manifested in your photography?

PE: I have certain political views, but I've never really thought of myself as a socialist photographer or really trying to make any political points with my work. But if you look at the work of any photographer, their interests and their views are recognizable. I've thought of what I do as trying to capture what I think is important in our built environment, but I suppose I could not deny that I am influenced by my beliefs or values.

Today I sometimes think of myself as a small "c" conservative as much as a socialist; I'm certainly not a neo-liberal. Anyway, modern politics is pretty messed up. When I started out as a photojournalist for the *Chevron*, I took quite a few photos of people, and the idea was always to complement the text or story. The *Chevron* and another community paper I worked at, *On the Line*, were fairly left-wing, but since those days I think I've looked at photography more as simply recording my environment. Of course there are powerful forces at work which are shaping our built environment, and so everything we see around us is the result of a political process, thus it's hard to separate out. And I know that some of my photos in my first book have made people angry because of the folly or greed captured, or both, but that is not my main goal.

AC: I've got to jump on your last phrase: What then do you see as your main goal?

PE: To a large extent my goal is, like Atget, to make a record of what is disappearing or likely to do so.

AC: Someone with a more neo-liberal bent might look at your photos and say—ah, what they capture is capitalism in action! The layers of the city that so attract you are the product of the "creative destruction" associated with capitalism and, if anything, the ongoing growth of those layers would be hindered, not helped, by heritage regulations that would have the effect of freezing development. How would you respond?

PE: I would not say that development and redevelopment are necessarily either good or bad. It's rather a matter of degree affected by the circumstances. And sometimes there are nefarious motives, such as destroying a community with wholesale "slum" clearance; however, I would say that the development of property for the sole intent of making money and which has no connection to the community can be bad. I try to understand development in the 19th century, and I guess that most of it had a direct connection to the community. So when people were having commercial buildings put up for their own use, there was a great deal more pride taken in what was done. A good example to study would be the commercial block on the southeast corner of King and Erb Streets in Waterloo. I believe the merchants who had the block built had all worked and lived, and continued to do so, within blocks of that corner. So the building was an expression of pride in the community, of their success in business and in their continuing faith in advancement. I'm pretty sure it was all local materials, and local craftsmen. I think of Haussmann's mid-19th-century intervention in Paris, which is now well appreciated, even though it displaced thousands of people and destroyed parts of medieval Paris. This was an arbitrary exercise of power on the part of the self-declared Emperor Napoleon III and Haussmann, whom he had named Prefect of the Seine. And then think of the old Kitchener City Hall and its public space that was replaced by a mall, which failed in not much more than a decade while bleeding downtown Kitchener retail business practically dry. This was the result of influence of a property development company on Kitchener City Council. For present-day actions of capitalism in real estate, I would recommend the documentary film *Push* (2009) by director Fredrik Gertten, which describes in harrowing detail how real estate has become an investment asset with no regard for people's housing needs.

Good development would create places where people feel physically and socially comfortable, where their needs can be met reasonably easily, and where they can make connections with others in their community as they wish, without barriers. These places could be heritage areas, or new.

AC: Beyond its familiarity from your work at the *Chevron*, what was the appeal of the Pentax Spotmatic over other contemporary options?

PE: At the time it was not an expensive camera, and the built-in light meter was a really good feature. Otherwise, you either had to guess at exposures or use a hand-held light meter. I appreciate the simplicity now, compared to modern digital cameras. There were just aperture, speed, and focus to deal with, whereas today digital cameras have a menu of 50 options and a multitude of buttons and dials. You can use digital cameras in a manual mode, but it doesn't seem quite as simple. Another aspect that was important to me was being able to establish a darkroom at home. Circumstances changed, my daughter got a bigger room, and her room which had been the upstairs kitchen when the house was a duplex was available to me. So, I had counter space and running water for a darkroom.

AC: How many photos have you developed and printed over the years?

PE: I've never really kept track. I have seven binders of negs in my office, not sure how many in each. There are 6,300 black-and-white negatives that I have digitized in my computer, but some are duplicates. My habit was to print a contact sheet, and then to make smaller test prints of anything promising. When I got the camera I had access to other darkrooms, but colour slide film was popular because printing was not necessary to view them. My slides are fairly disorganized. After I started the cabinetmaking business with my brother in 1975, I began to document our work. I got two more Pentax bodies, so I always had black-and-white, slide, and colour negative film handy. I did learn to print in colour, but it is bothersome and expensive unless you do a lot.

AC: When it comes to the pictures themselves, what are your attitudes to framing and cropping? Are you trying to "get" the photo you want when you take it, or do you anticipate doing so later, when cropping the developed image?

PE: Framing is an interesting question. When I was printing with an enlarger I would crop to a small degree. In photojournalism, images were often cropped severely, depending on space and the editor's whim or, rather, direction. Now I barely crop at all. I had never used zoom lenses before I got a digital camera, and after not too long a time I realized I was becoming pretty lazy with regard to framing, or perhaps I should say composition. With a zoom lens you can frame an image from almost any vantage point, so you don't have to think about the context—just the subject. So, I went back to using in fact the same 50mm prime lens that I had used with film (with an adapter). With a prime lens I find I may have to cross the street, or basically think about where I want to stand before I take a picture. I have used longer focal length lenses when I have tried to show the contours of the landscape.

AC: I find interesting what you say about context. Am I understanding correctly that you avoid a zoom lens to essentially compel yourself to think about context?

PE: Yes, that's right. A 50mm lens gives an angle to view similar to what one sees with the eye. There's a small range where it doesn't matter too much, but with wide angle or telephoto lenses, the view becomes "unnatural". As a rule, but not always, I try to include some setting or context, rather make building portraits. In looking at historic photos, I've come to realize that they contain much valuable information beyond the subject that the photographer intended.

AC: This seems a good time to bring up (or return to) your thinking about verisimilitude. You've referred to your work as documentary, and to an important extent in your photos you are trying to "capture" a moment that is fleeting—a cast of light, the position of people in relation to one another and the buildings around them, a building about to be demolished. And yet the photos can't of course fully capture a moment—they capture aspects of the visual in a static image (as opposed to, say, the moment's sounds and smells), and a static image that is also composed, cropped, and developed in a particular way by you. What do you see as the relationship between your subjective position as a photographer and the objective reality that you're seeking to catch?

PE: There is no doubt that my photos and the photos of others are the result of some subjective process. It is not possible to do otherwise, whether I (or others) think they are being objective or not. I've realized that a viewer will see different things in an image; and that an image can evoke memories or feelings in a viewer which are unanticipated by the photographer. I'm not sure I'm trying to capture an objective reality. I think it is just my reality, and hopefully others can share it or appreciate it.

AC: A very interesting part of "your reality" as captured in the photos is that they are colourized. How does the colourization work, and why do you choose to add colour to black-and-white images as opposed to using colour film?

PE: I was exposed to the idea of colouring photos when in 1978 a friend gave me a hand-coloured print of the Bluenose by Wallace MacAskill. From then I started collecting coloured black-and-white photos primarily from second-hand shops. I also read about the process. So when I had my own darkroom for black-and-white, I bought some watercolour dyes, which is one method of colouring photos. More common is using oil-based colours. It was appealing for several reasons. First is that even the smallest amount of colour radically changes the character of the photo. It's also cheap—and relaxing for me. And the detail and the forms in the image are predominant because the colour saturation does not overwhelm the subject matter. Another factor was painting with oils, which I took up as a teenager. My subjects then were streetscapes and landscapes. Colouring photos seemed an easier way of achieving what I tried to do with oils.

Where possible I research the colour of objects if I don't remember. I did learn colour printing from my friend Gary Robins, a professional photographer and instructor of photography in Regina, but for reasons of equipment and expense I never really considered setting up a colour darkroom.

However there are advantages to using black-and-white film, and when I had the ability to process and black-and-white film, I explored the possibilities. There are a number of factors to consider. First, black-and-white film is generally sharper than colour, because it has one layer of emulsion, where colour has three. I also looked for the film and developer combination that would produce the finest grain; and with developer, there are factors of temperature, strength, and time which affect the grain characteristics. Also having read about Ansel Adams' zone system, I decided that the sky was not important. So, in order to get better detail in the darker areas, I would slightly over-expose the film, and burn out the sky to white.

For my 2016 exhibition at Schneider Haus and for the subsequent publication, I began digitizing the old negatives and colouring them on my computer, rather than directly colouring the prints. I could make prints still, but it saved steps in preparing work for publication.

AC: If the addition of even small amounts of colour radically changes the image, doesn't colourization contradict the documentary aspects of your photos?

PE: By changing the image I mean that the viewer will begin to interpret it as a colour image. I don't think the result is any less documentary than colour photography.

AC: Your photos sometimes feature people, but they are not generally characterized by the relationship between buildings and people in the way, say, of many of the American photographer Walker Evans' photos. How do you see people fitting in to your work?

PE: I generally prefer not to have people in the photos, or not many, although sometimes they are quite interesting. My camera is at eye-level, so when one views the photos they can imagine themselves as stepping into the scene, and relate to the place rather than to other people.

AC: Somewhat similarly, while your general focus is the built landscape, trees and other natural elements are featured prominently in some of your works. What is the significance of these elements in the photos that feature them?

PE: I am quite interested in natural landscapes and have many such photos, but I guess I think of them as personal, rather than something I want to present to others. Although the relationship between the natural and built environments is fascinating. Some photographers have been interested in cloud formations, and such photos stimulate feelings of amazement and an appreciation of beauty, but they are completely transitory. One can use an orange filter to accentuate the cloud formations with black-and-white film, but this approach does not appeal to me.

AC: You began your career in the late 1960s when Ontario artists such as London's Greg Curnoe responded to American cultural imperialism by expressing a kind of regional Canadian nationalism in their works. Was this a movement with which you identified or came to identify?

PE: As a youth I was swept up in Canadian nationalism around Canada's centennial, for sure, and was an enthusiastic supporter of the replacement of the Red Ensign with a truly Canadian flag. I have spent a lot of time studying and admiring Canadian art of the 20th century generally, but I don't think it has had a direct influence on my photography, although I was and still am a great fan of the Group of Seven. I never felt part of a Canadian art scene even though as a young adult I made many friends who were artists. Music has always been a huge part of my life, playing the viola from my teenage years, and taking up the electric bass guitar in the late sixties, so I identified as a musician rather than an artist. In the late sixties I had many friends who had criticisms of Canadian society and government, so my feelings of nationalism waned.

AC: Walker Evans' democratic approach to photography was at once radical and a consciously American alternative to what he saw as a more hierarchical, and previously dominant, European tradition. Do you identify with this?

PE: In the late 19th and early 20th centuries in America and Europe there was a movement or style of photography called Pictorialism in which photography tried to imitate older forms of art such as painting. So the question of whether photography is art or not has been a longstanding one. I'm not quite sure about Evans, but my interpretation of Abbott (and her view of Atget) is that if photography was art, it would stand on its own merits, and not try to be like painting or etching or whatever. For a long time, though, Abbott was shut out of photo exhibitions by Pictorialists. In any event, most art has attempted to be realistic for centuries up until Cubism and other modern movements. I do identify with Atget, Abbott, Evans, and other photographers for whom the subject has greater importance than the artistic impact of the image.

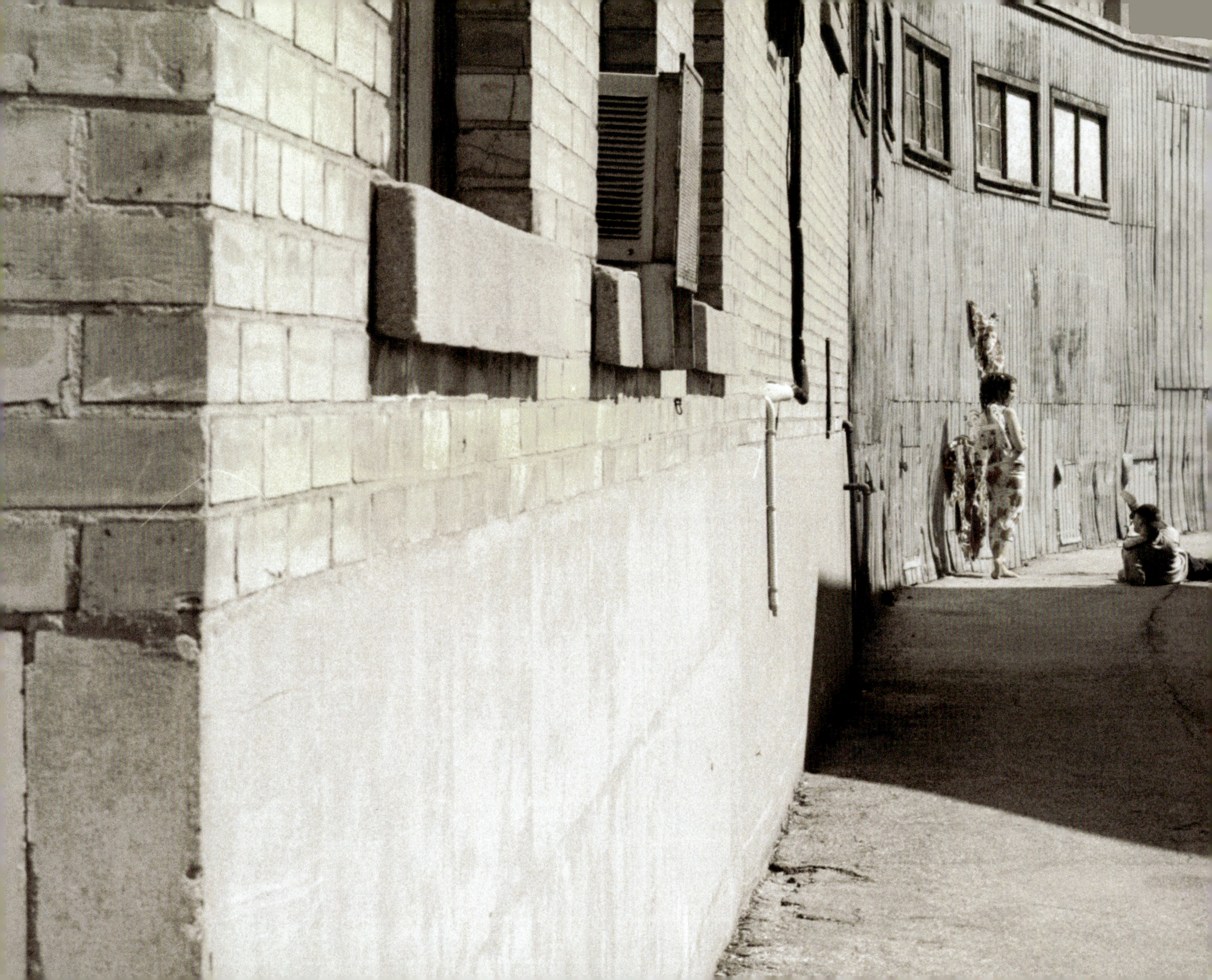

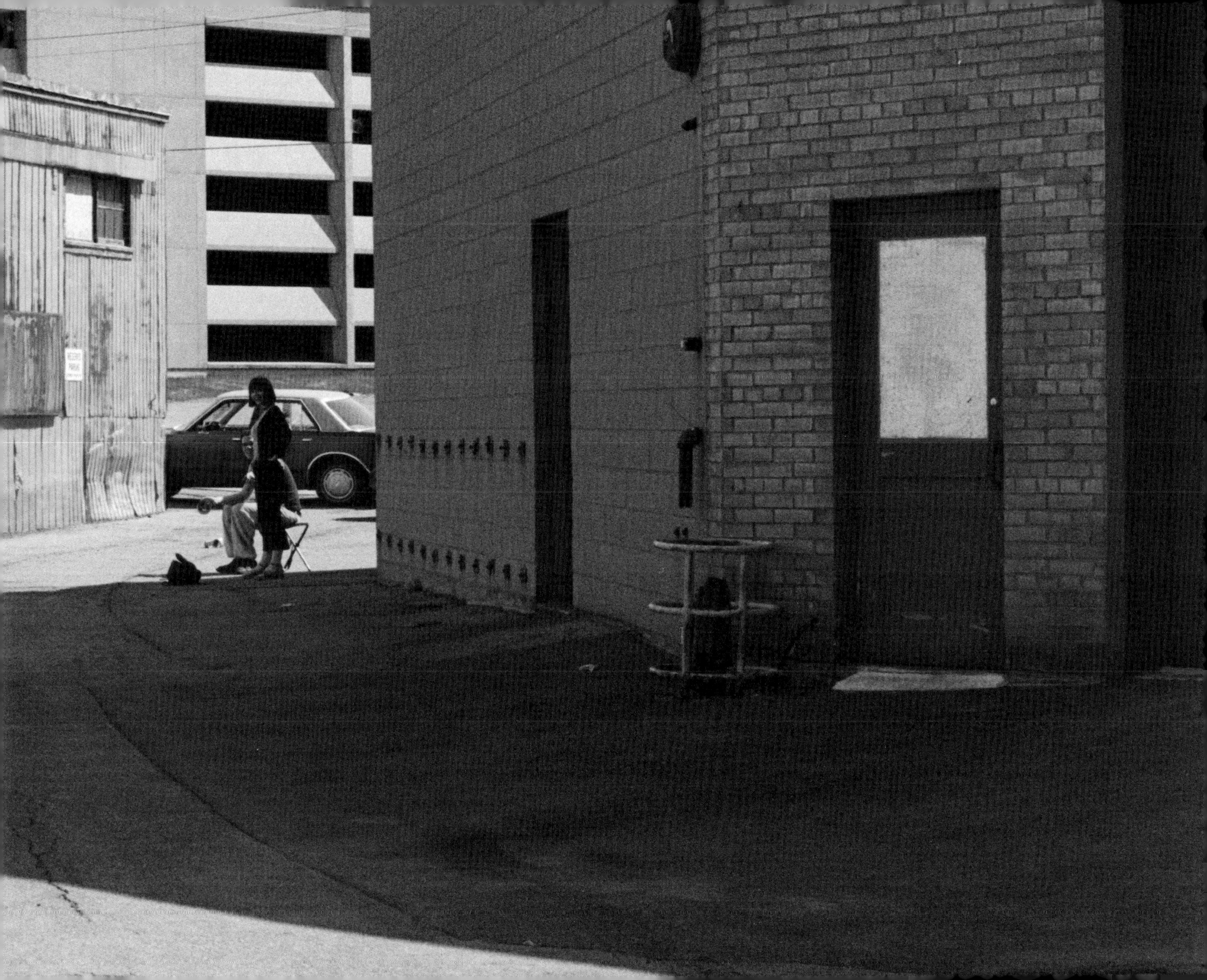

AFTERWORD

Adam Crerar

Through a Changing Landscape takes me on two journeys. The first has me travelling roughly north to south through Waterloo, Kitchener, Preston, and Galt with Philippe Elsworthy as he has walked his community for more than a half-century. The second has me moving backward and forward in time across that period as I turn the pages. In these deceptively ordinary images, I see the various pasts of when the photos were taken, the further pasts of when the things in them—cars, buildings, fashions—were imagined and made, and even the past imagined futures of Intercosmetics and Orion Electronics and Travel. I seek to fix each image in time, and the cumulative effect is vertiginous.

In the local specificity of these photos, we're given a social and cultural history of Waterloo Region. There is Jimmy's Lunch when it was open for nearby factory workers. The Maritime Store's offer of "Newfoundland Foods" conjures homesick post-war migrants who "came down the road" in search of opportunities in a small Ontario city. As recently as the 1990s the central city of Waterloo appears at once industrial—in the shadows of furniture factories, Seagram's, and Labatt's—and rural, with country lanes and unfinished sidewalks just feet from the main street and a bingo hall on the main street itself.

Yet this is more than local history. Modern North American urban history more broadly, and the relentless capitalism associated with it, are captured in a picture and a phrase. A Tim Hortons that was once a garage is now a condo. Corner stores built out from residences become residences again, and Kmart welcomes Sunday shoppers as Seagram's crumbles. Idling Chevettes and Lincolns recall the oil crisis of the 1970s and point to the climate crisis of our own era. The signs of the times—all times, it seems—are for liquidation services and buildings for sale and lease. Canada Trust and Woolworth's are long gone; I'll never have a Tin Roof donut. It's unsettling to find comfort from the stability offered by glimpses of signs for Coke and Yamaha.

At times there is a suggestion that nature's broader cycles transcend this flux. Vehicle and architectural styles come and go, but there are always trees. Even their leafless branches enfold and incorporate utility poles and their wires, and houses can seem to grow up among them. There are limits, however, to the reassurance this provides when you realize that since that winter day the trees by the Bethel Chapel have been cleared.

Phil has a position on all of this. He is a heritage activist who is fascinated by older buildings—by how they were made and by how they relate to the history of the region and to the history of architecture more generally. In several of these photos he captures their demolition, though not in the way of photographers who seem to delight at the sight of theatres crumbling in Buffalo and of trees growing from Art Deco skyscrapers in Detroit. Most of us walk past the shells of mid-century factories and Georgian taverns as they are coming down. Phil pauses to document their bones and sinews and to reflect on the loss of urban variety that comes with their destruction.

But this is far from a book of heritage or otherwise "special" buildings. Views of distinguished-looking buildings—aren't those the ones most interesting to heritage activists?—are often cut off in the frame in favour of homely ones, or blocked altogether by trees. A caption mentions an award-winning architect, but the accompanying photo doesn't show that person's work. Sometimes Phil's attention seems to be more on road and parking lot surfaces than on a particular structure or structures. Always it is on context: how buildings relate to one another and to the people who live among them. Why leave the earth-moving machine in the frame when it blocks part of the view to the right? Because that's what it does when you stand there and look that way. This is Stephen Shore's photography that "feels like seeing."

That the seeing in question is Phil's is self-evident. But what makes it especially so is his fascinating choice to colourize his images—black-and-whites and de-colourized ones alike. There is no effort to prettify or otherwise alter; Phil's intent is to capture the colours of brick and grass, jackets and dumpsters, and late-season snow exactly as he saw and remembered them. It's a bracing subjectivity in an art that promises verisimilitude.

Shore's photographs of ordinary "uncommon places" in American towns and cities in the 1970s are not the only ones that come to mind when viewing Phil's work. In the late nineteenth and early twentieth centuries Eugène Atget documented the streets and storefronts of what remained of pre-Revolutionary Paris in the wake of Baron Haussmann's urban renewal; Phil's shot of storefront mannequins is a sly homage. Atget in turn inspired Berenice Abbott to capture what she saw as "the past jostling the present" in older street-level shops and tenements and towering new skyscrapers in the Manhattan of the 1930s. And early in our century Zse Tsung Leong's photography reflected on the power of market forces to erase Ming and Qing architecture in Chinese cities in ways even more total than those imagined by the ideologues of the Cultural

Revolution. Phil is in good company here, but, like Alice Munro, has been committed to telling stories about ordinary circumstances in places without the broader cultural cachet of New York, Paris, Shanghai, and even small-city America.

Also like Munro, Phil is non-judgmental and relentlessly curious. There are limits to this equanimity, of course; Waterloo's post-war suburbs are off-frame, and a certain parking garage draws fire. But here are strip malls and strip clubs, tire-factories and nail salons, spires and satellite dishes, Albert Kahn and postmodern hodgepodge—all noted and confronted without winking comment. People made these things, and we should give them the attention they deserve. Phil's socialism is not on overt display here, but his attentiveness is the basis for an empathetic and compassionate politics.

It seems strange to say that this book is about people when people are rarely the focus of the photos and, when present, are often off to the side and not particularly relevant at first glance. But this off-to-the-sidedness gets me thinking about how people lived in and around these spaces. I feel the cold feet of those milling cadets and wonder about the anxieties of the payday borrowers. And the felt presence of absent people sometimes has me staring at a photo as if at a Breughel. Who's going to climb that ladder? Who sits in that chair outside the Hydro house? Who installed the cooling unit on the meat processing plant? What flirtations occurred between the auto refinishers and the hair stylists on University?

We are in the middle of the flow of time as people enter doors and turn away from conversations, as cars move into or just out of frame. All is flux as steam rises, birds fly, and light fades. If you're a certain age, you yourself are in the photos, turning circles on your bike in the summer sun, fumbling for change in the phone booth, hurrying to the Dustin Hoffman movie in the gloaming, waiting for the bus in the rain as the cars hiss by. Across the street, perhaps behind a ragged sidewalk tree or an off-kilter traffic sign, a building sits, familiar and unremarked upon by most, awaiting its coming transformation.

Further Reading

Barberie, Peter. *Looking at Atget*. Philadelphia: Philadelphia Museum of Art in association with Yale University Press, 2007.

Barthes, Roland. "Rhetoric of the Image," in *The Photography Reader: History and Theory*, 2nd ed., edited by Liz Wells, 128–38. London and New York: Routledge, 2019.

Clarke, Graham. *The Photograph*. New York: Oxford University Press, 1997.

English, John, and Kenneth McLaughlin. *Kitchener: An Illustrated History*. Waterloo: Wilfrid Laurier University Press, 1983.

Jussim, Estelle. "The Eternal Moment: Photography and Time," in *The Photography Reader: History and Theory*, 2nd ed., edited by Liz Wells, 161–71. London and New York: Routledge, 2019.

Leong, Sze Tsung, and Stephen Shore. *History Images*. Göttingen: Steidl, 2006.

McLaughlin, Kenneth, and Sharon Jaeger. *Waterloo: An Illustrated History, 1857–2007*. Waterloo: City of Waterloo, 2007.

McEuen, Melissa A. *Seeing America: Women Photographers Between the Wars*. Lexington: University Press of Kentucky, 2004.

Moore, Kevin. *Old Paris and Changing New York: Photographs by Eugène Atget and Berenice Abbott*. Cincinnati: FotoFocus and the Taft Museum of Art in association with Yale University Press, New Haven and London, 2018.

Shore, Stephen. *Uncommon Places: The Complete Works*. London: Thames & Hudson, 2014.

Wollen, Peter. "Fire and Ice," in *The Photography Reader: History and Theory*, 2nd ed., edited by Liz Wells, 195–98. London and New York: Routledge, 2019.

Worswick, Clark. *Berenice Abbott, Eugène Atget*. Santa Fe: Arena Editions, 2002.

BIBLIOGRAPHY

Abbott, Berenice. *The World of Atget.* New York: Horizon Press, 1964. Reprinted in Clark Worswick, *Berenice Abbott, Eugène Atget*. Santa Fe: Arena Editions, 2002.

Bird, Michael S., and Terry Kobayashi. *A Splendid Harvest: Germanic Folk and Decorative Arts in Canada.* Toronto: Van Nostrand Reinhold, 1981.

Blake, Verschoyle Benson, and Ralph Greenhill. *Rural Ontario.* Toronto: University of Toronto Press, 1969.

Borcoman, James. *Eugène Atget, 1857–1927.* Ottawa: National Gallery of Canada, 1984.

Ellard, Colin. *Places of the Heart: The Psychogeography of Everyday Life.* New York: Bellevue Literary Press, 2015.

Gehl, Jan. *Cities for People.* Washington: Island Press, 2010.

Greenberg, Ken. *Walking Home: The Life and Lessons of a City Builder.* Toronto: Random House, 2011.

Harris, David. *Eugène Atget: Itinéraires parisiens.* Paris: Éditions du patrimoine, 1999.

Jacobs, Jane. *The Death and Life of Great American Cities.* New York: Vintage Books, 1961.

Johnson, Amanda, Troy Glover and W. Stewart. "Attracting locals downtown: everyday leisure as a place-making initiative." *Journal of Park and Recreation Administration* 32, 2014. https://www.semanticscholar.org/paper/Attracting-locals-downtown%3A-everyday-leisure-as-a-Johnson-Glover/de817b2652fde5c2696a07089af154431427d649.

Kunstler, James Howard. *The Geography of Nowhere: The Rise and Decline of America's Man-Made Landscape.* New York: Touchstone, 1994.

MacRae, Marion, and Anthony Adamson. *The Ancestral Roof: Domestic Architecture of Upper Canada.* Toronto: Clarke, Irwin & Company, 1963.

Pevsner, Nikolaus. *Pioneers of Modern Design: From William Morris to Walter Gropius.* London: Penguin Books, 1960.

Rempel, John I. *Building with Wood and Other Aspects of Nineteenth-century Building in Ontario.* Toronto: University of Toronto Press, 1972.

Ritchie, Thomas. *Canada Builds, 1867–1967.* Toronto: University of Toronto Press, 1967.

Sullivan, George. *Berenice Abbott, Photographer.* New York: Clarion Press, 2006.

Szarkowski, John (introduction). *Walker Evans.* New York: The Museum of Modern Art, 1971.

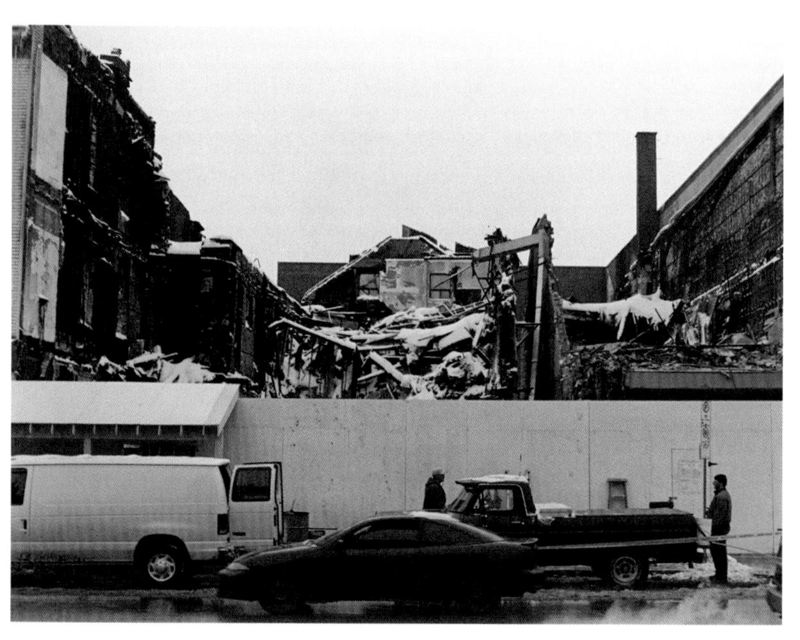

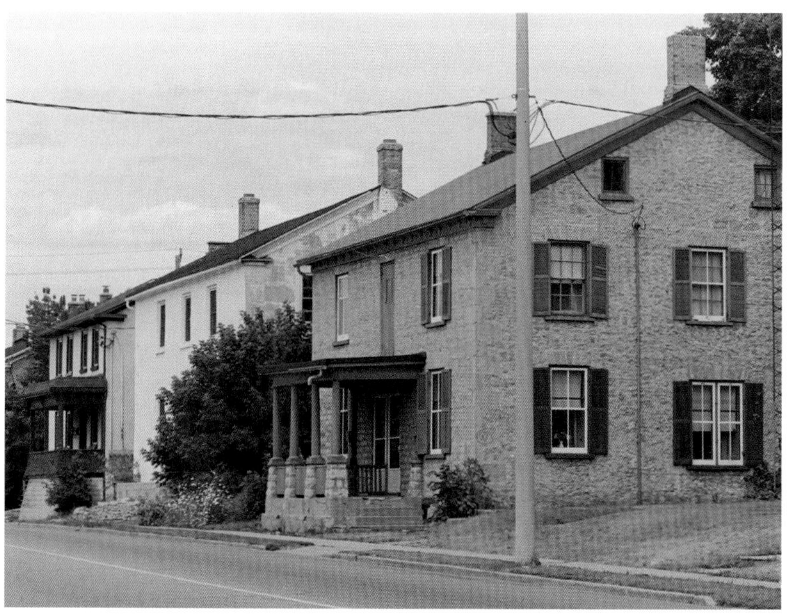

BIBLIOGRAPHY

Abbott, Berenice. *The World of Atget.* New York: Horizon Press, 1964. Reprinted in Clark Worswick, *Berenice Abbott, Eugène Atget.* Santa Fe: Arena Editions, 2002.

Bird, Michael S., and Terry Kobayashi. *A Splendid Harvest: Germanic Folk and Decorative Arts in Canada.* Toronto: Van Nostrand Reinhold, 1981.

Blake, Verschoyle Benson, and Ralph Greenhill. *Rural Ontario.* Toronto: University of Toronto Press, 1969.

Borcoman, James. *Eugène Atget, 1857–1927.* Ottawa: National Gallery of Canada, 1984.

Ellard, Colin. *Places of the Heart: The Psychogeography of Everyday Life.* New York: Bellevue Literary Press, 2015.

Gehl, Jan. *Cities for People.* Washington: Island Press, 2010.

Greenberg, Ken. *Walking Home: The Life and Lessons of a City Builder.* Toronto: Random House, 2011.

Harris, David. *Eugène Atget: Itinéraires parisiens.* Paris: Éditions du patrimoine, 1999.

Jacobs, Jane. *The Death and Life of Great American Cities.* New York: Vintage Books, 1961.

Johnson, Amanda, Troy Glover and W. Stewart. "Attracting locals downtown: everyday leisure as a place-making initiative." *Journal of Park and Recreation Administration* 32, 2014. https://www.semanticscholar.org/paper/Attracting-locals-downtown%3A-everyday-leisure-as-a-Johnson-Glover/de817b2652fde5c2696a07089af154431427d649.

Kunstler, James Howard. *The Geography of Nowhere: The Rise and Decline of America's Man-Made Landscape.* New York: Touchstone, 1994.

MacRae, Marion, and Anthony Adamson. *The Ancestral Roof: Domestic Architecture of Upper Canada.* Toronto: Clarke, Irwin & Company, 1963.

Pevsner, Nikolaus. *Pioneers of Modern Design: From William Morris to Walter Gropius.* London: Penguin Books, 1960.

Rempel, John I. *Building with Wood and Other Aspects of Nineteenth-century Building in Ontario.* Toronto: University of Toronto Press, 1972.

Ritchie, Thomas. *Canada Builds, 1867–1967.* Toronto: University of Toronto Press, 1967.

Sullivan, George. *Berenice Abbott, Photographer.* New York: Clarion Press, 2006.

Szarkowski, John (introduction). *Walker Evans.* New York: The Museum of Modern Art, 1971.

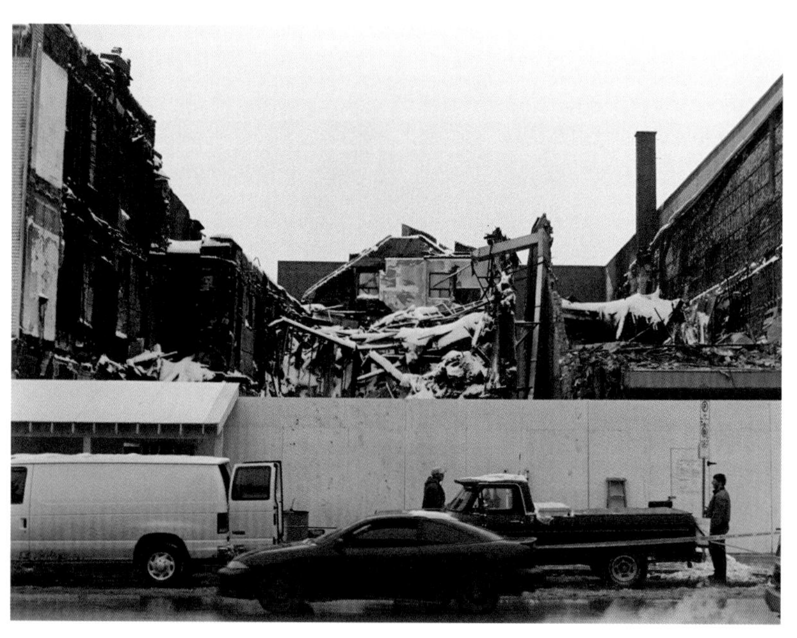

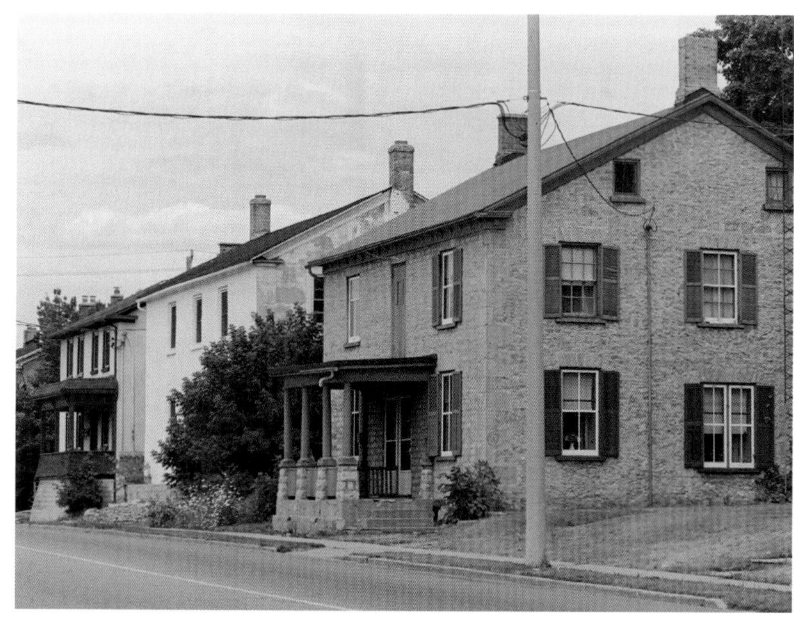

PHILIPPE ELSWORTHY is an artist, musician, and retired cabinetmaker. His first book, *Evolving Urban Landscapes*, received the Waterloo Region History Prize in 2017. As well as numerous awards for furniture and musical instrument construction, he received the Waterloo Regional Heritage Foundation's Award of Excellence in 2014.

ADAM CRERAR teaches Canadian history in the Department of History at Wilfrid Laurier University.

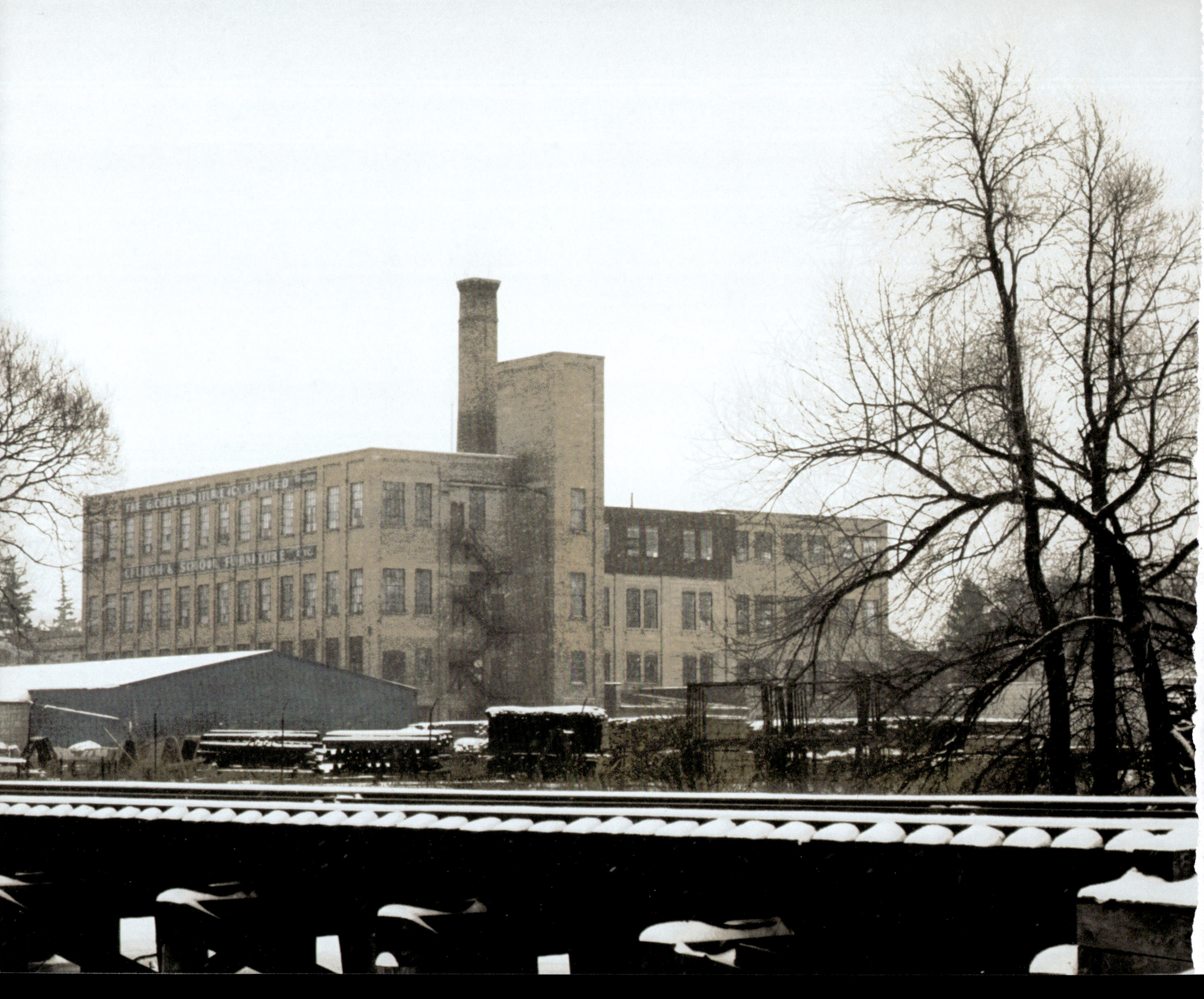
LIMITED
SCHOOL FURNITURE